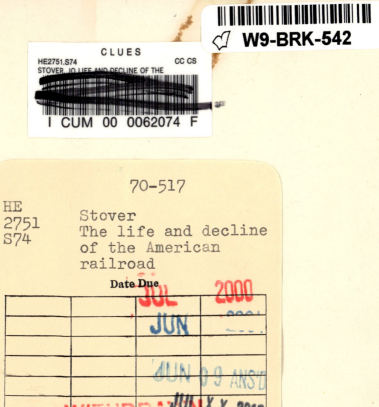

70-517

HE
2751
S74

Stover
The life and decline
of the American
railroad

Date Due

		JUL 2000
		JUN
		JUN 0 9 ANS'D
WITHDRAWN		JUL X X 2015

 PRINTED IN U.S.A.

The Life and Decline
of the American Railroad

The Life and Decline
of the American Railroad

John F. Stover

NEW YORK OXFORD UNIVERSITY PRESS

1970

Copyright © 1970 by Oxford University Press, Inc.
Library of Congress Catalogue Card Number: 77-83054

Printed in the United States of America

For my Mother and Father

Foreword

No doubt the year 1969 will best be remembered for the voyage of the Apollo XI and the moon walk of Neil Armstrong and Edwin Aldrin. As the nation, and the world, celebrated the completed moon mission, few remembered that just a century before, the spring of 1869 marked another landmark in American transportation history. On May 10, 1869 a golden spike had completed the railroad to the Pacific—an iron trail fashioned and built by the plans and schemes of such men as Leland Stanford and Thomas Durant, and the harder labor of countless crews of Chinese and Irish track men. For a century Americans were proud of their railroads and the transportation they furnished for an expanding industrial economy. But by the era of lunar orbit and space travel American railroads were in decline, both in service and in the mind of the public. On the very day of the Apollo XI blast-off, July 16, newspapers were reporting that in Pennsylvania some thirty-five rail passengers from the *Spirit of St. Louis* sat down on the track in front of the locomotive until a work crew repaired the faulty air-conditioning on their coach.

The railroads of today certainly do not rate the attention of those of an earlier day. Today's rail mileage is less than that of 1904, and the level of railroad employment is below that of the mid-1880's. Once the only Big Business on the American scene, our railroads have long since been dwarfed by a number of industrial and utility concerns. While rail freight ton-mileage is currently at a record high, it is still below the combined traffic of intercity trucks and pipelines. The decline of passenger service has been so precipitous in recent years that dozens of cities are being faced with the disappearance of their last passenger train. Tulsa, Oklahoma faced such a prospect in the summer of 1969, and a few weeks earlier Dallas, with a total population of nearly a million, earned the dubious distinction of being the largest city in the nation without any rail passenger service.

While many Americans today may consider their railroads to be hopelessly out of date, it has not always been so. Once the whistle of a locomotive was the most exciting sound in America. Throughout the nineteenth century, railroads played a dramatic and significant role in nearly every facet of American history. Most enduring of the competing forms of transport used in the era of internal improvement, the railroad speeded the growth of Atlantic seaport cities, and helped to people and supply the early West. As lines were built to the Pacific, the iron rails hastened the settlement of the trans-Mississippi frontier and shaped the lives of western cowboys, miners, and farmers. In the decades after the Civil War, American railroads helped to transform an agrarian-based, second-rate industrial economy into the industrial giant that we know today. As railroads in this century have become controlled by a stringent and complete federal regulation, they have also faced increasing competition from new highway, barge, air, and pipeline facilities. Even so, the inherent economy of the flanged wheel running on a steel rail would suggest that there still remain in America many transportation jobs that can most efficiently be performed by railroads.

J. F. S.
West Lafayette, Indiana
October 10, 1969

Contents

Maps and Illustrations

Illustrations follow page 148.

The Life and Decline
of the American Railroad

1

"A Perfect Passion for Railroads"

It was a bright crisp July morning and reasonably cool by the standards of the upper Chesapeake. There was an unprecedented bustle about the city, for Baltimore was about to experience a very special Independence Day. The pavements and walks were crowded at an early hour with the hundreds of country folk seeking vantage points to view the parade scheduled for eight o'clock. Inns were jammed, especially the May Pole, the Golden Lamb, and the White Swan out on Paca and Franklin streets on the way to the Frederick Pike and the National Road. The taverns in the center of town, like the Fountain Inn with its famous swinging sign, were crowded too. Farm wagons, carts, and gay stage coaches had brought hundreds of visitors in from all directions over the seven hard-surfaced pikes that converged upon the city. In the days just past, hundreds of artisans and their apprentices had put in long hours of extra labor designing and fashioning dozens of floats which would represent the trades and guilds of the city: the bakers, the victuallers, the tailors, the blacksmiths, the bleachers, the glass cutters, the Windsor chair makers, the rope makers, and the ship captains, mates, and seamen. Later it was generally agreed that the high point of the monster two-mile long parade was the exhibit prepared by the ship captains, mates, and seamen, the good ship *Union*—twenty-seven-foot miniature brig, with rigging, sails, and flags in place, and manned by a crew of distinguished city shipmasters. Crowds, parade, and celebration—all because Baltimore was about to build a railroad!

The parade made its way out to James Carroll's estate, on the edge of town, where the officials and directors of the Baltimore & Ohio Railroad had resolved to lay the first stone of their new project. In the year since the organization of their company the dozen directors and officers of the B. & O. had considerable difficulty in deciding upon the entranceway to the city, the exact route that should be taken to the distant Ohio, and the type of power to be used upon their rails. But on one point they had been quite agreed: there was to be a commemorative cornerstone—and it was to be laid on Independence Day, 1828. All the major canals built, or building, in the nation had been started on the Fourth of July, and the officials of the B. & O. did not propose that their great endeavor be in any way inferior to the major internal improvements of New York, Pennsylvania, or Ohio. And so in mid-morning of this bright holiday the venerable Charles Carroll, sole surviving signer of the Declaration of Independence, pushed his heavy spade deep into the ground to turn the first earth. The Grand Master and other officials of the Masonic Order brought and placed the square granite block in its intended resting place. The *Baltimore American* reported that the ninety-year-old Carroll refreshed himself from his labors with only a glass of water. Since whiskey was but three cents a glass in some of the local taverns, many of the celebrants that Fourth of July were not so temperate.

The promoters and sponsors of the B. & O. had decided to build a railroad because they were afraid—afraid that Baltimore's recent growth and prosperity were being threatened by commercial rivals to the north. Certainly Baltimore a few years earlier had had nothing to fear. No major American city had grown more rapidly than Baltimore in the 'teens, from 35,000 in 1810 to nearly 63,000 by 1820. Now the third city in the nation, Baltimore boasted a theater lighted by a new illuminating gas, and a newly dedicated cathedral. The pretty harbor was crowded with beautiful tall copper-hulled ships from Amsterdam and Liverpool, from Bordeaux and Le Havre. Swift schooners unloaded their cargoes on wharves crowded with goods from

Boston, Halifax, Havana, and southern American coastal ports. Baltimore dominated the tobacco and grain trade of Virginia, Maryland, and much of the Susquehanna Valley in Pennsylvania. Steamboats gave daily service to Annapolis, Norfolk, and Washington.

But one of Baltimore's great advantages was her geographic advantage relative to the western trade. The bankers and businessmen of the town, meeting in their new Exchange, noted with approval local editorial claims that Baltimore was two hundred miles closer to the navigable western waters than New York City, and had a comparable advantage of a hundred miles over Philadelphia. Baltimore's western trade connection was the National Road, which had been completed in 1818 from Cumberland, Maryland, a small town on the upper Potomac, to Wheeling, on the Ohio River. Connecting turnpikes with Baltimore, thus gave that city a relatively fast and direct connection with steamboat service on the upper Ohio. Changing horses every dozen miles, stage lines were soon carrying passengers and the U.S. mail from Baltimore to Wheeling in three and a half days. Long lines of blue and red canvas-topped-wagons groaned heavily behind teams of large draft horses driven by rough-voiced cigar-smoking teamsters. Both the huge wagons and the cigars (shortened to stogies) took their name from the Conestoga Valley of Pennsylvania. This great highway, which the merchant-traveler John Melish had described as "one of the finest roads in the world," was bringing great prosperity to Baltimore by the early 1820's. The wise old merchants and men of business would naturally be concerned with any development which might challenge the turnpike commerce of their busy city.

The challenge had appeared with the new canals in New York and Pennsylvania. On November 4, 1825, Governor DeWitt Clinton marked the completion of the Erie Canal, eight years in the digging, by slowly pouring a keg of Erie water into the Atlantic in the lower harbor of New York City. During the next year, 1826, more than 15,000 canal boats passed through the Erie locks near Schenectady, and the tolls collected on the entire 364-mile canal during the year came to $765,000! The merchants of Baltimore knew that a barrel of flour, worth five dollars on the dock in Baltimore, would net but a dollar in Wheeling because of the freight charges over the National Road. Canal freight charges were but a fraction of those found in the turnpike traffic. A further worry to the men of Baltimore was the news that on July 4, 1826, construction had started on the Pennsylvania Grand Canal to the west.

During the winter of 1826–27 the interested businessmen of Baltimore met several times to discuss the problem of this new northern commercial competition. One of the more articulate in the group was the Quaker, Philip E. Thomas. This pleasant hardware merchant and president of the Merchants' Bank in Baltimore had for a year been the Maryland commissioner in the newly revived Chesapeake and Ohio Canal Company. By the fall of 1826 Thomas was convinced that the proposed canal, since its intended route would be several miles distant from Baltimore, could never materially aid the commercial position of his city. Evan Thomas, a brother of Philip, had recently returned from England, where he had inspected the operations of the newly opened Stockton & Darlington Railroad. By early February 1827 the two Thomas brothers were convincing such friends as William Patterson, shipowner and merchant, Alexander Brown, one of Baltimore's best-known mercantile figures, and George Brown, the banker son of Alexander, that the commercial future of their city lay in the construction of a railroad. They at once approached the Maryland legislature, and received a charter to incorporate the Baltimore & Ohio Railroad on February 28, 1827. The 15,000 shares of capital stock available for individual subscription were quickly oversubscribed during March, and the company was formally organized on April 24, 1827. Philip E. Thomas was made president, George Brown became treasurer, and the board of directors included such men as Alexander Brown, William Patterson, and Charles Carroll.

The B. & O. soon employed prominent engineers such as Jonathan Knight, Colonel Stephen H. Long, and Major George W.

Whistler to survey and plan the new route to the West. Knight, a self-taught civil engineer and former federal commissioner for the extension of the National Road, was appointed chief engineer of the B. & O. in 1829, a position he held until 1842. Both Long and Whistler were U.S. Army engineers. Late in 1828 the company sent Knight and Whistler to England to make a careful study of the two railroads already in operation; the Stockton & Darlington, and the Liverpool and Manchester. The engineers returned with many ideas concerning both construction standards and the most effective motive power. Knight and Whistler preferred heavy solid construction, including masonry bridges and stone foundations under the track. Colonel Long, on the other hand, favored lighter more economical construction, and wooden rather than stone bridges. The B. & O. started out using iron rail on wooden sleepers or ties placed on stone or granite sills, but with the passage of a few years increasingly shifted to iron rail on wooden ties without benefit of a stone foundation. All of the engineers agreed that they should use the English standard track gauge: 4 feet 8½ inches.

Track was laid west of Baltimore starting in October 1829, and by late May 1830 the thirteen miles to Ellicott's Mills were opened for the transportation of passengers and freight. The directors had never seriously considered any other motive power for their early operation than horse power. Horses were certainly adequate for this early local service, especially since Ross Winans had invented his easily drawn "rail wagon." Winans was a New Jersey horse trader who had come to town to sell horses to the B. & O. He never returned home, but stayed on in the city to become a practical mechanical engineer for the railroad, designing and making innumerable improvements in railroad rolling stock and motive power during the next thirty years. Ross Winans assisted Peter Cooper, glue-maker and part-time inventor from New York City, when that gentleman brought his small experimental locomotive, the *Tom Thumb* down to Baltimore. Cooper was interested in the B. & O. because he had some money invested in Baltimore real estate, and he did not wish to see the railroad fail simply because of inadequate motive power. The little locomotive lost its famous race with a little gray horse during a return run from Ellicott's Mills in the summer of 1830, but the engine's speed and general practicability convinced president Thomas and his fellow officials that the B. & O. should turn to steam. Early in 1831 they announced a competition for an American-built coal-burning locomotive suitable for use on their line. There were few entries in the competition, but the railroad did purchase from Phineas Davis, a Pennsylvania watchmaker, a three-and-a-half-ton locomotive which he had hauled down to Baltimore in an ox-cart. The new locomotive, the *York,* named for the watchmaker's home town, easily performed beyond the required specifications. It pulled fifty-ton loads, negotiated the line's sharpest curves, and reached the unheard of speed of thirty miles an hour.

On December 1, 1831, the line was opened to Frederick, sixty-one miles west of Baltimore. The special excursion train that day was filled with "VIP's," the very first car—the fine new coach *Frederick* built by the capable mechanic Richard Imlay —being occupied by high railway officials and the mayor of Baltimore. Next came a flat car to which was firmly attached the Governor's barouche, and in which sat the smiling Governor of Maryland. Possibly this was the first instance of railroad "piggyback" service on American railroads. In any event, some eighteen months later *Niles' Weekly Register* reported that a machine had been erected at Frederick which could lift loaded wagons (weighing more than two tons) onto railroad cars for shipment to Baltimore.

It was during the same spring of 1833 that Andrew Jackson became the first President of the United States to ride a railroad. Accompanied by Louis McLane, his secretary of state, and Lewis Cass, his secretary of war, the President and his party took a B. & O. train, pulled by a locomotive, from Ellicott's Mills into Baltimore on June 6, 1833. Later that same year, on November 8, a former President of the United States, John Quincy Adams, escaped unharmed when a broken axle on a

Camden & Amboy passenger car caused an accident which killed and injured several of his fellow passengers.

By April 1832 the Baltimore & Ohio tracks had been completed to Point of Rocks, on the Potomac, 69 miles from Baltimore, where steamboat connections were possible with Harper's Ferry, 12 miles upstream. Downstream one could take a packet boat on the Chesapeake and Ohio Canal to Washington City. At Point of Rocks the Potomac was contained and hemmed in by tall rugged hills on both banks. This was especially true of the Maryland side where the B. & O. end of track came up against the abruptly rising granite base of Catoctin Mountain. The bench of land between the base of the mountain and the water's edge was hardly sufficient for a wagon road, let alone a sixty-foot canal and a railroad roadbed. Boasting of a prior claim in the region, the Chesapeake and Ohio Canal Company had months before obtained in Frederick an injunction denying the B. & O. any track-laying privileges west of Point of Rocks. President Thomas had his lawyers take the railroad's case to court, but after long litigation the Court of Appeals at Annapolis found in favor of the canal company. The B. & O. next appealed to the Maryland legislature for relief. Here the chances for success were better, since public opinion in the state and in Baltimore, now a city of over 80,000 people, favored the railroad. A compromise was reached which permitted the railroad to share the limited Potomac bank with the canal.

The B. & O. completed its line to Harper's Ferry late in 1834, entering the little hill-set Virginia city over a new combined railroad-highway bridge which curved 900 feet across the Potomac. In the next decade and a half the B. & O. would slowly push construction through and over the hills and mountains in back of Harper's Ferry. The mountains proved too high for the canal, which was only built halfway up the slope, finally stopping at Cumberland in 1850.

In the fall of 1836 Philip E. Thomas retired from the presidency of the Baltimore & Ohio to be succeeded shortly by Louis McLane, a lawyer and diplomat who had held two cabinet posts under Andrew Jackson. During the Thomas regime the B. & O. had completed the 81-mile line to Harper's Ferry, where it connected with the Winchester and Potomac, a 32-mile line serving the lower valley of Virginia. In the late summer of 1835 the company also opened a 37-mile branch line to Washington, where a new depot was being built just below Capitol hill. A good passenger business on the line seemed assured since the railroad replaced a number of stage lines which daily carried an average of 200 passengers between Baltimore and Washington. When Thomas retired, the B. & O. had annual gross revenues of more than $260,000, and listed on its equipment roster 7 locomotives, 44 passenger cars, and 1078 freight or "burthen" cars. While admittedly the B. & O. had not reached its western river destination, by the mid-1830's it was the pioneer rail line in America, and a line whose experience and operations were widely viewed and heeded by the dozens of new and smaller roads.

The B. & O. was indeed the pioneer road in America, but by the early 'thirties many rival lines were also planned and building. The *American Railroad Journal* in January 1832 noted that nine different lines were being constructed in seven states. The projected lengths of the roads under construction ranged from 6 to 250 miles. The completed mileage for the entire group of companies was only 135 miles, with the B. & O. the longest road by far. But another twenty railroads were being projected, and soon that number would grow. By mid-decade close to a thousand miles of line was in operation in the nation and the day of the railway promoter had arrived. These were the impressive gentlemen with frock coats, smooth silk top hats, and smoother tongues who brought the good word to city and town, state and county across the broad nation. State legislatures were busy giving papers of incorporation to new rail lines. Rival seaport cities planned rail routes to the interior, and interior towns anticipated commercial success through projected lines to lake, river port, or tributary area. Many unneeded lines were only built on paper, and other half-started roads never achieved a decent scale of operation, but dozens and dozens of railroads were completed. By 1840 only four of the twenty-six states had yet to complete their first mile of track. But more than 90 per cent of the nearly 3000 miles of line lay east of the Appalachians, stretching like a thin broken network from Portsmouth, New Hampshire, down to the Carolinas and Georgia.

Down in Charleston the city fathers were aware that the commerce of their fair city was in decline. Charleston was becoming of secondary importance in foreign trade, and her population had stood still during the 'teens while that of Baltimore had nearly doubled. Hoping to secure the trade of the cotton-growing region of their state and Georgia, the merchants projected a railroad to Hamburg, South Carolina, just across the Savannah River from Augusta, Georgia. Not wishing to close the door on possible new waterways, they obtained in 1828 a charter for the South Carolina Canal and Railroad Company. The new company obtained some modest local stock subscriptions and elected William Aiken president. Aiken and his directors soon employed the twenty-seven-year-old Horatio Allen of Pennsylvania to build their line. As chief engineer for the railroad Allen was young in years but mature in experience—he had served as engineer on the Delaware & Hudson Canal and Railroad Company. There in the summer of 1829 he had experimented with the seven-ton English-built *Stourbridge Lion,* and had found the locomotive too heavy and rigid for use on American track. But Allen was still sold on steam power, and he persuaded his directors to purchase a locomotive for their road.

Allen helped prepare the plans for the *Best Friend of Charleston,* constructed for $4000 in New York City, and the first locomotive built for sale in the United States. The sturdily built four-ton engine arrived in Charleston harbor aboard the steamship *Niagara* in late October 1830. On Christmas Day, 1830, the *Best Friend of Charleston,* pulling a short passenger train, headed out of town over the first six miles of completed line, to become the first scheduled steam-railroad train run in

America. After several months of successful operation the *Best Friend*, on June 17, 1831, suffered an accident when the Negro fireman, annoyed by hissing steam escaping from the pop value, tied down the offending valve. The resulting explosion tossed the engineer into the air, fatally scalded the fireman, and totally demolished the locomotive. In the weeks after the explosion, fearful passengers were slightly reassured when the company coupled between the locomotive and the first passenger car a flatcar upon which six bales of cotton were strapped as a protective barrier. The 136-mile line to Hamburg was finished by October 1833 to become the longest railroad in the world. The versatile Horatio Allen was rewarded for his diligence in building the road by being given the additional title of superintendent of transportation.

John Jervis, associated with Horatio Allen on the Delaware & Hudson Canal and Railroad Company, was the major builder of the first railroad in New York state. This was a seventeen-mile road, the Mohawk and Hudson Railroad, connecting Albany and Schenectady on the Erie Canal. The railroad was proposed by the English-born George William Featherstonhaugh, a wealthy gentleman farmer who lived west of Schenectady. Featherstonhaugh argued that the railroad would allow the canal packet passengers to avoid the tiring day-long forty-mile trip through the numerous locks in the final eastern section of the Erie Canal. The company received a charter from the New York legislature in 1826, selected that Old Patroon, Stephen Van Rensselaer of Albany, as president, and hired Jervis as engineer at an annual salary of $2000 plus expenses. In the summer of 1830 President Van Rensselaer, using a silver spade, broke ground for the line near Schenectady.

Jervis built the road during the next year, and also designed a locomotive to be built by the West Point Foundry. The *DeWitt Clinton*, a 7000-pound locomotive, had a horizontal boiler but lacked—as did all early engines—bell, whistle, headlight, and cab. Lest one think that the locomotive had been impudently named for the builder of the Erie Canal, it should be recalled that early in 1830 DeWitt Clinton had seriously suggested to several fellow New Yorkers the practicability of a railroad to be built from New York City, via Richmond, Augusta, and Mobile to New Orleans! The new engine was shipped by boat up the Hudson in late June 1831 and, after minor adjustments, was ready for its first passenger train run out of Albany on August 9, 1831. Passengers in the three-car train had a jerky unpleasant ride, for engineer Dave Matthews had had too little experience at the throttle, and the coupling chains between the cars had too much slack. Also the hot pitchpine in the firebox soon caused blazing cinders to spew from the stack back upon the passengers sitting in the open stagecoach type of car. Protective umbrellas were soon burned to the ribs, and more than one passenger found holes in his clothing at the end of the journey. The trip out to the end of track took an hour and forty-five minutes, but on the return run, even with two extra coaches added, Dave opened her up, and made the seventeen miles in a reported thirty-eight minutes. Most of the country folk onlookers who crowded the right of way were excited and enthusiastic about the new railroad, as were many rival rail promoters. Within half a year *Niles' Weekly Register* reported that two dozen new railroads were applying for incorporation before the New York legislature.

In Massachusetts the merchants and businessmen of Boston also eventually chose railroads. New textile factories in New England during and after the War of 1812 gave the area an economic boost, but Boston itself was not doing too well. Her population was lagging behind her commercial rivals to the south— New York, Philadelphia, and Baltimore. After 1825 the completed Erie Canal threatened her trade in western Massachusetts, and the turnpikes serving New Haven, Hartford, and Providence seemed to be attracting more and more of the commerce in the central sections of the state. Still, there was no early enthusiasm for railroads. Many seemed to pay heed to the warnings of the Boston *Transcript* that riding the cars would rob "passengers of manliness" and "death of half its terrors."

But canals had not brought prosperity to Boston. All the local canals were short and did not return any substantial dividends to their owners and sponsors. After all they were frozen up four or five months each winter. The merchants of Boston finally noted the success of the short Granite Railway, a two-mile broad gauge tramway built in 1826 in Quincy by Gridley Bryant to help transport granite for the Bunker Hill Monument. Also in May of the following year, 1827, many Bostonians bought tickets to view English locomotives shown at the country's first Railway Exhibition. Finally, in 1829, the merchants of Boston and the textile manufacturers of Lowell petitioned for the incorporation of a railroad from Boston to Lowell. A storm of protest came from turnpike proprietors, wagon freighters, and canal owners. But the promoters of the Boston and Lowell Railroad had a friendly ally in Governor Levi Lincoln, and they also retained one of the great orators of the age, Daniel Webster, to speak in their behalf. Webster in numerous public addresses had a good word to say for railroads in general, and soberly predicted that before many years his listeners could ride on railways that might extend as far as fifty or one hundred miles from Beacon Hill. The twenty-six-mile Boston and Lowell received its charter from the state on June 5, 1830.

During the following year several other Massachusetts lines were chartered, including the 44-mile Boston and Worcester to the west and the Boston and Providence to the south. All three of the roads serving Boston, like spokes on a hub, were in service by 1835. Soon after the 41-mile road to Providence was put in operation, Commodore Cornelius Vanderbilt of New York had his Long Island Sound steamer *Lexington* ready for connecting service between Providence and New York City. It was the same *Lexington* which met a calamitous death by fire, an event in 1840 which was portrayed in a garish lithograph prepared by Nathaniel Currier and entitled: "The Awful Conflagration of the Steamboat Lexington in Long Island Sound by which Melancholy Occurrence Over 100 Persons Perished." Before the catastrophe it was possible to have lunch in Boston, journey by train to Providence, embark at four on the *Lexington,* and arrive in New York the next morning before the opening of the Exchange.

But the most important of the three early lines was the Boston and Worcester, which celebrated its completion to Worcester on July 4, 1835, with four special trains crowded with some 1500 passengers. The president of the road, nephew of the Revolutionary War patriot and editor of the *Boston Daily Advertiser,* Nathan Hale, had for some time been urging that his railroad be built on to the west. Abbot Lawrence, New England textile manufacturer, Josiah Quincy, Jr., president of Harvard, and Edward Everett, Unitarian clergyman and orator, all joined with Hale in promoting the new 150-mile Western Railroad to run from Worcester, via Springfield and Pittsfield, to Albany. The line was chartered in 1833, and Boston men subscribed to most of the contemplated two-million-dollar stock issue.

Private money proved inadequate for the costly construction, and the Commonwealth of Massachusetts had several millions invested in the project before it was completed to Springfield, on the Connecticut River, in 1839. George W. Whistler, formerly of the B. & O., husband of the good lady portrayed in "Whistler's Mother" and builder of the first locomotive with a steam whistle, was chief engineer and superintendent of the line as it was built westward through the rugged Berkshires to the Hudson River and Albany. Freight trains on the new western line often needed one or even two extra "helper" locomotives, more because of the heavy grades than the crush of traffic.

Enthusiasm ran high when the line was completed to Albany in December 1841. Rail officials and prominent Boston businessmen celebrated the event with a three-day round trip junket to Albany just after Christmas. In Albany the notables held a banquet and grand ball. The head table was lit by new whale-oil candles produced that very morning back in New Bedford as the assemblage listened to the wit of Josiah Quincy. Returning home, the Boston delegation brought back with them table salt mined the day before in the deep mines near Syracuse and barrels of Rochester flour, which were used for bread baked for their final banquet in Boston. Unfortunately, the new railroad never gave Boston any substantial part of the Erie freight at Albany. Most of it went down the Hudson to New York. Probably Charles F. Adams, Jr., had been correct when he claimed that the railroad across the Berkshires was built upon "the fallacy that steam could run up hill cheaper than water could run down."

And other Bostonians were no more enchanted with the early railroads of New England. Of a trip on the Boston and Providence in 1835 one traveler wrote:

> This morning . . . I took passage on a railroad car to Providence. . . . Other cars were attached to the locomotive, and uglier boxes I do not wish to travel in . . . made to stow away some thirty human beings, who sit cheek by jowl as best they can. The poor fellows . . . squeezed me into a corner, while the hot sun drew from their garments . . . smells made up of salt fish, tar and molasses. . . . The rich and the poor, the educated and the ignorant, all herded together in this modern improvement in traveling . . . and all this for the sake of doing very uncomfortably in two days what could be done delightfully in eight or ten.

Certainly there was an opposition voiced against most early railroads. Out in Ohio in 1828 a school board gave reluctant approval to a railroad discussion to be held in their schoolhouse with this caution: "If God had designed that His intelligent creatures should travel at the frightful speed of 15 miles an hour by steam, He would have foretold it through His holy prophets. It is a device of Satan to lead immortal souls down to Hell." A persuasive and fluent divine in Connecticut, lecturing on the menace of railways, claimed that the sight of rapidly moving locomotives might drive the viewers insane, and up in Boston it was argued that travelers going at high speed on a railroad would suffer "concussion of the brain." Farmers feared for their livestock, which reminds us of George Stephenson's answer, when asked what would happen if a cow strayed in front of his early English locomotive—"it would be uncommonly awkward for the cow." Locomotives were hard on cows until Isaac Dripps, top mechanic on the Camden and Amboy, invented the first "pilot" or cowcatcher in the early 1830's.

Canal owners, tavern keepers, turnpike and bridge companies, stagecoach lines, and assorted timid citizens all came out in opposition to the new form of transportation. Often the hostility was reinforced by state legislative action. The Utica and Schenectady, by the provisions of its New York charter of 1833, was not permitted to carry any property except the personal baggage of passengers. Only in 1844 was it allowed to handle freight. All this in deference to the Erie Canal, as was the early New York law which forced all rail lines parallel to the Erie to pay tolls equal to those on the waterway. Comparable legislation in Ohio and Pennsylvania was enacted in favor of canals and against rail traffic. Turnpike companies also furiously opposed new railroads, which they described as "cruel turnpike killers." Some new roads, such as the seventy-eight-mile Utica and Schenectady were ever required to buy up the capital stock of a competing turnpike as a prerequisite to their original charter from the state of New York. The opposition finally moved that friend of railroads, Josiah Quincy, to declare: "the believer in railroads was not only to do the work and pay the bills for his shortsighted neighbor, but, as Shakespeare happily phrases it, 'Cringe and sue for leave to do him good.' "

But really not too many Americans felt like Philip Hone, one-time mayor of New York City, who expressed his favor for leisurely ways to his diary: "This world is going too fast . . . Railroads, steamers, packets, race against time and beat it hollow. . . . Oh, for the good old days of heavy post-coaches and speed at the rate of six miles an hour." The great majority had a visionary enthusiasm about railroads. Soon hundreds of lines were being planned, even some in the West. By 1837 Kentucky, Ohio, Indiana, and Illinois had collectively chartered dozens of lines to build hundreds of miles of track. Those with money, like impetuous children, often committed it to rail ventures, even though they had never seen a locomotive or a section of track. Those with but pennies joined the craze by buying wall-paper or glassware decorated with the new steam cars. In the 'thirties the French economist Michel Chevalier, sent by his government to report on the status of internal improvements in America, was not guilty of overstatement when he wrote: "The American has a perfect passion for railroads."

While the iron rail, the flanged wheel, and the steam locomotive did not provide perfect transport, they did answer a number of deficiencies apparent in the turnpike, the canal, and river steamers of the day. Rail freight rates, on average, never were as low as water haulage, but they were several times cheaper than turnpike wagon freight. Canals could never challenge the railway in dependability or regularity of service. Canals were closed with ice four or five months each winter season and also, on occasion, were subject to problems of too much or too little water. An 1831 account in *Niles' Weekly Register* reported that while nearby canals had been closed nearly five months during the previous winter, bad weather had stopped travel on the B. & O. only a single day during the same period.

Shippers certainly welcomed a carrier basically unaffected by seasonal changes and vagaries of the weather. Railroads also could build short lines and sidings right up to a shipper's mill or loading dock, something difficult or impossible for the average waterway. Soon railroads were being planned and built into interior parts of country that had never known the sound of the stagecoach or canal packet horn, or the whistle of a sternwheeler steamboat. Finally the new rail lines could provide both freight and passenger service that was significantly faster than that available by packet boat, the stage coach, or the Conestoga wagon. Well before the Civil War steam railroads were moving freight three or four times as fast as was usual by canal boat or wagon. While the best sidewheeler packets on the Mississippi or Hudson were about as fast as early passenger trains, rail routes were often more direct than the winding river beds, again giving the railroad an advantage.

Many technical advances were made in rail operations and equipment in the generation prior to the Civil War. This was to be expected since the new form of transport was so popular with the traveling and shipping public. A fairly rapid development came in motive power, as the steam locomotive on practically every railroad relegated the horse to reserve status. One of the early major locomotive builders was Matthias Baldwin, a Philadelphia watchmaker-machinist, who built a crowd-charming miniature locomotive in 1830 for the Franklin Peale Museum. Officials of the newly incorporated Philadelphia, Germantown and Norristown Railroad liked the model and ordered a full-sized engine to replace the horses on their six-mile road. Baldwin built *Old Ironsides* during the next year, and the new locomotive was soon put in regular service whenever the weather was good—horses were used for rainy days and for snow. The officials didn't want their brand new engine to get wet! When the company complained of the engine's heavy weight (seven tons instead of a specified five) and tried to pay him $3500 instead of the agreed upon $4000, the disgusted Baldwin turned to a friend and said: "This is our last locomotive." In fact, he never really did anything else, and at the time of his death in 1866 had built 1500 engines. His company, the Baldwin Locomotive Works, was to become the largest producer of locomotives in the world, building nearly 60,000 steam engines by 1950.

Improvements in locomotives came quickly. Baldwin may not have been the first man to use a bell on a locomotive, but he can be credited as the first builder to so equip a new locomotive. The first whistle was added to the *Susquehanna,* a locomotive built in Lowell, Massachusetts, in 1836 by George Whistler for the Wilmington & Susquehanna Railroad. Down in South Carolina, Horatio Allen was probably the first to equip trains for night travel when he had a fire of pine knots bedded in sand on a small car in front of a Charleston and Hamburg engine. An improved light was soon being built by that mechanical genius up in New Jersey, Isaac Dripps. The bell, whistle, headlight, and even Isaac Dripps's cowcatcher, as warning and protective devices, were all rather essential for early American railroads since the lines were so commonly built through great open spaces without benefit of fencing. A plague of grasshoppers in Pennsylvania in 1836 almost brought trains to a halt in the area, until a sandbox was added to locomotives to provide greater wheel traction. And up in Massachusetts the incidence of frostbite among the engine men facing New England's bitter winter weather soon made crude wood and canvas cabs appear on the rear of locomotives.

By the 'fifties the most common style of engine was the eight-wheeled American-type locomotive, with a swiveled "bogie" truck under the stack and four larger drive wheels under the fire box and cab. John B. Jervis, with some help from Horatio Allen, had designed the bogie truck back in the 'thirties. The prototype American locomotive had been designed and built in 1836–37 by Henry R. Campbell, chief engineer of the Philadelphia, Germantown and Norristown, and James Brooks of Philadelphia. From 1850 on, first-class American-type locomotives were available from a number of builders for $8000 to $10,000. They came equipped with a name rather than a number, boasted a large balloon stack and a painted headlight, used wood or possibly coal for fuel, and cost well under a dollar a mile to operate. Needless to say such an engine was the pride and joy of the men assigned to it, and the engineer and fireman took care in keeping spotless the headlight, whistle, bell, and other brasswork gleaming.

In the generation before the Civil War, railroad travel was not too comfortable but the novelty of rail travel was for most Americans sufficient to make up for some inconvenience. It was the rare trip that escaped delays—waits for belated passengers or connecting trains, perhaps while a horseman went on ahead to locate the tardy cars. Other delays occurred because of a de-railed car, or too steep a grade, or an empty tender which forced not too eager passengers to commandeer a nearby rail fence for an auxiliary fuel supply. But early trains could show some speed. When Davy Crockett wished to test the speed of his train, by spitting out of an open window, he discovered that he "overtook it so quick, that it hit me smack in the face." Many of the first passenger cars had no heat, but urchins along the way often earned small change by selling passengers hot stones or bricks for foot warmers.

Fanny Kemble, the English actress who toured America in the early railroad years, described her passenger car as looking "like a long greenhouse on wheels." She was not much impressed, either with her accommodations or with her traveling companions. Nor was Charles Dickens enthusiastic over a trip made a few years later. In his *American Notes* he wrote:

> There are no first or second-class carriages, as with us, but there is a gentlemen's car and a ladies' car; the main distinction between which is that in the first, everybody smokes; and in the second nobody does. . . . On, on, on, . . . tears the mad dragon of an engine with its train of cars; scattering in all directions a shower of burning sparks from its wood fire; screeching, hissing, yelling, panting, until at last the thirsty monster stops beneath a covered way to drink, the people cluster around, and you have time to breathe again.

Dickens's "thirsty monster" could be dangerous, for accidents were quite frequent. Cars could derail, axles did break, and trouble sometimes came from poor coupling of the cars or excessive slack between them. Faulty rail caused many accidents. Often the spikes holding down the iron strap rails would work loose under the weight of passing trains to form "snakeheads." A twenty-foot snakehead could easily derail an engine, or if it broke through the floor of a passenger coach it would create almost unbelievable havoc and injury. No real solution to this problem appeared until Robert L. Stevens, engineer and president of the Camden and Amboy line, designed his heavier solid iron T-rail while on a locomotive buying trip in England. It was on a Camden and Amboy train that Cornelius Vanderbilt, owner of the steamer *Lexington* and many other New York boats, had a serious accident in the early 'thirties. The smash-up had broken several of the Commodore's ribs, and may help explain his long-time distrust of "them things that go on land," his name for railroads.

But in spite of accidents, passenger travel in the generation before the Civil War was much more important in producing railroad revenue than it has been in the twentieth century. Some early lines, such as the Utica and Schenectady, were almost exclusively passenger roads. In its first years the B. & O. obtained 40 per cent of its revenue from passengers. In the 'forties and 'fifties passenger traffic across the nation probably produced nearly a third of the total rail revenue. By mid-century, passenger fares in New England and the Middle Atlantic states were close to three cents a mile, and probably a cent or more higher in the rest of the country. Mail was increasingly carried by rail after the 1834 contract, when Postmaster General William T. Barry agreed to have several lines jointly carry the "Great Eastern Mail." Within a decade a pioneer railway-express business was undertaken when two Yankees, William F. Harnden and Alvin Adams, rented space in baggage cars for their parcel delivery service. By the eve of the Civil War the rail passenger could buy a coupon ticket good for a trip from New Orleans to Bangor, Maine, check his trunk for the entire trip, and check the performance of his train against the recently available railroad schedule books.

Railroad mileage in the nation had grown by 1850 to 9021 miles. Every state east of the Mississippi could point to at least a few miles of track, but the great bulk of the mileage was still east of the mountains. Nearly 60 per cent of the total in fact was located in the Middle Atlantic states and New England. The only states claiming over a thousand miles of road were New York, Pennsylvania, and Massachusetts. New England had a fairly complete rail network by mid-century, and some Yankees were even complaining that their region was overbuilt. The early maturity of rail development in the area probably helps explain the claim that New England led the nation in the original training of many railroad leaders.

During the 'fifties four major eastern railroads completed their lines across the mountains to the Ohio River or Lake Erie. The first of the four to cross the mountains was the New York and Erie Railroad. The man who first dreamed of a railroad to cross New York state from the Hudson River to Lake Erie was William C. Redfield, a Connecticut-born saddle maker with a great interest in meteorology and railroads. Two New York businessmen, Henry L. Pierson and Eleazor Lord, agreed with Redfield that a road through the so-called Southern Tier of counties in the state of New York would be a fine thing. Pierson and his young bride had been a honeymoon couple riding the cars behind the *Best Friend of Charleston* on its initial trip on Christmas Day, 1830, and he had been enthusiastic about railroads ever since. Shortly after the New York legislature gave a charter to the New York and Erie Railroad, the company organized with Eleazor Lord as the first president. Lord was to be president of the Erie three different times, 1833–35, 1839–41, and 1844–45. President Lord had some very decided opinions about how a first-class road should be built. For one thing he insisted on a broad 6-foot gauge when nearly all the lines in New England and the mid-Atlantic states were built to a standard 4 feet 8½ inches. Lord argued that with the broad gauge the Erie could prevent any connecting lines from stealing any trade from New York City. This was a preposterous notion, but the Erie clung to its off-brand gauge until 1878. Lord also had a fetish about building his road on piling, claiming that such construction would be impervious to floods, frost, and snow drifts. For months Lord had eight noisy Crane's Patent Pile Driving Machines (each with a crew of thirteen men) pounding white oak piling into miles and miles of proposed roadway. Lord had his way on gauge, but his pile-driving scheme was a total waste, since no permanent line was ever so constructed.

In the 'thirties and early 'forties the Erie had its troubles.
Many of the major Erie stock subscribers were ruined by a dis-
astrous fire in New York City, the Panic of 1837 further slowed
progress, and eventually the road was sold under foreclosure.
On one occasion an irate Goshen farmer, Adrian Holbert by
name, built a fence across the rails and stretched himself out on
the broad-gauge ties in front of a train to force company payment of money owed him for ties, piling, and right-of-way acres.
Finally, in 1845 a new president, Benjamin Loder, a forceful
and wealthy dry-goods dealer from New York City, put the
road on its feet. For the next six years Loder relentlessly pushed
his tough contractors to build more and more miles of road
across the state. Thousands of Irish workers, driven from their
homeland by the great potato blight of 1845, built the line. The
Irish fought with their own countrymen, the rival German work
crews, and the nearby canalers but they laid track. They dug
and blasted a road bed out of the rocky cliffs of the Delaware
River bank near Port Jervis, and occasionally their powder
blasts threw rocks down on the coal canal boats on the Delaware & Hudson Canal. The Irish stripped the fruit from nearby
orchards, stole chickens, and rioted in their drunkenness, but
they built mile after mile of line. When the road was finished in
the spring of 1851, the 483-mile route from Piermont-on-Hud-
son to Dunkirk-on-Lake Erie was the longest railroad in the
world. It had cost $23,500,000, several times earlier estimates,
but the pride of New Yorkers in the road's magnitude was such
that on June 13, 1851, the Board of New York City Aldermen
saluted the directors of the Erie with the resolution: "That we
hail the Completion of this gigantic and stupendous work as em-
phatically THE WORK OF THE AGE . . . "

Ben Loder insisted upon a celebration to match the length of
the Erie. A two-day excursion to Dunkirk was planned, and so
many governmental, civic, and railroad dignitaries accepted invitations that two trains were required. President Millard Fillmore, his secretary of state, Daniel Webster, three other cabinet
members, and assorted governors, senators, mayors, and rail-

road directors all crowded the cars, and the local press claimed that as many as six presidential candidates were on board. The aging Daniel Webster insisted on having a seat where he would miss none of the scenery, and obliging company officials placed him in a heavy rocking chair securely fastened to a special flat car at the end of the second train. Protected by a buggy robe Daniel had a bottle of Medford rum for company between frequent stops for speech making. The party stopped to view the Starrucca Viaduct with its eighteen graceful stone arches, was greeted by sixteen whistling locomotives at Susquehanna, and finally pulled in for an overnight stop at Elmira, where a seven-hour banquet and public levee left guests and the local populace exhausted and groggy.

The excursion party reached Dunkirk on Lake Erie at four the next afternoon, and the two trains, now coupled together, rolled to a stop just past a pedestal upon which was placed the plow that had been used for the first ground breaking more than a dozen years before. The crowds ate from a 300-foot table set up along Railroad Avenue, and which held, according to the official program:

> Chowder, a yoke of oxen barbecued whole, ten sheep roasted whole, beef à la mode, boiled ham, corned beef, buffalo tongues, bologna sausage, beef tongues (smoked and pickled), one hundred roast fowls, coffee, etc.

Pork and beans in 50-gallon tin vessels, barrels of cider, and giant loaves of bread ten feet long by two feet wide completed the feast. Daniel Webster observed to Attorney General John J. Crittenden that the clam chowder would have been improved with a more generous dash of sherry and port.

One of the officials on board the special excursion train was the new general superintendent, the portly and efficient Charles Minot, a Yankee hired away from the Boston & Maine Railroad by President Loder. Minot, in his first months with the Erie had persuaded Ezra Cornell, a New York telegraph promoter, to string telegraph wires along the length of the Erie. On the first day of the excursion trip, when one of the engines failed, Minot used the new facility to wire ahead for a reserve locomotive. Later that summer Minot used the telegraph for train dispatching when the passenger train he was riding was delayed at Turner's Station, New York. When the engineer of Minot's train refused to run his engine by telegraphic order, the general superintendent relegated the engineer to the rear of the train, mounted the cab, and piloted the locomotive into Port Jervis, where they met the opposing train. Within a short time the practice of telegraphic train control was adopted by most American railroads.

A second rail line across New York had given a through service of sorts from Albany to Lake Erie since the early 'forties. The line consisted of the Mohawk and Hudson, opened in 1831, the Utica and Schenectady, opened in 1836, and several other roads built later on west to Buffalo. By 1850 the ten short connecting lines, arranged from city to city like beads on a string, advertised fourteen-hour service between Albany and Buffalo; often the connections were so imperfect, however, that the 290-mile trip might take twice the announced time, or even longer.

By late summer 1853, under the leadership of Erastus Corning, president of the Utica and Schenectady, the ten independent roads were merged into a new company, the New York Central Railroad. Corning, nail maker and Albany mayor, had never received any salary during his twenty years as president of the Utica and Schenectady, being well satisfied with an arrangement whereby he supplied most of the rails, steel, and iron products needed by the road. Corning was the first president of the New York Central, but the cozy procurement arrangements that had been so profitable on the Utica line were not long permitted him on the New York Central. It was really too big a railroad for that sort of thing. The new line could boast of 542 miles of road, including main line and branches, 150 wood burning locomotives, some 300 passenger cars (first-class, second-class, mail, and baggage) and over 1700 assorted freight cars.

The new through line was prosperous and paid good dividends, even after the Panic of 1857.

Two other railroads finished their original planned routes to the West, both reaching the upper Ohio River late in 1852. The B. & O. finally reached the Ohio River not quite twenty-five years after Charles Carroll's early efforts as a cornerstone layer. In 1848 Thomas Swann had replaced McLane as president of the road, and he pushed construction through and over the mountains. By 1851 a force of some 5000 men and 1250 horses was building the road's last lap to Wheeling. Monthly payrolls exceeded $200,000, but the bankers and merchants of Baltimore assured themselves that the prize was worth the price. Tunnels, bridges, cuts, and fills smoothed the iron way through the final hills, and on Christmas Eve, 1852, the last spike was driven at Roseby's Rock, some eighteen miles east of Wheeling. The B. & O. was finished. Iron rails, 379 miles in length, at last connected Baltimore and the Ohio River. The first through train entered Wheeling on January 1, 1853. Passenger service between Chesapeake Bay and the Ohio was now available; a trip that earlier had taken several days by stagecoach on the National Road could now be made in 16 hours.

The last of the four trans-Allegheny roads was the Pennsylvania Railroad. In the 'forties Philadelphia had been lagging behind its rival seaport cities to the north and south. At the beginning of the Mexican War freight was crossing Pennsylvania via a clumsy and inefficient combination of canals, short rail lines, and inclined planes. The whole process was so costly that Pittsburgh sometimes sent goods to New York City by riverboat down the Ohio and Mississippi to New Orleans. There was increasing public pressure for an all rail route across the mountains, especially after the B. & O. offered to build a branch up to Pittsburgh. In April 1846 the Pennsylvania Railroad was incorporated by several businessmen of Philadelphia, with Samuel V. Merrick as the first president. Merrick at once employed J. Edgar Thomson, a well-trained civil engineer of old Quaker stock, to be chief engineer. Thomson had worked on the Camden and Amboy Railroad, and had just spent fifteen years as the very effective chief engineer of the Georgia Railroad. Thomson could be abrupt and even rude at times, but he did know railroading. Experts had said a rail line over the Alleghenies could never be built, but Thomson, after a rather quick survey, built practical grades including tunnels and the famous Horseshoe Curve. By 1849 he was made general superintendent, and in February 1851 was elected president, a position he held until 1874. Thomson completed a through rail line from Philadelphia to Pittsburgh on December 10, 1852. Several inclined planes were in use for two years on the route, but by 1855 the entire trip was being made with locomotive-drawn trains.

Like all the other east-west trunk lines north of the Potomac and Ohio, the Pennsylvania was interested in western connections on toward Chicago and the Mississippi River. Even before Thomson had seen the completion of his main line to Pittsburgh, he was urging upon his board of directors a program of financial aid for railroads in Ohio and Indiana. Three roads connecting Pittsburgh with Chicago, via Mansfield, Ohio, and Fort Wayne, Indiana, were built in the 'fifties, with the Pennsylvania investing $600,000 in the capital stock of the western lines. The three western roads were merged into the Pittsburgh, Fort Wayne & Chicago Railroad in May 1856, and the through line into Chicago was finished on Christmas Day, 1858. The management of the Pennsylvania decided they should have a closer look at their new western connection, and accordingly planned a two-week inspection tour or excursion for early October 1859. President Thomson did not make the trip, but ten of the thirteen directors did, headed by vice-president William B. Foster. Wives, children, and guests accompanied many of the directors, and the party roster eventually reached a total of forty-seven. Foster, formerly an engineer associate of Thomson's, had the president's daughter, Ada Thomson, and Harriet Buchanan as his guests. The 2180 mile excursion started in Philadelphia on October 3, 1859, with overnight stops at Altoona, Pittsburgh, Fort Wayne, Chicago, St. Louis, Cincinnati, Wheeling, Cumberland, and Baltimore. The arrival home in Philadelphia was delayed a day, when the party's B. & O. train was detained in Virginia as John Brown was making his famous raid on Harper's Ferry.

The Pennsylvania directors, once they had rested up from their seventeen-day junket, were able to report to J. Edgar Thomson upon the resources and trade prospects in the western states, a region which might furnish business for their road. It was by and large a thriving, booming region only temporarily slowed by the Panic of 1857. In the 'fifties the Midwest and the railroads had grown up together. By the Civil War the American enchantment with railroads had created a network which went far beyond anything made available by earlier forms of internal improvement. The eastern half of the nation was fairly well served, and the western fingers of the iron network were not far from the frontier line in Wisconsin, Iowa, Missouri, Arkansas, and Texas. As the guns of war sounded in 1861 most Americans already knew the sound of a locomotive whistle.

2

The Iron Pony
on the Prairies

The dozen years between the Mexican War and the firing on Fort Sumter represented a period of dynamic growth for American railroads. A broken skein of short railroads stretched from Georgia to Maine in 1850. West of the Allegheny Mountains only a few stray rail lines partially connected the Ohio River with the Great Lakes. The prairie region of the Mississippi Valley lay as yet untouched. West of the Missouri River the Great Plains, or the "Great American Desert," seemed so desolate and distant that a decade later both Horace Greeley and Abraham Lincoln were to predict that it might require a century to settle this last frontier.

These prophets were to be proven quite wrong as the railroad reached the prairies of mid-America. In 1850 the frontier line was well west of the western fingers of the rail network. By the end of the Civil War the western edge of the rail system had nearly reached the frontier in Texas, Arkansas, Missouri, Iowa, and Wisconsin. In the generation after the Civil War as competing rail lines raced to the Pacific they pulled millions of Americans into the western territories at a rate that would have astounded both Greeley and Lincoln. As iron rail reached the lake port of Chicago, the frontier state of Wisconsin, and the Mississippi River in the decade of the 'fifties, America caught a preview of the role the railroad was to play on its prairies.

The wind off the lake was chill, but the workmen and townspeople experienced a heartwarming pride as they watched the puffing black locomotive on the raw new tracks of the Galena and Chicago Union Railroad. The *Pioneer,* a third-hand engine purchased from the Michigan Central, weighed only ten tons and boasted but a single pair of driving wheels. But to the citizens of Chicago it held high promise. The busy lake port was getting a railroad. On that cool October day in 1848 a dream was coming true for William Butler Ogden, well-to-do real estate man and first mayor of the city.

Most of Ogden's fellow businessmen had believed that Chicago's bustling growth and prosperity were firmly based on lake shipping and the network of plank roads reaching out of the city to the north, west, and south. Two hundred wagons a day reached the city, and the civic leaders saw little need to help sponsor Ogden's dream rail line. They had even refused Ogden the right to build a depot within the city limits. Deprived of urban backing, Ogden had taken his dream to the farmers whose homes were scattered along the plank roads of the flatlands to the west. The farmers liked Ogden's plan, and with their small savings helped to fill his stock subscription books.

The line was eventually built, and when the first carloads of wheat started to arrive from the western prairies the city fathers quickly granted Ogden his depot. By 1850 the line was 43 miles long and grossing $1000 a week. Ogden had his new depot with a cupola from which, with the benefit of a marine telescope, he spotted arriving trains for the passengers in the waiting room below. In little more than a decade Ogden's much expanded system was known as the Chicago & North Western. Chicago, served by eleven different lines, had become a major western rail center. Within a lifetime Chicago was *the* rail center of the nation, with more than a score of trunk lines converging from all directions on half a dozen giant railroad stations.

Further north, up in Wisconsin, the decade of the 'fifties saw other farmers help in the financing of railroad construction. Finding local capital inadequate and Congress slow with land grants, the Milwaukee and Mississippi Railroad turned to the farmers of Wisconsin for help. Byron Kilbourn, president of the road and mayor of Milwaukee, had first favored plank roads and canals to bring prosperity to his city, but by 1849 he viewed the railroad as the transport of the future. Kilbourn hoped that Milwaukee could outstrip Chicago and push a railroad to the Mississippi before its southern rival. His dream was graphically portrayed by a chart that long hung on his office wall, a map showing Milwaukee's future rail connections with St. Louis, Dubuque, La Crosse, St. Paul, and the western regions beyond.

Cash was needed for this dream to become a reality. The early grading of the road in 1849 was partially paid for in kind, with harness, carts, oats, beef, timber, and labor—but if iron rails were to be placed on the grade of the Milwaukee and Mississippi hard money was required. In the spring of 1850 a meeting of the sponsors of the road was called to discuss the financial crisis. Little new was suggested until a farmer, Joseph Goodrich, from Milton (60 miles west of Milwaukee) rose from his chair and said, "See here; I can mortgage my farm for $3000, and go East, where I came from, to get money for it." The idea was appealing, especially since the directors felt they could find 100 farmers on the line of the road who might do likewise.

An ingenious scheme was worked out in which the farmers along the intended right of way were invited to buy stock paying 10 per cent dividends, in exchange for their personal notes, secured by mortgages on their farms, payable in ten years, and bearing but 8 per cent interest. The railroad promised to pay the interest from the dividends, with the remaining 2 per cent to accumulate and cover one-fifth of the principal debt. Naturally the railroad planned to dispose of the mortgages back East to obtain cash and credit. In the prosperous early 'fifties the plan looked foolproof to the Wisconsin farmer, who figured that in ten years both the railroad stock and his farm would appreciate in value. The chance to get railroad stock for practically nothing was so appealing that soon hundreds of farmers were buying not only the stock of the Milwaukee and Mississippi but of many other lines that created comparable farm mortgage stock purchase plans. Between 1850 and 1857 nearly 6000 Wisconsin farmers subscribed to $5,000,000 of railroad stock.

With its $900,000 of new farm mortgage credit Kilbourn's line bought its rail, and soon had a railroad in operation. Early in 1851 the first twenty miles out of Milwaukee were finished, and on Tuesday, February 25, 1851, the first formal trip was made out to the end of track at Waukesha. Round trip tickets at $1.50 included not only the music of the Hess band, which accompanied the train, but also a free dinner in the company's new car house at Waukesha. The line was extended to Madison by May 1854 and to Prairie du Chien on the Mississippi by April 1857. Kilbourn's dream was beginning to come true.

But the dreams of the 6000 farmers of financial security and profit were soon to turn sour. With the Panic of 1857 every railroad in the state was near bankruptcy, and the stock purchased so hopefully was soon nearly worthless. Extravagance, mismanagement, and often outright fraud compounded the rail failures. When the railroads failed to pay their bond interest the eastern holders of the farm mortgages started to seek foreclosures on the farms of Wisconsin. The anger of the farmers was the greater where altered rail routes or fraud resulted in the total absence of an operating rail line in their community. The anti-railroad attitude of much of rural Wisconsin was deepened when it was revealed in 1858 that Byron Kilbourn two years before had been guilty of wholesale bribery in obtaining a state land grant for his La Crosse and Milwaukee Railroad. More than $800,000 of railroad bonds had been delivered to the greedy state officials in Madison, with $50,000 going to Governor Coles Bashford, $175,000 going to thirteen state senators, $335,000 more going to fifty-nine assemblymen. During the next decade the railroad issue was a very active one in Wisconsin politics. The farm mortgage question plus the land grant scandal formed a solid base upon which the Granger movement of the 1870's was to be built in the state.

A happier occasion took place in the spring of 1856, when the people of Iowa gained their first complete rail connection with the East. On April 22 the people of Davenport, Iowa, and Rock Island, Illinois, cheered vigorously as three locomotives pulled eight passenger cars across the Mississippi on the newly completed bridge of the Chicago and Rock Island Rail Road. Three years of planning and hard work had gone into the six huge spans constructed out of a million feet of timber and more than 600,000 pounds of cast and wrought iron. There were a few who wished to scoff and ridicule the achievement—the stage drivers, the river men, and those who favored the steamboat interests— but most of the crowds on the river banks were enthusiastic in their praise of the new service. A citizen of Iowa could now reach New York City by rail in no more than forty-two hours. Perhaps the proudest man in the throng was the impressive and clean-shaven Henry Farnam, president and builder of the Rock Island.

Farnam had reason to be proud. This self-taught surveyor from New York and Connecticut had with his partner, Joseph E. Sheffield, finished the Chicago and Rock Island a year and a half earlier than the time specified in the contract. When the 181-mile line from Chicago had been formally opened two years earlier, in June 1854, the cost of less than $4,500,000 had included 28 locomotives, 28 passenger cars, and some 350 assorted freight cars.

Business soon was booming in Rock Island, and in Davenport across the Mississippi. J. M. D. Burrows, early produce merchant of Davenport, in recalling the new rail service wrote:

> When the railroad got in operation, produce men were as thick as potato bugs. If a man could raise two hundred and fifty dollars he could begin business. That amount would buy a carload of wheat. In the morning he would engage a car, have it put where he could load it, and have the farmer put his wheat in the car. By three o'clock in the afternoon the car would be loaded and shipped.

Things had moved more slowly over in Iowa. Farnam had promised that the subsidiary line west of Davenport, the Mississippi and Missouri Railroad, would quickly be built to Muscatine and to Iowa City, the capital of the state. Even with the financial support of the easterners John A. Dix and Thomas C. Durant, the rate of construction was exasperatingly slow. Fearing that perhaps the main line was planned for the rival town of Muscatine, the citizens of Iowa City made Farnam an offer: "Get your railroad into our city, put a train into our depot on or before midnight of December 31, this year (1855), and you get a $50,000 cash bonus."

Rails had been laid out to Wilton, 23 miles west of Davenport, by midsummer 1855, and Muscatine was reached before Thanksgiving. But the 55-mile line to Iowa City went slower. December came with colder weather and the closest rails were still miles away from the capital. On December 31 it was thirty below zero and the railhead a thousand feet distant. The exhausted workers desperately laid ties and rails on the frozen earth, and by midnight a track of sorts lay in front of the new wooden depot. It was so cold that the locomotive had frozen up, but pinch bars and the tired muscles of the spent track gang pushed the engine into town just as the church bells marked the passing of the old year. Farnam and his tired crews had earned the cash bonus.

Now it was the spring of 1856, and Iowa had its rail connection with the East across the new Mississippi bridge. Two weeks after the opening of the bridge a new steamboat belonging to the New Orleans & Louisville Packet Company, the *Effie Afton*, made her first trip north of St. Louis. After passing the bridge, her wheels stopped, and as she swung against a central bridge pier a stove was upset on the boat. The fire on the boat quickly spread to the bridge, but the efforts of the volunteer firemen of the river towns saved everything but the central bridge span.

The owners of the *Effie Afton* refused to pay damages for the "accident" and, claiming the bridge to be a menace to navigation, brought suit against the Rock Island Railroad. Upon the advice of Norman Judd, the railroad's attorney, Henry Farnam engaged a well-known Springfield trial lawyer to help with the case. Abraham Lincoln went to Rock Island, conversed with a twelve-year-old boy about river currents, and studied a report on that section of the river earlier made by Robert E. Lee. In presenting his case before the trial judge in Chicago, the lanky Springfield lawyer argued that "people have as much right to travel east and west as north and south." The case crept through the courts and was finally appealed to the United States Supreme Court, which held in favor of the railroad. Iowa thus retained its rail connection with the East. Shortly thereafter the Rock Island, in recognition of its own western ambition, changed its name and became the Chicago, Rock Island & Pacific.

In the decade before the Civil War many Americans were dreaming about and planning for an iron trail to the Pacific. Back in 1845 Asa Whitney, world traveler and New York City merchant, had unsuccessfully argued before Congress that a railroad should be built to the western coast. Now in the 'fifties the recent acquisition of California and the Mexican cession, the discovery of gold, and the pleasant prosperity that followed, all pointed to a new and lively interest in a Pacific railroad. Western frontier cities from the Gulf to the Great Lakes all sought the honor of being the eastern terminus of the projected line. The city fathers, merchants, and realtors of Milwaukee, Chicago, St. Louis, Memphis, Vicksburg, and New Orleans all sponsored their favorite cities.

The popularity of the Pacific railroad resulted in Congressional legislation in the spring of 1853 which provided $150,000 to be spent by the secretary of war, Jefferson Davis, in surveying possible routes to the Pacific. Wagon trains led by West Point-trained army engineers and carrying surveying instruments and equipment soon headed west. In the two years 1853–55 they exhaustively surveyed five major routes: (1) St. Paul to Vancouver; (2) Council Bluffs, Iowa, to San Francisco; (3) Westport, Missouri, to San Francisco; (4) Fort Smith, Arkansas, to San Pedro; and (5) New Orleans to San Pedro. The third route soon was considered by all to be impracticable because of the high mountains of Colorado. The announced practicality of the other four has since been proven, for today the Northern Pacific, the Union Pacific, the Santa Fe, and the Southern Pacific in general follow the several surveyed routes.

During the same years railroad building in the region east of Chicago was a scene of action and accomplishment rather than mere planning. In Ohio, Indiana, and Michigan railroad construction proceeded at a hectic pace as nearly 4800 miles of new road were completed during the 'fifties. Beginnings had been made even before 1850. In 1848 a railroad connection across Ohio had been finished from Sandusky on Lake Erie to Cincinnati on the Ohio River, with the completion of the Mad River and Lake Erie. The next year the Michigan Central was opened from Detroit to New Buffalo, giving direct rail service between Detroit and Lake Michigan. The Michigan Central was built on into Chicago by May 1852 by a trio of eastern Yankees—John Murray Forbes, John W. Brooks, and James F. Joy. The three rail officials had just won a "railroad war" with a number of local Michigan farmers who had objected to being paid only half the value of livestock killed earlier by Michigan Central locomotives. The farmers retaliated by firing buckshot at passing trains, greasing rails, tampering with switches, and finally burning a railroad depot. A legal battle ensued and several farmers received jail sentences, even though they were defended by an imported lawyer, William H. Seward of New York. Another Michigan line, the Michigan Southern, also was giving service to Chicago by 1852.

South of Michigan railroads were being constructed so rapidly that the Buckeye State by the eve of the Civil War had more rail mileage than any other state. The 2946 miles in 1860 formed a network that covered most of Ohio, and only a few residents, in the southern counties, lived more than 25 miles from a railroad depot. Cleveland, Toledo, and Cincinnati each were terminals from which several lines radiated. Unlike her sister states north of the Ohio River, where standard gauge track was normal, the Buckeye State built the great majority of her railways in an off-brand gauge of 4 feet 10 inches.

Like the Pennsylvania, with its western connection to Fort Wayne and Chicago, the B. & O. soon was planning a western line across the state. Down river from Wheeling the B. & O. built a second line, the Northwestern Railroad of Virginia, from Grafton to Parkersburg, Virginia. At Parkersburg a transfer by steamer was made across the Ohio to Marietta, where the Marietta and Cincinnati Railroad was opened by 1857. West of Cincinnati the broad gauge 6-foot Ohio and Mississippi was built in the same year across Indiana to Vincennes and on to East St. Louis.

In June 1857 President Chauncy Brooks of the B. & O. was host for a giant excursion celebrating the opening of the American Central Line from Baltimore to St. Louis. The guest lists and crowded "official trains" headed westward were reminiscent of the great Erie party of half a dozen years before. President James Buchanan had to decline, sending instead his secretary of state, Lewis Cass of Michigan, who headed a large delegation from the District of Columbia. So many uninvited guests boarded the excursion trains that at an overnight stop at Grafton, up in the mountains of Virginia, the hotel accommodations were sufficient only for the ladies in the party. The next afternoon at Cincinnati the huge assemblage was greeted by the several rival fire companies of the city, who were eager to honor not only the new western rail route but also to call attention to their acquisition of several new steam fire engines. In the demonstration of their prowess with ladders, new engines, and full streams of water, one errant fire crew managed to douse the honorable Secretary of State Mr. Cass, sending his fine silk hat rolling into a Cincinnati gutter.

In Indiana nearly 2000 miles of new rail were laid in the 'fifties, with the centrally located capital city of Indianapolis being the focal point for seven different lines. One of the longer lines in the state was the New Albany & Salem Railroad, a southern Indiana road that was to be built from New Albany on the Ohio River to Michigan City on the Lake Michigan shore. Running the length of Indiana, this 288-mile road was to be known in the twentieth century as the Monon or the Hoosier Line. Most of the north-south line was built in 1853 and 1854, and in the earlier year Horace Greeley, the editor of the *New York Tribune,* rode the line during a western temperance speaking tour. Greeley boarded the New Albany & Salem cars at Lafayette for La Porte, his next tour stop in northern Indiana. Trouble plagued the entire 90-mile trip. North of Lafayette the engine was derailed, and when once again on the track both wood and water soon ran out. Greeley joined a train crew who set out in the chilly autumn night on a hand-car in search of another locomotive. He finally reached La Porte some twenty-one hours after his departure from Lafayette.

Another important north-south line serving Chicago was the Illinois Central, a road laid out in the shape of a thin wishbone running the length of the state. One line ran south from Chicago to Centralia, where it was joined by a second line running down from Dunleith on the Mississippi. The main line continued on down to Cairo. When the road was finished in 1856 its 700 miles of track probably made it the longest railroad in the world. One of the lawyers retained by the Illinois Central was the same lanky trial lawyer from Springfield who had helped the Rock Island keep its Mississippi bridge. Lincoln aided the Illinois Central in winning a vital county tax case, and then presented the company with his bill for $2000. As his law partner and biographer, William H. Herndon, recalled the incident, the railroad official who received Lincoln's bill for legal services exclaimed in surprise: "Why, sir, this is as much as Daniel Webster himself would have charged. We cannot allow such a claim." Lincoln departed without his fee, but later sued the railroad for a new bill, this time for $5000. He won his suit, and the money thus received certainly helped finance Lincoln's increased activity in politics in the late 'fifties.

But most of the railroads built in the Old Northwest in the decade before the Civil War were east-west lines, connecting the

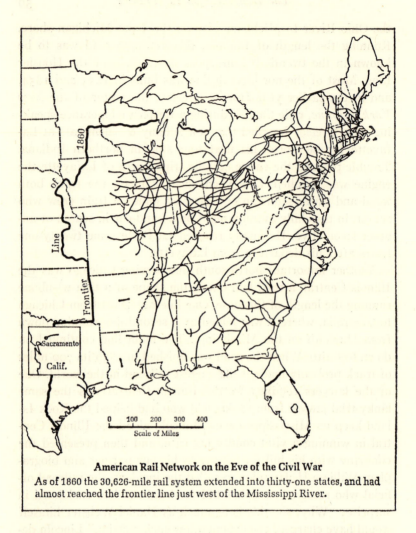

American Rail Network on the Eve of the Civil War

As of 1860 the 30,626-mile rail system extended into thirty-one states, and had almost reached the frontier line just west of the Mississippi River.

western markets and economy with the major seaports on the mid-Atlantic coast. When Lincoln, as President-elect, left Springfield on a rainy Monday morning for his twelve-day inaugural trip to the nation's capital he intentionally took a roundabout route via Indianapolis, Cincinnati, Columbus, Pittsburgh, Cleveland, Buffalo, Albany, New York, Philadelphia, Harrisburg, and Baltimore. He traveled 1904 miles when the direct rail distance to Washington was much less than half as long. Certainly Lincoln had a wide choice of routes for his trip east: the Illinois-Indiana border was crossed by seven routes east, and the Indiana-Ohio line by eight.

In the two decades prior to 1850 the Erie Canal packets and the Mississippi-Ohio sidewheelers had reached a virtual standoff in their competition for the trade and economic allegiance of the Old Northwest. The numerous east-west rail lines built between the Atlantic and the Mississippi Valley in the 1850's clearly broke that stalemate in favor of the railroad. Hundreds of miles of iron track built over the rocky barrier of the Alleghenies into the western states had given the economic and commercial victory to the Northeast. Had the Civil War come a decade earlier, certainly the military and economic contributions made by the upper Mississippi and Ohio Valleys to Union victory would have been much smaller. In the decade the western rail construction had clearly created what the historian Allan Nevins calls a "web of transport" binding together the mercantile and industrial East with the agrarian West. Puffing locomotives, and the iron network built in the 'fifties, definitely helped the states of the Old Northwest decide that they should support the Union.

When war came in the spring of 1861 the rival northern and southern rail systems offered more in the way of contrast than similarity. The eleven Confederate states with about 9000 miles of road had not quite one-third of the national rail mileage. But the average cost of the more lightly constructed southern lines at $28,000 per mile was two-thirds that of the northern average cost. Southern roads had less and lighter traffic and employed no more than one-fifth of the nation's railroad workers. Many Yankees were employed on the southern railroads in the 'fifties, since in the South there was a dislike for mechanical pursuits. When war broke out some of these northerners returned home, and many of those who stayed with the Confederacy were viewed with distrust. There was also a tremendous disparity between northern and southern lines in motive power and rolling stock. The entire Confederacy had hardly any more locomotives than those on the combined roster of the Erie and Pennsylvania railroads. Certainly in 1861 those two lines plus the B. & O. and the New York Central could put more motive power and rolling stock on the road than could be found on all the rail lines south of the Ohio and Potomac. The Confederacy was also woefully weak in its facilities for producing new locomotives, cars, and rail. A dozen Yankee locomotive plants could be found for every one in the Confederacy, and the southern production of new rails in 1860 was only one-ninth that of the North.

The Civil War was the first American conflict in which railroads had an important role to play. Both sides had a great dependence upon river and water transport, but railroads were also quickly used. Just a few days after Fort Sumter, Lincoln's secretary of war, Simon Cameron, was ordering troops to converge on Washington by railroad. The heavy rail movement of armies and their supplies in the summer of 1861 was common both in the North and the South. Southern roads serving the Virginia and Tennessee fronts were crowded with trains filled with excited young volunteers and their antiquated ordnance.

In 1862 the line coming into Richmond from the south had a record-breaking operating ratio (the ratio of operating expenditure to operating revenue) of but 28 per cent, and the connecting road on south, the Wilmington and Weldon, paid a record dividend of 31 per cent in 1863. Some of the Confederate rail prosperity was false because of the rapidly rising prices for supplies and wages. Between 1861 and 1864 coal went from 12 cents to $2 a bushel, lubricating oil from $1 to $50 a gallon, and mechanics' wages from $2.50 to $20 a day. The old senator from Georgia, John P. King, complained that his Georgia Railroad had been losing money for two years because of high prices. In his annual report for 1864 he wrote of his line: "The more business it does, the more money it loses, and the greatest favor that could be conferred upon it—if public wants permitted—would be the privilege of quitting business until the end of the war!"

In neutral Kentucky, no man's land, the Louisville & Nashville had prosperity of a more permanent kind. The builder and president of the road, the lame and uncouth but highly respected James Guthrie, made capital of his line's strategic location—the only line offering direct connection to Confederate railroads. In the early weeks of the war the Confederacy, anticipating future scarcities, feverishly bought supplies in the North and shipped them south over the L. & N. This prosperous trade continued until September 1861, when the crafty Guthrie rather reluctantly decided he was a Union man. He soon had so much federal traffic that he was obliged to rent extra locomotives from the United States government. The gross earnings of Guthrie's line increased fivefold during the war years and dividends reached a high of 16 per cent in 1864. Other northern lines did almost as well. So many trainloads of recruits, horses, ordnance, and wounded and returning veterans crowded the Illinois Central that that road, even with its reduced land-grant government rates, paid 8 per cent dividends in 1863 and 1864, and 10 per cent in 1865. Even the normally financially embarrassed Erie declared a dividend in 1863, and the soberly managed New York Central raised its rate to 9 per cent in 1864.

Rail movements of troops and supplies continued throughout the war, and on occasion massive troop movements were made by both the North and the South. Late in July 1862 the entire army of General Braxton Bragg, some 30,000 men, was moved by rail 775 miles over an indirect route from Tupelo, Mississippi, to Chattanooga. The largest single Union troop movement was to the same city in the early fall of 1863. Secretary of War Edwin M. Stanton proposed to Lincoln that 30,000 men be sent from the Army of the Potomac in Virginia down to Tennessee to lift the Confederate siege of Chattanooga. Stanton thought the total move would take only five days, but the skeptical Lincoln objected: "I will bet that if the order is given tonight the troops could not be got to Washington in five days." Stanton was not too far off, for in less than twelve days 30 trains of 600 cars moved 25,000 men and all their gear from the Potomac some 1200 miles to the upper Tennessee via Harper's Ferry, Indianapolis, Louisville, and Nashville. South of Chattanooga in the spring of 1864 the railroads gave another boost to the Union cause when 1600 tons of supplies (in 16 trains) were forwarded daily to General William T. Sherman as his army of 100,000 men sought to capture the strategic city of Atlanta.

Both sides suffered railroad destruction, but the greatest damage was felt by the Confederate lines. Perhaps the first attempted major destruction was the Andrews raid on the Confederate line between Chattanooga and Atlanta in the spring of 1862. The Union raiders stole the locomotive, the *General*, but the raid itself, while exciting, was frustratingly ineffective. Nathan Bedford Forrest was about as effective a railroad raider as the Confederacy possessed, but the high command of both armies discovered that you could not destroy a railroad from horseback. It was the tough foot soldiers of Sherman's army who made railroad destruction a fine art, as they slogged through Georgia and the Carolinas in the last months of the war. The war left Confederate railroads a shambles. Gutted depots, twisted rails, and lost or dilapidated cars and rolling stock were the rule for the typical southern line by 1865. When Chief Justice Salmon P. Chase toured North Carolina in May of that year the military provided him with a train described by a press correspondent as "a wheezy little locomotive and an old mail agent's car, with all the windows smashed out and half the seats gone."

Northern lines suffered far less than the Confederate roads for several reasons. Most of the campaigning and raids were in southern states rather than northern states; the Union forces were better equipped to repair damage when it did occur; and finally the North was aided in rail rehabilitation and system management by a pair of very capable railroad men, Daniel C. McCallum and Herman Haupt. McCallum, former superintendent of the Erie, was commissioned a colonel in the Union Army in 1862 and placed in charge of the United States Military Railroads, a system largely composed of ex-Confederate roads which grew to 2100 miles by the end of the war. Colonel Haupt returned to the Army in 1862 after years of civilian engineering experience with numerous railroads. His job was railroad construction and bridge rebuilding. His magic in rapid bridge-building was such that Lincoln once described a Haupt-built bridge as "the most remarkable structure human eyes ever rested upon . . . there is nothing in it but beanpoles and cornstalks."

American railroads were strengthened in the war experience. Northern lines gained a new prosperity, learned a new spirit of corporate cooperation, and successfully experimented with such innovations as coal for fuel, steel rails instead of iron, and new techniques of mail handling on trains. In making their contribution to victory, the northern lines had also achieved a substantial degree of maturity.

In some ways the Pacific railroad really started in the Sierra foothills east of Sacramento, California. An eastern engineer, twenty-eight-year-old Theodore Dehone Judah, was engaged in the spring of 1854 to be the chief engineer of the Sacramento Valley Railroad, a line that was to connect the California capital with nearby mining camps up the American River. Judah quickly surveyed the route, and by February 1856 the short 21-mile road to Folsom was in operation. In the process the energetic Judah had started to dream of a railroad across the Sierras.

Supported by the friendly editorials of the Sacramento *Union*, Judah talked to all who would listen about the desirability of building a railway across the mountains to the east. He managed to convince the California legislature to call a state railroad convention. This convention of a hundred delegates met in San Francisco in September and October 1859 and, won over by the engineer's ample statistics, charts, and pictures, appointed Judah to carry its petition to Congress. Judah's lobbying efforts in Washington in the early weeks of 1860 were not successful, but dozens of Congressmen visited his Pacific Railway Museum which a friendly Illinois representative, John A. Logan, had permitted him to set up in a small room in the Capitol.

Not discouraged by failure, Judah returned to California certain that his road would eventually be constructed. Surveying in the mountains above the mining town of Dutch Flat in the fall of 1860, Judah found the pass he was certain would provide the best possible route through the Sierras. Going to the mining camp drug store of his friend Dr. Daniel W. Strong, Judah at once drew up a rough draft of the "Articles of Association of the Central Pacific Railroad of California." Stock subscriptions were slow, but several Sacramento merchants such as Leland Stanford, wholesale grocer; Charley Crocker, dry goods; and Mark Hopkins and Collis P. Huntington, partners in a hardware firm; finally ventured their money. On April 30, 1861 the organization was complete, and the Central Pacific Railroad Company of California was a fact.

Meanwhile Abraham Lincoln had been elected President and the Republican party had come to power in a nation threatened by secession and conflict. The brief Congressional session in the summer of 1861 was naturally devoted to war measures, but the regular session in the winter of 1861–62 turned its attention again to the domestic matters of the tariff, free land for farmers, and internal improvements. Since the Republicans wished to be true to their platform promises of 1860, the Pacific Railroad bill met with little opposition. With the southerners no longer in Congress it was easy to agree on a central route, a line that would be equally fair to Chicago and St. Louis. In its deliberations Congress was aided by the facts and figures supplied by Judah, who had returned to Washington. The railroad was also staunchly supported by James A. McDougall, the Democratic senator from California. McDougall, who was an effective orator when sober, spoke frequently in behalf of the project. The two houses finally passed the legislation late in June, and Abraham Lincoln signed the bill on July 1, 1862.

The Pacific Railroad Act authorized two companies to build a line to the Pacific: the Central Pacific to build eastward from Sacramento, California, and the Union Pacific to build westward from the Missouri River. Unlike the Central Pacific, which operated originally only under a state charter, the Union Pacific Railroad Company was created under a federal charter. This provided that the new company was to be capitalized at $100,-000,000, and more than 150 commissioners were selected to solicit stock subscriptions. The government was to grant ten alternate sections of public lands (later increased to twenty sections in 1864) for each mile of completed track. In addition, a thirty-year government loan in United States bonds was available to the two railroads. The size of the loan was to vary with the difficulty of the terrain: $16,000 of bonds were to be lent for each mile of railroad built on the plains, $32,000 for each mile built in hilly or desert regions, and $48,000 for each mile in the really difficult mountain regions.

Ground-breaking was not immediately possible for the Union Pacific, for when the entire nation was given the opportunity in 1862 to purchase stock in the line only seven subscribers came forward. By the fall of 1863 the necessary stock subscriptions had been obtained and the company was organized with Major General John A. Dix as president. Dix, a prominent New Yorker, had earlier had a financial interest in the Mississippi and Missouri Railroad in Iowa. Since Army administration kept General Dix quite busy, the real direction of the railroad fell into the hands of its vice-president, Dr. Thomas C. Durant. Like Dix, Dr. Durant had been interested financially in several western roads, including the Chicago, Rock Island & Pacific, and the Mississippi and Missouri. Thomas Durant held a medical degree, but he was always better known for his stock manipulation than for his medical practice.

Finally, ground was broken for the new railroad on December 2, 1863, out on the bleak Nebraska prairie at Omaha. Durant spent the meager funds of the new company with abandon, sending dozens of telegrams to editors, bankers, Federal officials, and state governors inviting them to attend the "gala ceremony and banquet." No doubt many were included in the crowd of more than a thousand that followed Nebraska Territorial Governor Alvin Saunders up the trail north of the ferry landing to the spot selected by Durant and the company engineers. Militia companies from Iowa and Nebraska fired salutes from their brass cannon, the Governor dug up a few clods of cold clay, and the chief orator of the day, George Francis Train, promised the audience that millions of immigrants would "settle in this golden land in twenty years."

For a while it seemed that every major figure associated with the Union Pacific had a last name beginning with the letter D —to Dix and Durant were added Dillon, Dodge, and Dey. Sidney Dillon, a distinguished New York financier of long railroad experience, was soon a director of both the Union Pacific and its corrupt construction corporation, the Credit Mobilier. Back in the early years of railroading Dillon, Dix, and Durant, along with Judah, Crocker, Stanford, and Huntington, of the Central Pacific, all had been youngsters in or near the then-pioneer rail centers of Troy and Albany, New York. General Grenville M. Dodge, who became the chief engineer of the Union Pacific after the Civil War, was to work with the road until the day of the golden spike. The first chief engineer of the line, Peter A. Dey, was not to remain so long with the company.

The round-faced and dour Peter Dey did not wholly approve of the way Durant was running the road. Dey had seen Durant's rail operations back in Iowa before the war, and now in Nebraska the cautious engineer deplored the manner in which the doctor was planning the new line. After the ground breaking Dey busied himself with the surveys and construction estimates for the first hundred miles of road west of Omaha. He made what to his professional eye seemed liberal allowances for the currently high costs of materials and labor and arrived at an estimated cost of $30,000 a mile.

After a "consulting engineer," Colonel Silas Seymour, a

brother of Governor Horatio Seymour of New York, had visited Nebraska, Dr. Durant instructed Dey to raise his cost estimates to permit broader embankments and lower grades. Engineer Dey complied with the request, changed the specifications, and soon arrived at an estimated cost of $50,000 per mile. Durant then arranged a contract with Herbert M. Hoxie, who really represented the corrupt Credit Mobilier. The construction contract called for a payment of $60,000 per mile for a line that was to follow the specifications originally drawn up by Dey. When Dey saw a copy of the contract he was indignant. Shortly thereafter he sent in his resignation to General Dix

But in spite of delay, inadequate financing, and crooked construction contracts, the railroad was finally started. The years 1863 and 1864 had seen only grading accomplished—1865 was to see some actual track laid. The first supply of rails had come clear from Pittsburgh on the little steamer *Elkhorn*, which had pushed two loaded barges down the Ohio and up the Mississippi and Missouri Rivers to Omaha. The rails were light—only 50 pounds to the yard—but Durant felt that they were sufficient for a prairie road. Ties and bridge timbers were cut far up the Missouri and floated downstream by raft to the Omaha railhead. Most of the ties were of soft cottonwood, but some were of oak or cedar.

The first two locomotives for the road, the *General Sherman* and the *General McPherson,* had come from the East via the Hannibal and St. Joseph R. R. and a hazardous steamboat trip from St. Joseph up to Omaha. Later two dozen passenger cars and a large number of freight cars arrived by steamer from St. Louis. Many of the later supplies came across Iowa on the Chicago & North Western R. R., using ox-teams for the final haul across the hills of western Iowa.

The first rails were laid in Omaha on July 10, 1865, and the inexperienced crews took eleven days to put down the first mile of track. By late September they had laid a dozen miles, and in November the end of track was some thirty miles west of the Missouri River. Dr. Durant decided it was time for a simple celebration. General Sherman and a handful of other guests were invited to accompany Durant on a brief inspection tour. The accommodations were so primitive that Sherman sat on a nail keg on one of the two flatcars that was coupled to the locomotive that bore the general's name. A few speeches brightened the stop at the end of track, but Sherman no doubt felt a private skepticism as he listened to the confident predictions of success. The treeless terrain, the unpopulated territory, the laggard rate of track laying, and the threatening Sioux and Cheyenne did not incline the general to any optimism.

But the new year brought a spurt in construction on the Union Pacific. The two years since the ground-breaking had seen only 40 miles of road completed. The year 1866 was to see the track laid out to North Platte, 290 miles west of Omaha. The need for speed was soon imperative, for in June 1866 Congress, no doubt prodded by the legislative counseling of Collis P. Huntington, agreed to remove the clause in the legislation of 1864 which forbade the Central Pacific to build more than 150 miles east of the California-Nevada border. The Union Pacific was ready to accept the challenge from the western road, for in February 1866 Dr. Durant had signed a contract with the Casement brothers of Painesville, Ohio.

The Casements, General Jack and his younger brother Dan, were small but active men. A friend once called them "a pair of the biggest little men you ever saw—about as large as twelve-year-old boys, but requiring larger hats." The 37-year-old Jack, only 5 feet 4 inches tall, had a gruff manner which in no way was diminished by a full beard. But he had a way with men and was able to command their respect and loyalty. His brother Dan, who had helped Jack build track for several midwestern lines prior to the Civil War, was clever with figures and was in charge of supplies and logistics in the construction operation. The Casements in early February 1866 offered to "lay and fill" track for the Union Pacific at the basic rate of $750 a mile with the company furnishing a graded way and all supplies, materials, and transportation that might be needed. Durant gave them a favorable reply, and the Casements at once started to recruit their workers and build a special construction boarding train.

The construction train contained cars supplying every conceivable service: blacksmith shop, feed store, wash house, carpenter's shop, saddler's shop, water storage, telegraph office, dining rooms, kitchens, and several sleeping cars, each with bunks for over a hundred men. Fresh beef was supplied from a herd of cattle which plodded along the newly laid track.

Most of the men in the Casement crews were veterans of the Civil War. Many of them were Irish but probably more were "Galvanized Yanks," men whose army service had been with Lee, Jackson, or Joe Johnston. But whether they were veterans or recent immigrants recruited in Chicago, they all came to know the military discipline demanded both by General Jack Casement and by the presence of the lurking Cheyenne or Sioux. Rifles were generally nearby to answer the first thud of Indian arrows. The work train could become a real fortress, for several of the boarding cars had special ceiling racks holding hundreds of extra rifles.

The Casements quickly succeeded in speeding up the laying of track. Singing helped the rhythmic use of the track sledgehammer, but a prize offered by Jack Casement was even more effective. He promised his workmen a pound of tobacco per man if they could lay a mile of track in a day. Soon they earned their tobacco, and Dan proposed an extra half-day's pay if they could lay a mile and a half in a shift. The pace of construction quickened, and by the end of the summer of 1866 a single month was to see 65 miles of new iron added to the line running up the broad valley of the Platte.

When the end of track reached the 100th meridian, some 240 miles west of Omaha, the exuberant Doctor Durant felt an urge to celebrate. The vice president wished an elaborate commemoration of the event, and sent off invitations in September 1866 to most of the important people in the country, including President Andrew Johnson, his cabinet, and the entire Congress. Many found it impossible to accept, including Andrew Johnson who was perhaps still tired from his recent political campaign trip to the Midwest. The tour group did boast of several congressmen and senators, including Benjamin F. Wade and Rutherford B. Hayes of Ohio, and James W. Patterson of New Hampshire. A certain cosmopolitan flavor was given the junket by the presence of such foreigners as the Earl of Arlie of Scotland and the Marquis de Chambrun, a bewhiskered descendant of Lafayette. The group left Chicago on the Burlington road, riding down to the Hannibal and St. Joseph in a "magnificent train of Palace Sleeping Cars" furnished by George M. Pullman. From St. Joseph they traveled to Omaha on two large Missouri steamboats, the *Denver* and the *Colorado*.

Once in Omaha, the excursion was under the complete direction of General Grenville Dodge, who had been chief engineer of the Union Pacific since the previous May. Dodge quickly obtained sufficient bedding and tents from the Army to provide the trainload of guests with fairly restful October nights on the Nebraska prairie. Two locomotives were needed to get the nine-car train over the heavy grade out of Omaha, but once the broad Platte Valley was reached, the *Idaho*, an eight-wheeler trimmed with flags and a pair of buckhorns, easily pulled the cars to the end of the line. At the end of the train was the ornate new directors' car, which had been set aside for high federal officials and other guests of distinction. Vice-president Durant and his favorites used the "Lincoln car," which the Union Pacific official had purchased from the government some months after its somber funeral trip from Washington to Springfield, Illinois.

Out of Columbus, where the travelers spent their first night on the open prairie, Dodge had an aide assemble fifty or sixty dependable Pawnee braves who put on a war dance around the evening campfire. Well after midnight Dodge himself led the eager warriors in a mock raid on the sleeping circle of tents. The "raid" was so realistic that the general was forced to reassure quickly the terrified and alarmed guests. Later the Union Pacific provided for more sedate entertainment which included vaudeville acts, a buffalo hunt, a first-hand view of Jack Casement's Irish track laying experts, and finally, on the last day, a specially set prairie fire which lighted up the lower Platte valley for miles.

Some thirty months later a group not much larger than the Union Pacific's 100th Meridian Excursion gathered in a barren valley north of the Great Salt Lake to help celebrate the final joining of the Central Pacific and the Union Pacific. Judah's dream of a rail line across the Sierras was now a fact. The Chinese brought from the Orient by Charley Crocker had made giant earth fills with hand barrows, drilled the Summit Tunnel, and eventually learned to lay track with a speed which impressed even the Casement boys. A special train from California brought President Stanford to the little construction town at Promontory Point so that he could share with Dr. Durant the honor of driving home the final spike.

Speeches of self-endorsement and approval accompanied the placing of special spikes in the tie of polished California laurel. On their first try both Durant and Stanford missed the golden spike, much to the amusement of the professional trackmen who had driven home spikes from Omaha to the Pacific. As the spike, which had been fashioned out of $400 worth of pure gold, was at last tapped into place a waiting nation heard the news from clicking telegraph instruments from Maine to the Golden Gate. A seven-mile parade began to move in Chicago, dozens of firebells rang out in San Francisco, and a magnetic ball dropped from a pole on top of the Capitol dome in Washington, D. C. Back at Promontory the popping of champagne corks was drowned out by the shrieking whistles of at least four locomotives. Stanford invited his guests back to his private car for a multi-course dinner. Champagne, food, and the general festivities for the day were listed as a $2200 expense item in the books of the Central Pacific. Out in San Francisco the new editor of the *Overland Monthly*, Bret Harte, hastily composed a poem:

> What was it the engines said,
> Pilots touching, head to head,
> Facing on a single track,
> Half a world behind each back?

On May 10, 1869, Collis P. Huntington was in the New York City office of the Central Pacific when the battery down at Castle Garden began its crashing 100-gun salute. As vice-president and eastern financial representative for his company, this canny Yankee wondered if the new transcontinental line could really be made to pay. His partner Leland Stanford that afternoon out at the Golden Spike celebration had boasted: "The day is not far distant, when three tracks will be found necessary to accommodate the commerce and travel which will seek a transit across the continent." Huntington was not so sure.

The Union Pacific-Central Pacific remained but a single track for some time, but other Pacific railways were soon to try to duplicate the original engineering feat. The following February 1870 saw the first rails of the Northern Pacific laid in Minnesota. Construction on the new road was rapid, and nearly 500 miles of line were complete when the Panic of 1873 forced the failure of Jay Cooke, Philadelphia banker and chief sponsor of the new transcontinental. Receivership and delayed construction plagued the road during the middle 'seventies, but the Bavarian immigrant, Henry Villard, with strong financial support from New York capital, managed to complete the line across the mountains by late summer 1883. While the Northern Pacific was stalled by depression and receivership out on the Dakota prairie, still another northern road started to expand. The canny James Jerome Hill and a group of Scotch-Canadian associates purchased the bankrupt and rusting St. Paul and Pacific in 1878. Building slowly and substantially wherever they saw a profitable traffic, the Hill group during the 'eighties expanded their road, now called the Great Northern Railway, toward the Pacific. In 1893 the line built by the "Empire Builder," Jim Hill, was finished to Seattle, and continued in good financial health while most competing roads were at least flirting with bankruptcy or receivership.

South of the Union Pacific other roads were also building across the mountains in the 'seventies and 'eighties. Cyrus K. Holliday, the "Free-Soiler" who had helped found Topeka, Kansas, was one of the first railroad builders in the American

Southwest. Two years before the Civil War started, Holliday pushed through the Kansas Territorial legislature, sitting at Lawrence, a charter for the short Atchison and Topeka Railroad Company. In 1863 he managed to obtain a land grant of three million acres from Congress, but the first construction was delayed until 1868 when a pile bridge was thrown across the Kaw River to connect Topeka and the westward building Kansas Pacific.

The Kansas farmers smiled that blustery October day as the first dirt was moved to the accompaniment of a prediction by Colonel Holliday that someday his road would reach both the Pacific and the Gulf of Mexico. Twenty-eight miles of track were laid down in 1869, and three years later the road, now with the word Santa Fe added to its title, had been pushed up the Arkansas River valley to Dodge City. This southwestern Kansas outpost was soon to become the most famous cow town in the West. As the line reached Colorado it soon came into conflict with the narrow-gauge Denver and Rio Grande being built south of Denver by General William Jackson Palmer. The 3-foot line ultimately won out in the violent fight for the narrow mountain gateway west of Pueblo, the Royal Gorge of the Arkansas. A few weeks before the Santa Fe had beaten General Palmer's crews to Raton Pass, the easiest entrance into New Mexico.

William Strong, a rugged Vermonter who had learned railroading in Wisconsin and points west, became president of the Santa Fe in 1881. Through a combination of leases, purchases, and construction, the energetic new president expanded his road by the time of his retirement in 1889 to a 7000-mile system reaching from Chicago to the Gulf and the Pacific. A few weeks after his retirement his line was used by Nellie Bly of the *New York World* in her famous 72-day trip around the world. She made the 2577 miles from San Francisco to Chicago in 69 hours, and out on the prairies of Colorado and Kansas her special train of a single Pullman plus a baggage car frequently reached speeds of 75 to 80 miles an hour.

The last of the transcontinentals completed in the generation after the Civil War followed a route important in the earliest plans to span the continent, following as it did the entire length of the Gadsden Purchase. After completing the main line of the Central Pacific in 1869, the Big Four started to build a major branch into southern California. Using a new name, the Southern Pacific, Huntington, Stanford, Crocker, and Hopkins pushed their new road down to Yuma, Arizona, by 1877. Difficulties in crossing the Yuma Indian Reservation delayed the line for a while in Arizona but construction was soon continued on eastward into New Mexico. In 1882 the Southern Pacific made a junction east of El Paso, Texas, with the Texas and Pacific, a line built by Thomas A. Scott of the Pennsylvania Railroad. Shortly thereafter the Big Four completed a second line across southern Texas which gave them their own through service to New Orleans.

In the generation after the Civil War the prairie states built railroads far more rapidly than the mountain states further west. In the eleven prairie states west of the Mississippi (in two tiers, Minnesota to Louisiana and North Dakota to Texas), the rail lines built and building were soon to form a network running in every direction. Further west in the mountain and coastal states, where there was more scenery than population, the rail lines were farther apart, and most of them were east-west roads. The typical prairie state by the turn of the century had far more rail mileage than the mountain or high plateau states further west. In 1900 Iowa, only slightly more than a third of Montana in area, had, with its over 9000 miles of line, more than three times the rail mileage of the larger state. Nebraska had more than four times the mileage of Wyoming; and Kansas, with not quite 9000 miles of line, had as much rail mileage as the combined total of Arizona, New Mexico, Nevada, Utah, Idaho, and Oregon.

Several of the prairie states were of course served by one or more of the major Pacific or transcontinental lines. In addition the northern prairie region was served by four major "Granger" lines—the Chicago & North Western; the Chicago, Milwaukee & St. Paul; the Chicago, Rock Island & Pacific; and the Chicago, Burlington & Quincy. In the last decades of the nineteenth century, the Granger area in mid-America might be described as the grain growing states from Kansas, Missouri, and Illinois north to Canada. Of these nine states seven were west of the Mississippi, while the remaining two, Wisconsin and Illinois, were to the east. The entire region was subservient in an economic way to Chicago and to a lesser degree to such satellite cities as St. Louis, Kansas City, or Omaha. Chicago was the main eastern terminal for each of the four Granger railroads. The lines brought prosperity both to the city and themselves in carrying the grain, beef, and pork of the prairie states to the elevators and stockyards of Chicago.

Oldest of the four lines was the Chicago & North Western which had grown out of William Butler Ogden's little Galena and Chicago Union Railroad. The North Western had been the principal connecting line east for the Union Pacific ever since January 1867, when an unusually severe winter had permitted temporary track to be built on the thick Missouri River ice between Omaha and Council Bluffs. Twenty years later, when the Union Pacific inaugurated its new deluxe train, the *Overland Limited*, the tracks of the North Western carried the train in and out of Chicago. The second Granger road, the Chicago, Milwaukee & St. Paul, had started out as Byron Kilbourn's dream of a rail empire serving Milwaukee. When Alexander Mitchell, the poor Scotch immigrant youth who had prospered in insurance and banking in Milwaukee, became president in 1864 the line started to grow. It was built into St. Paul shortly after the Civil War and was extended south to Chicago by 1873. By the late 'eighties the annual gross revenue of the Milwaukee averaged about $25,000,000, and it was the longest of the Granger lines.

While the Rock Island had been the first line to bridge the Mississippi, its race across the rolling hills of Iowa to be the first line into Council Bluffs had been lost to the Chicago &

North Western. The Rock Island's gleaming silver locomotive, *America*, entered Council Bluffs on May 12, 1869, but it had been preceded two years and four months earlier by the rival Chicago road. Nevertheless the Rock Island could boast in the early post Civil War years a prudent management and low fixed charges which normally permitted dividends of 7 or 8 per cent. It had been one of the first western roads to try steel rails, and in 1880 was proud of being the only line between Chicago and the Missouri River to have an all-steel track.

The last of the four Granger lines was the Burlington, a road whose early history was dominated by a group of Yankees led by John Murray Forbes. This merchant from Boston had been interested in Chicago ever since his Michigan Central had reached the Windy City in 1852. The Burlington was built to two points on the Mississippi in the decade before the Civil War, and extensions in Missouri, Iowa, and Nebraska were added in the 'sixties and 'seventies. Later the expanding and well-managed line reached Denver, Colorado in 1882, St. Paul, Minnesota in 1886, and Billings, Montana in 1894.

All of the Granger roads just reviewed, and all but one of the major transcontinental lines to the Pacific, received generous grants of land from the United States government. In the 1830's and 1840's the federal Congress had been accustomed to offer lands from the public domain as an inducement to the building and completion of projected internal improvements. By 1850 they had granted about 3,500,000 acres to turnpikes and highways, and roughly an equal amount to various canal projects. With 9000 miles of railroad in operation in the nation by 1850, many Americans believed the new form of transportation also deserved assistance from the federal government.

Out in Illinois a young senator, Stephen A. Douglas, was willing to try a land-grant bill for a railroad. His first efforts in 1848 were unsuccessful, even though he was aided in the lower house by Abraham Lincoln, who presented to Congress no fewer than a dozen pro land-grant memorials from his constituents. In

1850 Douglas was more successful. Douglas was seeking land for a projected railroad, the Illinois Central, a north-south line to run the length of the state from Chicago down to Cairo. Douglas soon obtained stalwart support from Senator William R. King of Alabama, who was seeking a comparable grant for the Mobile and Ohio in the states of Alabama and Mississippi. Eastern support was obtained when the western pro-railroad group agreed to tariff changes popular in the East. Soon eastern as well as western senators were supporting the measure. In Senate debate William H. Seward of New York contended that the national interest would best be served if the western lands were brought "into cultivation and settlement in the shortest space of time and under the most favorable auspices." The bill was finally passed and signed on September 20, 1850 by the new President, Millard Fillmore. It provided a grant of six alternate sections of land per mile of railroad to the Mobile and Ohio in the states of Alabama and Mississippi and to the Illinois Central in Illinois.

As the iron network spread west of Chicago into and across the broad valley of the Mississippi many other states naturally sought land grants for projected lines. Legislation in the spring of 1856 granted land for four east-west rail routes across Iowa with three of the four grants going, originally or ultimately, to the Granger railroads described earlier. In the decade of the 1850's at least twenty million acres were granted for railroads, much of the land being given to the first tier of trans-Mississippi states. Most of the grants were modest in extent, normally being of the same amount as the Illinois Central grant, six sections per mile of completed railroad.

The Civil War and postwar grants were generally more generous. The Pacific railroads normally obtained twenty sections per mile of line, but in a burst of extreme largess Congress provided forty sections for each mile the Northern Pacific constructed in the territories. Unlike the earlier grants of the 1850's, the transcontinental grants were usually given directly to the projected railroads rather than to the individual states. The last important railroad grant was given in March 1871, going to the Texas and Pacific, the road that Tom Scott was trying to build across the dry plains of Texas and New Mexico. In the twenty-one years between the Illinois Central-Mobile and Ohio grant of 1850 and the last grant in 1871 a generous Congress made more than 170,000,000 acres available to eighty-odd railroads. Since nearly half of the projected railroads proved to be merely dream lines that were never built or completed, some 35,000,000 acres were forfeited and ultimately returned to Uncle Sam.

By the time the national rail network was complete, the railroads of the country had received full and final title to 131,-350,534 acres of government land. Nearly nine-tenths of the grants were in states west of the Mississippi. Most of the railroads receiving land were prairie railroads. Dozens of railroads in Illinois, Wisconsin, Minnesota, Iowa, Nebraska, and Missouri received grants that made possible a construction which otherwise would have been long delayed. The Hannibal and St. Joseph in Missouri; the Kansas Pacific in Kansas; and the extension of the Burlington west of the Missouri in southern Nebraska, all had a more rapid construction because of the federal land-grant program.

The principal contribution of the grants to prairie railroading was that they furnished an early basis of credit so that construction could start. Typically the new line which obtained government land mortgaged its acres long before it completed final certification with the government. But the average railroad often also obtained some cash in outright sale of the land. The Union Pacific in the 1870's was selling its land to farmers in Nebraska at $3 to $5 an acre. Further east the Rock Island was selling its rolling Iowa farmland at an average of $7 to $8 an acre.

The pace of the westward movement clearly sped up with the coming of the railroad to the prairies of America. In the decade before the Civil War the locomotive and iron rail had reached Chicago and the rolling plains of Illinois, Wisconsin, and Iowa. The census of 1860 showed the frontier line in most places to have moved well west of the Mississippi—a railroad map of the same year would show the westward moving fingers of the growing iron network not far behind.

In the generation after the Civil War the prairies, the high plains, and the plateaus and mountains further west were to see the rapid building of thousands of miles of railroad, and the coming of millions of new pioneers and settlers. The railroads came first and quickly pulled the people into the territories that soon would be states. The flamboyance of the nation-wide celebration in mid-May 1869 truly marked an event of significance, for the completion of the iron road to the Pacific was as important to Americans as the opening of the Suez Canal in the same year was to western Europeans. Other parallel lines to the Pacific soon followed, and the network was strengthened between the foothills of the Rockies and the Great Lakes by the addition of the Granger lines and other railroads serving the Midwest. In the last decades of the nineteenth century the railroads of the American West had moved the Texas longhorn from the Kansas cow town to Chicago, had served the gold and silver miners of Leadville and Virginia City, and had moved to eastern markets the crops of the prairie farmer and homesteader. Long before the turn of the century the iron pony had come to stay on the American prairie.

3

Years of Integration, Corruption, and Service

In the half-century after Appomattox, America changed from an agrarian to an industrial nation. Between 1865 and 1917 the population increased nearly threefold, climbing from 35,700,000 to 103,400,000. In the same five decades the rail network increased sevenfold, and the gross operating revenues increased some twelvefold, rising from $300,000,000 in 1865 to about $4,000,000,000 in 1917. The iron and steel rail network expanded from 35,000 miles in 1865 to 53,000 miles in 1870; 93,000 miles in 1880; 164,000 miles in 1890; 193,000 miles in 1900; 240,000 miles in 1910; and pushed to a record 254,000 miles in 1916. By the early twentieth century few Americans did not enjoy at least some rail service, and almost all of the 100 million residents were literally within the sound of the lonesome wail of the locomotive whistle. At the turn of the century American rail mileage was greater than that of Europe, and railroading was still generally regarded as being the biggest business in an era of bigness.

The rate of rail construction naturally varied from region to region in the post Civil War decades. Western rail expansion, as we have already noted, was the most rapid. As additional rail routes were completed across prairies and mountains to the Pacific, their final spike celebrations invariably made the biggest headlines. At the other extreme was New England, where rail mileage only roughly doubled in the half-century. The rail industry in the six states was clearly dominated by two roads, the

New York, New Haven & Hartford; and the Boston and Maine. In the central trunk line region from New York, Philadelphia, and Baltimore on west to Chicago and the Mississippi River, the rail mileage expanded a bit more than fourfold in the half-century. Two giant systems, the New York Central and the Pennsylvania, each with about 10,000 miles of line, clearly dominated the region. Lesser roads in the trunk-line region, in a descending order of mileage, were the B. & O., the Erie, the Philadelphia & Reading, the Lehigh Valley, and the Delaware, Lackawanna & Western. Several of the important Granger lines out of Chicago also had substantial mileage east of the Mississippi.

South of the Potomac and Ohio Rivers construction after the war was more hectic than in any area except the West. The ex-Confederate states increased their rail network sevenfold by 1910 to a total of some 63,000 miles. Included in this mileage was Texas, a state almost more western than southern. Texas with 14,000 miles of track in 1910 was easily first in mileage among all the states, being well ahead of Illinois and Pennsylvania, in second and third spots respectively. Five railroads were dominant in the region east of the Mississippi and south of the Ohio and Potomac at the turn of the century. The new Southern Railway, a 6000-mile line organized by J. P. Morgan in 1894 out of the Richmond and Danville system, was the largest of the five. The oldest railroad of the group was the Louisville & Nashville, a line controlled by the arbitrary and strong-willed Milton Hannibal Smith, president of the line from 1891 to 1921. This southern railroad king would brook little back talk, whether from a weak-kneed state railroad commissioner or the much tougher Hetty Green, who once lectured Smith from her private car in the Louisville yards because he liked shiny brass on his locomotives. He did much to build up the freight traffic on his line, but he hated the passenger business and let his coaches become antiques. The remaining three major roads in the South were the Atlantic Coast Line, the Seaboard Air Line, and the extensive Illinois Central system between Cairo, Illinois, and New Orleans.

Two other themes ran parallel to the extension of the rail network in the long generation after the Civil War. A major development in the late nineteenth and early twentieth centuries was the new integration and uniformity in service, made possible by a host of technological advances and innovations in operating efficiency. Unfortunately the same post-war years were also years of retrogression. Railroad corruption, incompetent management, fraudulent stock market manipulations, and an entire spectrum of rate discriminations were so common in the last decades of the century that by the turn of the century increasing governmental regulation was to be but a natural result.

Certainly the American rail network in 1865 was neither integrated nor very efficient. At the beginning of the war the Mississippi was crossed by but a single railroad bridge, and no rail lines crossed either the lower Potomac or the Ohio. Important cities had inner city gaps in their rail service. No railroad in 1861 entering either Richmond or Philadelphia made a direct connection with other lines in the city. The great diversity of gauge across the nation made impossible any substantial cross-country freight movement without break of bulk. Manual braking and coupling of cars, the crazy-quilt pattern of innumerable local sun times, wooden bridges, iron rails, small cars, and inadequacies in train control all combined to make rail operations slow, dangerous, and inefficient. One of the first innovations made to improve post-war freight traffic was the introduction in 1866 of cooperative fast freight lines. In such a service several participating roads each contributed cars to an administrative pool for a fast freight service between major cities. Rates for such service were higher, but the delivery was faster and the shipper was saved the inconvenience of having to break bulk at transfer points. By 1874 most of the nation's through freight was moving via such fast freight lines as the Star Union, the National, the Empire, the Great Western Dispatch, and the White, Blue, and Red lines. Most large railroads were in several fast freight pools. The New York Central and the Pennsylvania each belonged to three. South of the Ohio the Green Line was organized in 1868. With twenty-one member lines in 1873 it was clearly the major fast freight line in the South.

During the 'sixties and 'seventies several techniques were introduced to permit the interchange of cars between lines of different gauge. One answer to the problem was the "compromise car" in which wheels with a tread five inches wide could be used on either standard gauge track or the wider 4-foot 10-inch gauge. A second expedient was a car with wheels which could be slid along the axle to fit two or more gauges. Careful railroad officials considered neither of these methods really safe. Both the Erie and the Illinois Central, with 5-foot trackage south of Cairo, used car hoists or "elevating machines" to lift a car from tracks of one gauge to a set of tracks of a different gauge. In a few places, such as the tracks west out of Cincinnati, the addition of a third rail created a "double gauge" which would permit trains of either of two gauges to use the line.

But there was really no substitute for the adoption of a single standard gauge for the entire nation. In 1861 more than 46 per cent of the total mileage varied from the 4-foot 8½-inch standard gauge. In the South the most common width was five feet, except for the small trackage of Louisiana and Arkansas (5 feet 6 inches) and some standard gauge in most of North Carolina and part of Virginia. North of the Potomac standard gauge was dominant except for New Jersey (4 feet 10 inches), New York (with its 6-foot Erie) and Maine (with a 5-foot 6-inch gauge to match the Canadian mileage). In the Old Northwest the standard gauge also generally prevailed except for the broader 4-foot 10-inch width which was widely used in Ohio and eastern central Indiana. Trackage west of the Mississippi was generally standard gauge except in Missouri, where all the lines out of St. Louis were built to the 5-foot 6-inch width. Eastern interests persuaded Congress in 1863 to authorize the standard gauge for the Pacific railroads, although Abe Lincoln had earlier favored the 5-foot gauge which was common in California. This western transcontinental building in the standard gauge gave that width a definite edge, and midwestern lines one by one shifted to standard gauge.

One of the major broad-gauge lines in the East to narrow its trackage was the Erie. This was accomplished during the presidency of Hugh Judge Jewett, a shrewd and honest Ohio lawyer who headed the line from 1874 to 1884. Jewett was really a second choice after Colonel Thomas A. Scott, the able first vice president of the Pennsylvania. Prior to his long Pennsylvania service as J. Edgar Thomson's right-hand man, Scott had brilliantly directed early Civil War rail operations as assistant secretary of war in the Lincoln cabinet. Now in 1874 when Scott was ready to accept the proffered Erie position the unexpected death of Thomson resulted in his being made president of the larger Pennsylvania. Jewett, who had had years of railroad experience in Ohio, was not too eager to accept the position, but finally did so at a record annual salary of $40,000 and a $150,-000 advance on a ten-year contract. He was worth the money. Jay Gould's control of the Erie from 1868 to 1872 had left the road in terrible financial shape. Jewett quickly moved the company's headquarters out of the garish Grand Opera House on 23rd Street where the flamboyant Jim Fisk and financial manipulator Jay Gould had plundered and exploited the road. The new president did not try to stop the impending bankruptcy and receivership, and in the spring of 1875 the Erie was reorganized as the New York, Lake Erie, and Western Railway. Jewett improved the new Erie in a number of ways, but his first wish was to rid his main stem of the unfortunate 6-foot gauge as quickly as possible. On Sunday, June 22, 1880, the entire Erie line across New York state was changed to standard gauge. Although other northern lines also had shifted during the 'seventies, 1880 still found roughly one-fifth of all American rail mileages to be other than standard gauge.

Most of the remaining off-size mileage was in the South. In that region the 5-foot gauge mileage had actually increased during the post-war years from 7300 miles in 1865 to 12,000 miles by 1880. The first major southern line to make the shift was the Illinois Central line south of Cairo: the Chicago, St. Louis & New Orleans. James C. Clarke, the general manager of the southern road, had spent weeks in preparation for the change. Two-thirds of the inside spikes on the rail to be moved 3½ inches had already been pulled, and every superintendent, road-master, and section foreman along the 547-mile line had been fully briefed on the operation. Finally, on Friday, July 29, 1881, between dawn and 3:00 p.m. some 3000 workers shifted the gauge of the entire main line. The *Railroad Gazette* called it the "greatest feat ever accomplished in gauge changing!"

A few years later the rest of the South agreed to the change. Southern road representatives worked out the details of the shift in an Atlanta conference on February 2, 1886. The dates selected for the shift were Monday, May 31, and Tuesday, June 1, 1886. During the spring of 1886 part of the southern rolling stock was shifted to the new narrower gauge. For some years in anticipation of the shift one major engine builder, the Baldwin Locomotive Works, had been building its locomotives to make the shift in wheel gauge relatively simple. In their track planning many southern lines leaned heavily upon the earlier experience of James C. Clarke of the Illinois Central. Using track gangs of from three to five men for each mile of track, ten railroads west of the mountains changed their track on May 31, and the eastern roads shifted the next day. On both days the work was completed by 4:00 p.m. The actual shift was but three inches, to the 4-foot 9-inch gauge of the Pennsylvania. This half-inch variation from standard gauge caused no practical operational difficulty, but during the next few years all roads with a 4-foot 9-inch gauge did shift to the official standard gauge which was soon to be required by the American Railway Association.

The achievement of a nearly uniform gauge throughout the country immediately permitted a more extensive interchange of freight cars by the rail lines of the nation. At first a car rental system with mileage rates was used, with the rates ranging from half a cent a car-mile for low-cost equipment, such as stock cars, to one cent a car-mile for refrigerator cars. This type of payment was not too satisfactory since the owning company had no easy way of checking the mileage. Also many railroads used "foreign" cars for storage purposes. Thus a per diem system of twenty cents per day per car was adopted in 1902. The per diem rates were raised several times during the early twentieth century and by 1920 were set at a dollar a day, a figure which was used for a number of years. A detailed code of car-service rules concerning the prompt return of cars to the home road and an equitable division of car repair costs was agreed upon early in the present century.

Great improvements in rail and track were made after the Civil War. By the 'sixties all new construction was using an iron T rail of the basic design created in the 'thirties by Robert L. Stevens of the Camden and Amboy. It was Stevens who had also designed the first hooked-head track spike. During the Civil War J. Edgar Thomson was trying some English-made steel rail on his Pennsylvania, but only in 1865 was the first domestic steel rail produced in Chicago. Acceptance of steel rail was not rapid, but by 1890 probably 80 per cent of all track was steel. The rail also increased in weight and length. Steel rails rolled in 1880 were 30 feet in length, and weighed no more than 35 to 40 pounds per yard. By 1925 the typical rail was 39 feet in length and the average rail in American lines weighed close to 85 pounds per yard.

In the same decade that America gained uniformity in its railroad gauge it also achieved a standard time. Uniformity in time or scheduling had not been important for the first railroads. In the early years no timetables were available to the general public, and train operating personnel and depot agents only had crude schedule sheets, which usually were more optimistic than accurate. With printed timetables the crazy-quilt variation of dozens of local sun-times still made any meaningful train scheduling most difficult. When it was high noon in Chicago it was 12:50 p.m. in Washington, D.C., 12:31 p.m. in Pittsburgh,

12:09 p.m. in Louisville, 11:50 a.m. in St. Louis, 11:41 a.m. in St. Paul, and 11:27 a.m. in Omaha. Railroads generally ran all of their trains by the local time of their major terminals. On the B. & O. Baltimore time was used for the eastern schedules, Columbus time for Ohio trains, and the Vincennes clock for everything west of Cincinnati. In the Buffalo station there were three clocks, each with a different railroad time. Trains arrived and departed in Pittsburgh by six different clocks. The *Chicago Tribune* claimed that Illinois had 27 different local times, Indiana 23, and Wisconsin 38. The major railroads across the country managed to run their trains on only 54 different times, and a traveler going from Maine to San Francisco might have to change his watch twenty times.

There was little support in 1870 for the suggestion of the *Railroad Gazette* that the entire nation be placed in a single uniform time zone. There was much more railroad support for a program of several broad time zones across the breadth of the nation as outlined by Professor C. F. Dowd, principal of the Temple Grove Seminary for Young Ladies at Saratoga Springs, New York. In 1872 in St. Louis a permanent organization was established by a number of railroad superintendents which was successively known as the Time-Table Convention, the General Time Convention (1875), the American Railway Association (1891), and the Association of American Railroads (1934). In 1876 William F. Allen, managing editor of the *Official Guide of the Railways,* became secretary of the General Time Convention. Allen at once began to work vigorously for nation-wide adoption of a system of standard time zones. He drew up a specific program in 1881 and early in 1883 submitted it to the General Time Convention. Allen's plan divided the United States into four time zones, the Eastern, Central, Mountain, and Pacific. Each zone was based on the mean sun time on the 75th, 90th, 105th, and 120th meridians, which, respectively, were near Philadelphia, Memphis, Denver, and Fresno. The railroads agreed to Allen's proposals in October 1883, and the plan took effect at noon on Sunday, November 18, 1883.

As the nation went on railroad time the *Indianapolis Sentinel* had this to say: "People will have to marry by railroad time, and die by railroad time. Ministers will be required to preach by railroad time, banks will open and close by railroad time, in fact, the Railroad Convention has taken charge of the time business, and the people may as well set about adjusting their affairs in accordance with its decree. . . . " Discussing the time change of Sunday, the 18th, James Gordon Bennett's *New York Herald* pointed out that: "The man who goes to church on November 18th will hug himself with delight to find that the noon service has been curtailed to the extent of nearly four minutes, while every old maid on Beacon Hill, in Boston, will rejoice to discover that she is younger by almost 16 minutes." But not all was calm. Many complained that they preferred to run their lives on "God's time—not Vanderbilt's." Down in Tennessee the good Reverend Mr. Watson from his pulpit castigated the Louisville & Nashville for the new railroad time, and to make his point to his congregation, used a hammer on his shiny Waterbury watch. But in spite of the editorials and the hubbub, depot clocks across America were changed to the new official Standard Time at high noon and the railroads of the nation started to follow a more sensible time pattern. It was strictly a railroad affair, and the attorney general of the United States, Benjamin H. Brewster, stated a few days before November 18 that no department need change their clocks until so authorized by Congress. No doubt it is an apocryphal story that the same official was astonished to find he had missed a late afternoon train to Philadelphia on Sunday the 18th by 8 minutes and 20 seconds.

The decade of the 'eighties also saw great improvement in railroad couplers and brakes. At the beginning of the decade rail traffic was still plagued by a pair of devices, the link-and-pin coupler, and the hand brake, that made all rail operations hazardous and slow. The link-and-pin coupler could, theoretically, be operated without the brakeman getting in between the cars, but the typical trainman was impatient and the coupler often obstinate. The result was a high incidence of crushed and injured fingers and hands. A missing finger or fingers on the hands of a boomer brakeman seeking a job would convince the normal yardmaster that the applicant was an experienced railroader. Slowing a train with handbrakes was only slightly less dangerous. As the cars had grown larger, clearances beneath overpasses and on bridges had often been reduced. When the engineer's whistle for "down brakes" signaled the freight brakeman to the top of the moving cars, the danger to life and limb was increased when the braking was done in snow, ice, or darkness.

In the post-war years hundreds of patents were issued for improved couplers, but none received any general acceptance. Many railroad presidents, like Henry B. Ledyard of the Michigan Central, were slow to adopt such innovations both because of the cost and also the difficulty of getting widespread acceptance and usage. Major Eli H. Janney, a Confederate veteran, used a knife to whittle out his version of a coupler while clerking in a Virginia dry-goods store. Janney's coupler, which worked like the hooked fingers of two hands, was first patented in 1868 and improved a few years later. About the same time the Master Car Builders' Association began a long series of tests of the hundreds of available couplers. Tom Scott's Pennsylvania Railroad adopted the Janney coupler for their passenger cars in the late 'seventies, and by 1887 the Master Car Builders' Association had approved the Janney automatic coupler as the standard for the country.

A 22-year-old Union Army veteran, George Westinghouse, was the inventor of the air brake. The young New Yorker had already invented a railroad track frog and a car replacer for derailed cars when he got the idea of stopping trains with air after reading about French tunnel engineers who cut rock with compressed air. He obtained a patent for his air brake in 1869, and later that year had his invention tested on the Panhandle Division of the Pennsylvania Railroad. Not far out of the Pittsburgh terminal the test train gave the new brake a dramatic test when a farmer's wagon was seen stalled on the crossing tracks dead ahead. The engineer whistled "down brakes" and also turned the lever for the new and untried braking system. Long before the trainmen could use their manual brakes, the power of air brought the engine to a screeching halt a few feet from the frightened team. The new brake needed improvements, and railroad men like the senior Vanderbilt were hard to convince, but by 1879 the Pennsylvania was using air brakes on all its passenger locomotives. Increasingly, Westinghouse turned to improvements in railroad signaling, but he did improve his brake system with a new "triple valve." The new valve gave the engineer control of his train at all times, and also automatically set the brakes should the train be accidentally separated. Extensive tests in 1886 and 1887 with the new system installed on freight trains running down a long hill near Burlington, Iowa, proved the Westinghouse brake to be effective even with long fast trains going downgrade.

Both Janney and Westinghouse were much aided by Lorenzo S. Coffin, a former schoolteacher who had been a chaplain with an Iowa infantry regiment during the Civil War. Returning to farm in Iowa, Coffin did a lot of traveling by train in the 'seventies. Coffin was riding a freight one day in 1874 when the train stopped to pick up a couple of box cars. In the required switching and coupling Coffin was present when one of the brakemen lost the two remaining fingers on his right hand in a familiar link-and-pin coupler accident. From that moment Coffin became a strong advocate of railroad safety. He discovered through experience that the train crews were correct when they claimed that the new available equipment—air brakes and automatic coupler—was not included on trains because of the costs involved. He discovered that many railroad managers simply took for granted the fact that railroad work was risky for life and limb. When Coffin tried to protest to the managers, many refused to see him, or were "in conference," or had "gone to Europe."

But the farmer from Iowa would not be still. For the cause of improved railroad safety Coffin traveled extensively, spoke often, and wrote for any journal that would print his material.

As the railroad commissioner for Iowa he helped arrange the
Burlington air brake tests, and eventually the Iowa legislature
passed laws requiring all trains in the state to use the improved
brakes and couplers. Coffin told his graphic story in the spring
of 1888 before a national meeting of state railroad commissioners which had been called by the newly established Interstate
Commerce Commission. He continued to lobby for railroad
safety, and Congress finally passed the Railroad Safety Appli-
ance Act, which President Benjamin Harrison signed on March
2, 1893. By 1900, 75 per cent of all American locomotives were
equipped with air brakes, and 96 per cent were fitted with automatic couplers. Lorenzo Coffin's long fight for improved railroad
safety was finally won.

In the last decades of the nineteenth century improvements
were also made in freight and passenger cars, in bridges, in signaling, and in locomotives. The locomotives purchased in the
'seventies and 'eighties were less and less likely to be eight
wheelers of the American type (4-4-0). William Mason, builder
of some of the most beautiful locomotives before the Civil War,
frequently had argued that it should be possible to merge
beauty and strength in the steam engine. He had once wryly
commented that locomotives ought to "look somewhat better
than cookstoves on wheels." But now the emphasis was on
strength, bulk, and tractive power. One change was an increase
in the number of driving wheels. The B. & O. increasingly
turned to the new ten wheelers (4-6-0) after their master of ma-
chinery, Thatcher Perkins, built several of that type in 1863 in
the company's Mount Clair shops. The Lehigh Valley shortly
after the war achieved still more tractive force with a fourth
pair of drivers in the Consolidation type (2-8-0). But a larger
firebox was really required if any great increase in power was to
be achieved. This was obtained by moving the firebox from between the rear drivers, making it broader, and placing it over a
trailing truck of smaller wheels. The first important locomotive
of this style was the Atlantic type (4-4-2), built for the Atlantic
Coast Line in 1895. A few years later another popular type, the

Pacific (4-6-2) was being ordered by the Missouri Pacific. The ultimate in new motive power was reached with the introduction of the articulated, or Mallet, engine, a steam locomotive with two sets of drivers powered by a single firebox and boiler. This was designed by Anatole Mallet from France, and the B. & O. ordered their first articulated engine in 1904. The Erie probably hit an all time high in wheel complexity in 1913 when Baldwin built for them three triplex Mallets (2-8-8-8-2) each engine weighing some 845,000 pounds. Reported to be the largest loco-motives in the world the huge Mallets were supposed to be cap-able of pulling freight trains of over four miles in length.

The freight train increased in size and variety of equipment in the half-century after the Civil War. In General Sherman's day the average freight car hauled 10 tons and the typical train had a net carrying capacity of 100 to 200 tons. By World War I car capacity was up to perhaps 40 tons and trains of 2000 tons were fairly common. New types of freight equipment were intro-duced in the same years. Wooden tubs on flatcars carried the first oil by rail out of Titusville late in 1865, but within three years horizontal cylindrical tank cars were in use. The first pat-ent for a refrigerator car was issued in 1867. The Illinois Cen-tral was shipping fresh strawberries from southern Illinois to Chicago in the crude cooled cars in the late 'sixties, and a few years later was using the iced cars for a growing banana traffic north out of New Orleans. Meat-packers in Chicago, and other meat-packing centers, purchased and used the new cars exten-sively, often painting them in brillant colors to advertise their products. Crude slat-sided freight cars had been in use for stock movement ever since the early cattle drives from Texas to cen-tral Kansas. The animals in such cars often received the most indifferent care enroute. One night in 1880 a young Chicago traveling man, Alonzo C. Mather, was much incensed at the suf-fering and death of animals he saw in a delayed cattle train. He at once sketched out plans for a stock car equipped with feed bins and watering troughs and later received a patent for the Mather Palace Stock Car. Before many years Federal legislation also forbade the transportation of stock by rail for more than twenty-eight hours without a five-hour layover for food and rest.

Passenger equipment did not increase in capacity, but many improvements and comforts were made in these same years. The coal or wood stove known by the young newsbutcher, Tom Edison, and his fellow passengers in the early 'sixties, gave way to hot water heaters in some cars in 1868, and steam heat from the locomotive was introduced a dozen years later. Electric lights replaced gas or kerosene lamps in the passenger cars of several lines by the late 'eighties, and late in the same decade passenger safety was much improved with the introduction of the vestibule, or a flexible covered passageway between the cars. And it was in these decades, of course, that George Pullman's sleeping and dining cars became so common that by the turn of the century the term "Pullman" was synonymous with first-class rail service. In Pullman's early days in Chicago he had made a reputation for himself in raising the all-brick four-story Tremont House several feet to the new street level by employing some 1200 workmen and over 4000 jack screws. Pullman's earlier pre-war sleeping car efforts were upgraded in the last months of the Civil War with a deluxe sleeper, the "Pioneer," with a record $20,000 price tag. The new car was first used on the last lap of Lincoln's funeral train, from Chicago to Springfield, at the request of the President's widow.

The new deluxe sleeping cars were soon in use on many roads, especially after Pullman, always the effective public-relations man, showed them to the country in several special excursion tours from Boston to California. Pullman organized the Pullman Palace Car Company in 1867, the same year he introduced his Hotel Car, which was a combination sleeping and eating car. Newspaper writers made much of the car's bill of fare, which included steak and potatoes at sixty cents and sugar-cured ham at forty cents. In 1868 Pullman put into service on the Chicago & Alton a deluxe dining car, the "Delmonico," named after New York's famous Swiss-born restaurateur. The dining car was a success, and in the following years Pullman turned out hundreds of sleeping cars, parlor cars, and diners, many of which were constructed in the newly built "company town" of Pullman on the southern edge of Chicago. Pullman's own competitive salesmanship was overwhelming and he succeeded in buying out all of his major competitors, including Theodore T. Woodruff, Edward Knight, and Webster Wagner. Wagner, whose sleeping cars were used for years by the New York Central after the old Commodore had helped set up the Wagner Sleeping Car Company, died in one of his own cars in a rear-end collision in 1882.

Pullman and the other manufacturers of parlor cars also outshopped hundreds of private cars, or "business cars," as defensive railroad executives might call them, for the tycoons and business moguls of the nation. Many of these "mansions on rails," as Lucius Beebe has so aptly described them, were the last word in luxury and elegance. Marble bathtubs, Venetian mirrors, hidden jewel safes, wine cellars, and English butlers were to be found in some of the best private cars. Mrs. Edward T. Stotesbury, wife of a Morgan partner, once told a reporter: "The only thing that's economical about our car, is the solid gold plumbing. It saves polishing, you know!" The range of prices for the fancy equipment ranged from a low of $20,000 in the 'seventies to an average of perhaps $250,000 per car in the prosperous 1920's. Several generations of Vanderbilts spared little expense in designing and outfitting their private cars. On the other hand the thrifty James J. Hill and his son Louis never paid above $16,000 for their own company or business cars that came out of the shops of the Great Northern. But such thrift was foreign to a railroad king like Jay Gould. Gould sometimes had a special train of four private cars with a personal physician on board plus a chef adept at baking ladyfingers for the financier's finicky stomach. Up front in a special baggage car was a fat milk cow whose butterfat content suited the banker's diet.

All passenger travel in the generation after the war was improved with the introduction of better signaling and train control. Ashbel Welch, engineer and vice-president of the Camden and Amboy Railroad, developed in 1865 the first manual block-signal after a tragic rear-end collision of two troop trains in New Jersey. In block-signal control, trains are kept apart a certain interval, or block of distance. A closed electric track circuit to control such signals was introduced in 1871. A manual interlocking system, in which it was impossible for signalmen to set signals and switches in conflict with each other, was first shown in 1876 at the Philadelphia Centennial Exhibition. By 1890 an electrically controlled compressed air switch was used on the interlocking at a Pennsylvania–B. & O. crossing. Speed and ease of train movement was also helped by new and improved bridges. Additional bridges across the Ohio, Mississippi, and Missouri rivers were opened in the 'sixties and 'seventies. Steel replaced iron in most bridges. After the failure of the Howe truss bridge at Ashtabula in 1876, bridge engineers put a new emphasis on proved margins of safety. The new emphasis on safety paid off, for railroad passenger safety (measured in deaths per millions of miles traveled) improved threefold between the early 'nineties and the years just prior to the First World War.

Better track, new bridges, safer rolling stock, bigger and more powerful locomotives, all combined to improve passenger schedules and the speed of travel. In the centennial year of 1876 the speed sensation was probably the special train run from Jersey City to San Francisco in a record-breaking 83 hours and 54 minutes in order for the producing team of Jarrett & Palmer to present Lawrence Barrett and company in *Henry V* in McCullough's Theater in San Francisco. Barrett, the matinee idol of the 'seventies, and his company were quartered in the Pullman hotel car "Marlborough," but the ride was so rough that few of the male troupers cared to shave during the three-and-a-half-day run. In 1887, a new deluxe train named the *Overland Limited* covered much of the western portion of the route over the tracks of the Union Pacific and the Southern Pacific.

East of Chicago the New York Central maintained one of the fastest routes, which was supervised by two very able railroaders, William Buchanan, the Central's superintendent of motive power, and George H. Daniels, the line's passenger agent. Daniels was a master of good public relations. In 1896 he was to gain much favorable publicity for his road with the introduction of *free* redcap baggage service. Earlier the two men combined to introduce extra fast passenger service between New York and Chicago on the line which Daniels was wont to call "America's Greatest Railroad." Daniels launched the *Empire State Express* as a fast deluxe train, and Buchanan supplied the motive power. He built a new series of American type (4-4-0) locomotives, the most famous of which was "No. 999." This speed queen, equipped with 86-inch drivers, hit a speed of over 100 miles an hour, running a mile in 32 seconds (112.5 miles per hour) on May 10, 1893, near Batavia, New York. Daniels, always the master publicity man, managed to have the "999" and the complete *Empire State Express* on display at the 1893 Columbian Exposition in Chicago. Later he even convinced the postmaster general that the train should be shown on a bicolor two-cent postage stamp.

The half-century before World War I was also a period of retrogression for American railroads. Inflated construction costs, incompetent managers, stock manipulations, rate discriminations, and general corruption were faults shared by many, possibly most, of the railroads in the post-Civil War era. Daniel Drew, Jay Gould, Jim Fisk, and others of their kind became adept jugglers of railroad securities and properties. Even the more sober members of the railroad managerial fraternity, men like James C. Clarke of the Illinois Central, James F. Joy of the Burlington, or James J. Hill of the Great Northern, all followed principles and practices of business ethics that would be unacceptable by the mores and the laws of the twentieth century. Inevitably, corruption, discrimination, and monopoly led to increasing state and federal railroad regulation in the late nineteenth and early twentieth centuries.

But it should be remembered that in these years the economic philosophy in the nation increasingly shifted from the laissez faire principle to growing governmental control and authority. Certainly, it would be unfair to judge the men and the methods in the age of Gould exclusively by standards which did not appear until the Progressive Movement several decades later. Also it should be recalled that the general impatience of an America which desired an immediate and complete rail network in the post Civil War period could not possibly help a situation in which many of the railroad managers lacked adequate construction and operating experience for the challenges facing them.

After the Civil War, especially as western lines were projected and built into desolate regions well past the settled frontier, the use of a "construction company" became a standard practice. The railroad construction company essentially provided the chance of a profit large enough to induce railroad promoters to undertake ventures despite the inherent financial risk involved. With this device the promoters, managers, and directors of the railroad company gave themselves the chance of an extra profit in a business that at best was filled with great risk. Oakes Ames of Boston, both a director of the Union Pacific and of the Credit Mobilier (construction company), once said that he would see the railroad finished even "if it took his last shovel." The U. P. was built, and Ames got his extra profit. Many perhaps remember the Credit Mobilier and the Contract and Finance Company of the Central Pacific because they made their owners fancy profits. Forgotten are the dozens of less fortunate contractors and construction companies that failed as they left roads unfinished and profits unmade. Since construction companies were paid for their work with the securities of the parent railroad, both bonds and stocks, the construction company might on occasion seem more interested in moving securities than in moving dirt. But the dirt was moved, even if the road was not always of first-class construction. Frederick Billings, president of the Northern Pacific, wrote his division engineer in 1880: "We have no money to spend in unnecessary work. We must get a cheap line and a safe road but at the out-

set we must in grades and curves try to save—and trust to the
future for the higher finish."

After the first road to the Pacific was completed the stench of
scandal soon emanated from the construction companies. Oakes
Ames had passed out shares in the profit-making Credit Mobilier to several members of Congress. The recipients of such
stock were those influential politicians where, as Ames saw it,
"they will do most good to us." The careers of such political
leaders as James G. Blaine, James A. Garfield, and Schuyler
Colfax were all splotched in the resulting investigation by Congress. But the owners and managers had made millions through
the activity of their construction company and Oakes Ames had
been well paid for his shovels. Estimates of their profits paid in
cash, stocks, and bonds ranged as high as $23,000,000, and crit-
ics claimed that perhaps half of the $100,000,000 capital struc-
ture of the Union Pacific was pure water.

The Big Four were more successful in hiding the operations
of their Contract and Finance Company which they set up in
1867. Finances and credit were not always easy for the California quartet. But generally, each of the four men: Stanford,
Crocker, Hopkins, and Huntington subscribed equally to the
new company. On one occasion, when there was need for still
more money, Hopkins asked his partner in New York City how
much they should subscribe. Huntington's terse reply was,
"Take as little as you can and as much as you must." The soul
of this thrifty Connecticut Yankee was also pained when he
made an inspection trip one winter up to the end of track in the
snow-bound high Sierras. The cold was so bitter that each camp
of workers was burning up to twenty-five ties per night to keep
warm—ties, which because of high haulage expense, were costing up to six dollars each! But in spite of high construction
costs the Central Pacific was completed, and the Big Four prospered. When Hopkins died in 1878 he left a fortune of $19,-
000,000, and Crocker's estate a dozen years later was estimated
at $24,000,000. When Collis Huntington came down to Wash-
ington to be questioned by the Wilson committee about the

finances of the Contract and Finance Company his memory grew hazy, and he answered the questions of the congressmen with, "I don't remember" or "Hopkins handled that." The four men had accounts which were really quite jumbled, and any worthwhile investigation was quite impossible, since the books of the construction concern had been lost in an unfortunate fire which had destroyed the offices of the company.

In another region of the nation, the South, there was also corruption in construction, but not much completed rail mileage. In the months immediately after Appomattox there had been a relatively rapid restoration of many of the ruined Confederate railroads, thanks to lenient bondholders and aid from the Military Railway Department of the federal government. But in the decade after 1865 the South lagged well behind the nation in its rate of new construction. This was in great measure the doing of corrupt railroad carpetbaggers from the North. Such northern gentlemen as Milton S. Littlefield, John Patterson, Hannibal I. Kimball, and the Stanton brothers, John and Daniel, were more intrigued with the notion of milking a railroad exchequer or receiving a handout from a state treasury than getting down to the hard work of building a railroad.

The bulk of the corrupt railroad carpetbag activity in the South was in the eastern coastal states from Virginia to Alabama. North Carolina issued more than $17,000,000 in state bonds for railroad construction, but obtained very little new mileage for the money. The money obtained from the bonds went into the hands and pockets of a railroad ring headed by a fellow from Illinois, the genial General Milton S. Littlefield. Littlefield had studied law in Lincoln's law office in Springfield in the 'fifties, but he had never picked up the Emancipator's characteristic of honesty. In the west wing of the statehouse in Raleigh the generous Littlefield worked his way with a pliable legislature by setting up a bar with free liquor, wine, and cigars available. With the money from the state bonds the Littlefield ring built a few miles of track on their Western North Carolina Railroad, but much more was spent on rail adventures in Florida or for gambling junkets in New York City. Rumor and gossip in New York placed some of the North Carolina bonds in the hands of the *demimonde* of the city, even in the chubby fingers of Jim Fisk's mistress, the buxom and unfaithful Josie Mansfield.

South Carolina, like North Carolina, built railroads in the first post-war decade more slowly than the South as a whole. In the Palmetto State the railroad gang was led by "Honest John" Patterson, former newspaperman, legislator, and henchman to Simon Cameron of Pennsylvania. Patterson claimed his nickname because once bribed he was honest enough to "stay bought." Using cooperative state officials and bribery in the state legislature Patterson and his associates plundered South Carolina of its state-held stock in the Greenville and Columbia Railroad and also the Blue Ridge Railroad.

In Georgia the major culprit was the former carriage and railroad car manufacturer from Connecticut, Hannibal I. Kimball. This handsome openhanded promoter was so persuasive that Georgians liked to say that you could resist him only by refusing to see him. Kimball was president of four of the seven railroads in Georgia which received substantial state aid, and he syphoned off enough of the state-endorsed bonds to help pay for Kimball House, a magnificent new hotel in Atlanta which was equipped with steam elevators and a well-paid French chef. Kimball also profited, along with his cohorts, from the corrupt mismanagement of the state-owned Western and Atlantic Railroad for several years. And in Alabama that state suffered in much the same way from the plundering of a pair of brothers from New England, John C. and Daniel N. Stanton. John Stanton never had the flair of Kimball, but his enemies accused him of trying to imitate both the Georgia carpetbagger and Jim Fisk up in New York. Carpetbag excesses in southern railroading clearly were responsible for a new low in business ethics in the post-war generation.

But while Kimball, Littlefield, and others in the Reconstruction South were stealing thousands of dollars, or even a million or two, from short southern roads, Jay Gould, Daniel Drew, and other financial buccaneers were taking millions or tens of millions from northern lines. The trunk-line railroads running west from New York, Philadelphia, or Baltimore were huge affairs, and when there was corruption it was also on the grand scale. Corrupt and dishonest management, watered stock, rigging of the stock market, rebating, and rate wars were all present in the northern railroad scene in the last decades of the nineteenth century.

Probably the best known of the post-war railroad barons in the North was Commodore Cornelius Vanderbilt, a man who by the Civil War had already accumulated an $11,000,000 fortune from his extensive steamboat operations. The Commodore had earlier made modest railroad investments, but his serious railroad interest began in 1862, first in the New York and Harlem and later the New York and Hudson, two rival roads on the eastern shore of the Hudson River. In 1862 Vanderbilt was 68 years old, an age that today is three years beyond obligatory retirement for the top executives of the New York Central. But a century ago, the Commodore was far from ready for retirement, and by 1867 he had maneuvered the larger upstate New York Central into a position where the leading stockholder requested Vanderbilt to take over the active direction of the line. The old man's statement: "Law! What do I care about law? Hain't I got the power?" is probably apocryphal, but convincing in the light of his obtaining authority from the legislature in Albany to combine his rail properties into the New York Central and Hudson River Railroad.

Vanderbilt, aided by his eldest son William H., ran his rail empire with both verve and financial acumen. His insistence that all motive power be a somber black, without brass or color, led some of his employees to call the locomotives "Black Crooks." Actually, the Vanderbilt labor policies were fairly reasonable, and during the summer of tough railroad labor violence in 1877 the strike by New York Central workers was rather mild. Early in his presidency of the New York Central, the Commodore had voted himself a bonus of $20,000,000 in watered stock plus $6,000,000 in cold cash. The other shareholders in the company of course also received some inflated watered stock, perhaps $20,000,000 worth. There were reports in these years that Wall Street brokers in one of their less serious moments had privately unveiled a statue of the senior Vanderbilt with a watering pot. But Vanderbilt had no monopoly on this type of finance, for the *Commercial and Financial Chronicle* in 1869 wrote that since 1867 some twenty-eight lines had increased their capital from $287,000,000 up to $400,000,000. The practice continued and in 1885 Henry V. Poor estimated in his annual railroad manual that perhaps one-third of all rail capitalization was water.

The Vanderbilts ran their road efficiently and had it paying honest dividends of 6 to 8 per cent on the inflated capital structure, even during the depression 'seventies. When the old man died in 1877, after a lingering illness, most of his $105,-000,000 fortune went to his prudent plodder of a son William H. The reporters wrote that in his last hours the old Commodore had quavered through a favorite hymn, one line of which ran: "I am poor, I am needy."

One of the few times that Cornelius Vanderbilt came out second best was in his struggle with the Erie. At the end of the war the man in control of the Erie, a railroad naturally in competition with the New York Central, was Daniel Drew, former cattle drover and long-time rival of the Commodore for the Hudson River steamboat traffic. Drew, who looked like a rustic deacon, was given to alternate periods of intemperance and piety whenever hard-pressed, and he was remembered both for his "lost weekends" and also for his gifts to a school of religion. By 1867 Drew, who never became president of the road, was aided in his running of the Erie by a pair of rascals out of New England, the brassy James Fisk from Vermont and Jay Gould, a quiet introvert from Connecticut. Fisk, former tin peddler and circus ticket-seller, was to become the Prince of Erie and to be known for being "first in the pockets of his countrymen," but the brainy

Jay Gould was a far better stock manipulator than either Fisk or Drew.

In eight years, 1864 to 1872, Gould showed his partners how to increase the book value of Erie common stock from $24,-000,000 to $78,000,000 without any new money or value being given to the road. Hoping to gain control of the Erie, Vanderbilt started to buy the pretty paper, but even his bags of money were no match for the printing presses of Gould and company. The Erie trio retreated to Taylor's Hotel over in Jersey City until Gould could hurry up to Albany, where a pliable and purchasable state legislature, with some prodding from Senator (and Boss) William M. Tweed, made the whole affair quite legal. Vanderbilt admitted defeat, grumbling that the Erie experience, "has learned me it never pays to kick a skunk." The Erie Railroad, now known as "The Scarlet Woman" of Wall Street, had a ruined credit rating and did not pay a dividend between 1873 and 1942. The flamboyant career of Fisk ended in 1872, when he was shot down by a rival for the favors of his mistress, Josie Mansfield. Drew was pushed out of Erie control by Gould and was ruined in the Panic of 1873, left with assets of little more than his gold watch, assorted hymnbooks, and a sealskin coat. In 1872 Gould gave up control of the Erie, hurried along by pressure from General Daniel E. Sickles and Tom Scott of the Pennsylvania. He left for broader rail opportunities in mid-America.

Gould, Vanderbilt, Tom Scott, men who controlled major competing railroads, engaged in periodic rate wars. These rate wars took place in all parts of the country but were the most often to be found in the trunk-line territory between Chicago and St. Louis in the west and the major Atlantic seaports. In that area the *Commercial and Financial Chronicle* wrote, such conflicts occurred with the regularity of "small pox or the change of seasons." The rate reductions were sometimes unbelievably great. In an early freight rate fight between the Erie and the New York Central, the Commodore finally cut the rate for cattle between Buffalo and New York City to a bankrupting level of a dollar a head. The crafty Jim Fisk at once made heavy beef purchases in Buffalo and shipped them to New York over his rival's line, and really at Vanderbilt's expense. Passenger fares in one rate war were so drastically cut that in the early 'eighties on one occasion a New York to Chicago ticket was only $5.00. Roads in receivership or near bankruptcy were often able to weather rate wars almost better than solvent lines because, at least for the time being, they did not have to pay bond interest or dividends on their stock. The Grand Trunk was such a line, and its frequent resort to rate cutting led one critic to observe that the railroad world almost seemed to reverse the rule of "survival of the fittest" to the "survival of the unfittest." Perhaps surprisingly during such rate wars the reaction of shippers and the mercantile group was not so much one of favoring the periodic bargain rates as it was general dissatisfaction with the frequency of rate change and fluctuation. Rate wars always disturbed "normal business." Shippers in the Chicago to Atlantic area claimed that during some years the published rates were shifted forty or fifty times within a twelve-month period.

One answer to the rate war was the railroad pool, wherein railroads in a given region decided to soften competition and maintain rates through an agreed upon division of the business. Essential to such an arrangement was the collection of statistics, and freight agents would cheat on a pool or attempt to build up their own traffic in the hope of claiming a larger share of the business the next time the percentages were allocated. Of such activities John M. Forbes, of the Michigan Central and Burlington, once wrote: "We can stand a great deal of cheating better than competition." And some pools worked quite well. The Iowa Pool, or "Great Pool," providing a sharing of the Omaha-Chicago traffic among three lines—the Burlington, the Northwestern, and the Rock Island—lasted from 1870 to 1884. Other successful pools were the Southern Railroad and Steamship Company in the middle 'seventies, and a little later a trunk line pool of the major roads between New York and Chicago. Commissioner of the former and chairman of the latter was Colonel Albert Fink, a German-born engineer with years of bridge-building and administrative experience on the Louisville & Nashville.

But even the persuasive Albert Fink could not keep peace for long among the warring eastern lines. Major competition in the 'eighties was between the Pennsylvania and the New York Central, the latter now run by the Commodore's son Willam H. Vanderbilt. In 1881 the Pennsylvania started to build and extend a parallel or nuisance line to the New York Central by chartering the New York, West Shore and Buffalo. Vanderbilt quickly retaliated with plans for the South Pennsylvania Railroad, to be built just south of the main line of the Pennsylvania. Supporting the Pennsylvania was George Pullman, who was unhappy because the Vanderbilt lines never used his sleeping cars; behind Vanderbilt was steel magnate Andrew Carnegie, who would have liked a little more rate competition in and out of Pittsburgh. The struggle became so intense that finally the nation's top banker, John Pierpont Morgan, decided to act as referee. Morgan invited Vanderbilt, Chauncey Depew, now president of the New York Central, and George B. Roberts, the successor to Tom Scott as top man of the Pennsylvania, to a peace parley in July 1885 on his yacht *Corsair*. After hours of cruising in the waters of New York harbor, Morgan brought the stubborn antagonists to a basic agreement wherein each agreed to dispose of the projected line which troubled his opponent. The House of Morgan received fees of somewhere between one and three million dollars for the yacht ride and the trouble of reorganizing the two abandoned railroads.

The rebate was one of the more hated types of rate discrimination. Henry Morrison Flagler, partner of John D. Rockefeller, obtained the first rebate for the Standard Oil Company in 1867, and before many years the giant oil company was getting not only refunds on its own freight charges, but also drawbacks or refunds on the higher rates paid by competitor firms. In a year and a half, four railroads paid the Rockefeller company more than $10,000,000 in freight drawbacks. The practice of rebates soon became normal for all large concerns, and William H. Vanderbilt, testifying before the Hepburn Committee in 1879, admitted that the New York Central had granted about 6000 such special rates in the first half of 1880.

But in spite of all the rate discriminations practiced by American railroads, there was still a marked reduction in freight rates during the last generation of the nineteenth century. Average rates dropped from about 2 cents a ton-mile at the end of the Civil War to roughly .75 cents a ton-mile by 1900. The Chicago to New York rate per 100 pounds of wheat dropped from 65 cents in 1866 to 20 cents in 1897, and the dressed beef rate per 100 pounds fell from 90 cents in 1872 to 40 cents in 1899. Part of the decline was caused by the general deflation, but rail rates dropped more rapidly than prices generally. Few freight rate wars ever saw a full return to the rate that had prevailed before the rate reduction. Railroad operating costs were of course also in decline in the generation. Steel rails which cost $50 a ton in 1877 were down to a bargain low of $20 a ton in 1897. But the major cause was clearly the great gains made in railroad operating efficiency. Steel rails, better signaling, larger and more powerful motive power, larger freight cars, longer trains, improved couplers and brakes, all had made their contribution to the general reduction in over-all freight rates.

Railroad labor made only modest gains in the post-war generation. Rail employment climbed sixfold, from 163,000 in 1870 to 1,018,000 in 1900, and the average annual wage of railroad workers increased from $465 in 1880 to $567 in 1900. In the same generation many railroad unions were formed, frequently as little more than fraternal or mutual insurance societies. Major unions of the operating personnel were the Big Four Brotherhoods: engineers organized in 1863, conductors in 1868, firemen and enginemen in 1873, and trainmen in 1883. A major railroad strike took place in 1877 during the depression and after most eastern lines had cut wages. When John W. Garrett, president of the B. & O., in July announced a second reduction for all workers making over a dollar a day, his firemen and brakemen struck. There were killings and violence in Baltimore and along the B. & O. in West Virginia, but greater violence hit Pittsburgh, where strikers against the Pennsylvania, and the mobs of unemployed eventually destroyed railroad and city property worth five million dollars. The strike spread to Buffalo, west to Chicago, Omaha, and St. Louis, and was finally broken only with the use of thousands of militia, GAR veterans, and regular army regiments.

A second dispute of major intensity came during the hard times that followed the Panic of 1893. In 1894 a powerful strike of rail workers followed labor difficulties at the Pullman works. George Pullman had refused to reduce the rent on company-owned houses occupied by his employees, workers who had recently had their wages cut 25 per cent. Pullman claimed that he was building cars at a loss, but his company was continuing to pay dividends. In sympathy with the Pullman workers, the members of the new American Railway Union headed by Eugene V. Debs refused to service any trains that hauled Pullman-built cars. Federal troops were brought in to guard the mails, Debs was jailed, and the rail workers slowly returned to work. The "Debs Rebellion," as it was called by the newspapers, was over. But thousands of the former members of Debs's union were in effect "blacklisted," for they found it difficult to obtain new railway employment on other lines. A close examination of their service letters from former employers often showed a secret watermark displaying a swan with a "broken neck."

In the 'seventies and 'eighties one of the more constant critics of the railroad was the farmer living in the trans-Mississippi West. He remembered the Erie War and Commodore Vanderbilt's affinity for watered stock. He did not like rebates, and he hated to see congressmen, state legislators, judges, assessors, other public officials, and newspapermen all ride the rails free with their annual passes. But he had other railroad problems which affected him more directly. He disliked it when railroad control of warehouse facilities or the local elevator resulted in the downgrading of his grain. Nor was he happy with the high prices he paid at the general or country store, prices he felt too high in part because of high local freight rates. But his biggest complaint was against the high freight rates charged against his crops as they were shipped to market. The rates were high. The farmers swapped stories about the family in Iowa that burned their corn crop for fuel because at 15 cents a bushel it was the cheapest fuel available; or about the farmer in Illinois whose wagon of grain brought him only enough to buy his son a pair of shoes. The farmers were angry about the discrimination of the long-and-short-haul. Many Minnesota towns had local rates of 25 cents a hundred pounds for grain moving to St. Paul, while the competitive longer haul from the Twin Cities to Chicago was 12.5 cents per hundred. The discrimination was not all in the West. An Elgin, Illinois, farmer could send a tub of butter to New York City for 30 cents, while the charge for the same tub from a small town in upstate New York where there was no competition might be 75 cents for a haul of no more than 170 miles.

The western farmers were especially angry because they had expected so much from the railroads, and because many had made sacrifices to obtain rail service. Some Wisconsin farmers had mortgaged their land to get railroads in the 'fifties, and further west the estimates of the total state and local governmental railroad subsidies had run as high as $60,000,000 in Iowa and $75,000,000 in Kansas. The western farmers often forgot the greater distances to market which applied to their commercial farming operations, as contrasted to an earlier farm frontier in the Old Northwest. Professor Frederick Logan Paxson once observed that these greater distances really made transportation costs an unavoidable tax upon trans-Mississippi farm operations.

The first significant regulation of American railroads, at the state level, came in the 'seventies as the result of farmer agitation expressed through a new farm organization, the National Grange of the Patrons of Husbandry. The Grange was founded in 1867 by Oliver H. Kelley, a former farmer from Minnesota who had become a clerk in Washington, D.C., in the Bureau of Agriculture. Kelley's success in establishing local Granges was at first slow, but the man had so much energy that a friend once called him: "an engine with too much steam on all the time." The depression after 1873 caused the organization to grow to 800,000 members in some 20,000 local Granges by 1875. The new members certainly could agree with the message found on a brightly colored lithograph hanging in many of their sparsely furnished Grange halls. The poster showed several men in characteristic poses: "I carry for all," said the railroad owner; "I fight for all," said the soldier; "I prescribe for all," said the doctor; "I legislate for all," said the statesman; "I plead for all," said the lawyer; "I trade for all," said the merchant; "I pray for all," said the preacher; and in the center stood a giant heroic figure, the farmer, who said, "And I PAY for all." By the early 'seventies the western farmer was ready for a change.

The first Granger railroad legislation was in Illinois in 1871, and two years later the railroad commission in that state was directed to prepare a schedule of reasonable maximum freight rates. Minnesota passed comparable legislation in 1874. In Wisconsin and Iowa, Granger railroad legislation was also passed in the same year. Iowa and Illinois were first in the nation in Grange activity and membership in the early mid-'seventies. In Wisconsin the Potter Law of 1874 set up some freight rates which were unreasonably low, and Albert Keep, president of the Chicago & North Western along with Alexander Mitchell, president of the Milwaukee road, told the state governor they intended to ignore the regulations. Compliance was forced by Wisconsin but the law was modified in 1876 to the general satisfaction of the railroads of the state. Granger legislation of much the same sort was also enacted in the adjacent prairie states of Missouri, Kansas, and Nebraska in the late 'seventies or early 'eighties. Georgia and some other southern states also had systems of state rail regulation which imitated the Illinois pattern. This western or Granger style railroad control had commissions which might be described as "regulative" or "strong." Of such regulation Charles Francis Adams, Jr., once remarked: "in the West the fundamental idea behind every railroad act was force; the commission represented the constable." In contrast, the railroad commissions in the eastern states, such as in Massachusetts and New York, were more moderate in action, and could be described as "weak" or "advisory." Naturally, railroad managers preferred the eastern style of control.

In the court cases brought by the railroads, the United States Supreme Court, in a series of decisions in 1876, favored the Grangers in the issue of laissez faire or public regulation. The decisions upheld the Granger railroad laws and further held that state-established maximum passenger and freight rates, in the absence of national legislation, would also apply to interstate commerce. In the early 'eighties the railroads of the nation continued to expand in mileage, and there was also a concentration of control as hundreds of small roads were leased to, purchased by, or merged with longer or larger lines. President Chester A. Arthur in 1883 urged Congress to pass a federal regulatory act, and Representative John H. Reagan of Texas, and Senator Shelby M. Cullom of Illinois, both urged such action. In 1886 the Supreme Court reversed its earlier opinion, and in the so-called Wabash case held that a state commission could not regulate any shipments beyond its own borders. Federal regulation was achieved when President Grover Cleveland signed on February 4, 1887, the Interstate Commerce Act which created a five-man Interstate Commerce Commission. The legislation also required that interstate freight rates be "reasonable and just" and further prohibited such railroad practices as pools, rebates, and drawbacks. The public reaction to the new law was generally favorable, and prices of railroad stocks even went up upon the passage of the act. As the law was being put into its final form the president of the Illinois Central, James C. Clarke, wrote Stuyvesant Fish: "The only thing left for Rail Roads to do is to largely increase the long haul or through rates. Act honestly with each other and be patient." Despite such optimism the 1887 legislation did not in any way end all railroad abuses, and much more stringent regulation was to be required and enacted in the early years of the twentieth century.

But the discrimination, the abuses, and the charges of monopoly, all of which brought a growing governmental regulation, were really minor when compared with the major contributions railroads made to the expanding American economy and society in the half-century prior to World War I. The half-century after the Civil War was in fact a Golden Age for American railroads. The capitalization of the rail network increased eightfold from $2.5 billion in 1870 to $21 billion by 1916. In the same period rail employment expanded tenfold from 163,000 to 1,701,000 workers, with the average annual wage roughly doubling in current dollars. Railroad operating efficiency and the total freight traffic both grew more rapidly than rail employment. The average railroad worker in 1916 was producing about two and one-half times as much freight ton-mileage as the rail employee of 1880. The year 1916 was also the year of peak railroad mileage —254,037 miles—an increase of 60,000 miles over 1900, and more than 200,000 miles above the 1870 figure.

Much of the new mileage was in the West where, with aid from a generous government, not one but several lines had been built across the dry plains and the high mountains to the far Pacific. The western railroad had helped the settler find a home in a land that was unique in its relative lack of wood and water. It had carried the Texas longhorns from Kansas cow towns to eastern markets, it had made more accessible the riches of the silver and gold mines of Nevada and Colorado. American railroads had done much to hasten the settling and the completion of the nation's last frontier.

During the first decade of the new century the trend toward rail merger and consolidation continued at a rapid rate. By 1906 almost two-thirds of the nation's mileage was controlled by a relatively few railroad magnates. Of the 224,000 miles of line in that year about 138,000 miles were controlled by seven groups: (1) Morgan roads, (2) Vanderbilt roads, (3) Pennsylvania group, (4) Hill roads, (5) Harriman lines, (6) Gould roads,

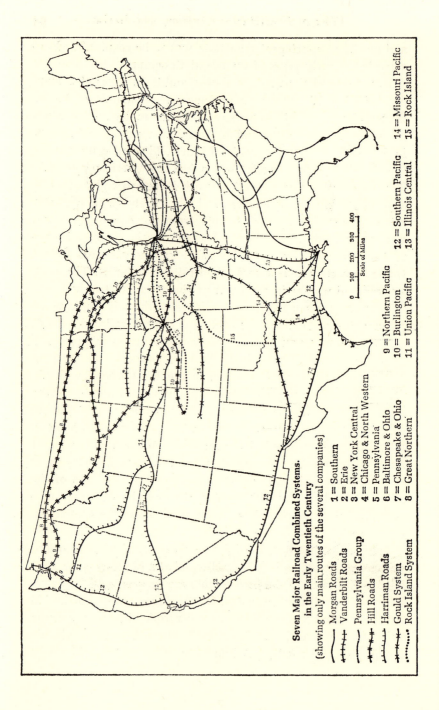

Seven Major Railroad Combined Systems.
in the Early Twentieth Century

(showing only main routes of the several companies)

Morgan Roads
Vanderbilt Roads
Pennsylvania Group
Hill Roads
Harriman Roads
Gould System
Rock Island System

1 = Southern
2 = Erie
3 = New York Central
4 = Chicago & North Western
5 = Pennsylvania
6 = Baltimore & Ohio
7 = Chesapeake & Ohio
8 = Great Northern

9 = Northern Pacific
10 = Burlington
11 = Union Pacific

12 = Southern Pacific
13 = Illinois Central

14 = Missouri Pacific
15 = Rock Island

Scale of Miles
0   100   200   300   400

and (7) the Rock Island system. The major banker involved in railroad management in those years was the New York financier and art connoisseur, John Pierpont Morgan. He had had a dominant voice in the control of the Southern Railway since his organization of that line in 1894, and he was also involved financially in several shorter southern railroads. Morgan had been a power in the Erie ever since he had reorganized that road in the middle 'nineties, and in 1901 he personally selected a new president for the road, the thick-set red-whiskered Frederick D. Underwood of the B. & O. In 1906 the various rail properties under Morgan domination probably came to a total of 18,000 miles. In the same decade this normally careful manager of railroads brought virtual financial ruin to the New York, New Haven & Hartford with policies which the I.C.C. report to the Senate in 1914 called, "loose, extravagant, and improvident."

The Vanderbilt lines included the New York Central in the trunk-line region and the Chicago & North Western, a Granger railroad west of Chicago. The system came to a total of more than 22,000 miles in 1906. The lines were still known as Vanderbilt lines even though a Vanderbilt was not always in the president's chair. The charming lawyer and raconteur Chauncey Depew was president of the New York Central from 1885 to 1898, and then continued as chairman of the board for thirty years more, until his death at the age of 93. From the 'eighties on Depew, William K. Vanderbilt (son of William H. and grandson of the Commodore), and F. W. Vanderbilt were on the board of directors of the Chicago & North Western.

A second major grouping in the trunk-line region was the Pennsylvania, which with its largely controlled B. & O. and Chesapeake & Ohio made a total system of about 20,000 miles. The seventh president of the Pennsylvania, Alexander Johnston Cassatt, early in his presidency decided that the troublesome problem of rebating might be resolved by a "community of interest" plan wherein one railroad controlled another. Accordingly, in 1900 the Pennsylvania acquired a major interest in the capital stock of both the B. & O. and the C. & O. lines. Reasonable and stable freight rates did result, and during his seven-year regime Cassatt nearly doubled the earnings of his company.

West of Chicago the two greatest rail combinations in the early years of the new century were those headed by Edward H. Harriman and James Jerome Hill. Hill, always building carefully and with financial prudence, did not complete his Great Northern Railway into Seattle until 1893. During the depression 'nineties his road continued to pay dividends while his major rival, the Northern Pacific, had financial difficulties so severe that the "Empire Builder" Hill was in effective control of the rival line by the turn of the century. Hill also secured direction of the Burlington early in the new century, and by 1906 the Hill roads came to a total of perhaps 21,000 miles. The Harriman rail empire came a little later, but was even a bit larger than Jim Hill's. Harriman had had a major financial interest in the Illinois Central since the mid-'eighties, and by 1906 he was so dominant a figure in the board of directors that he was able to replace the long-time president, the aristocratic Stuyvesant Fish. The new president was James T. Harahan, a man of humble parentage whose experience included more than a dozen different positions on half a dozen different railroads. In the mid-'nineties Harriman headed a financial syndicate which acquired the dilapidated Union Pacific in 1897 when it was facing foreclosure. Under his direction $25,000,000 was spent in a rehabilitation program upgrading track and rolling stock, and in 1903 he became president of a fully restored Union Pacific. In 1901, after the death of Collis P. Huntington, the last surviving member of the Big Four, Harriman had the Union Pacific buy into the Southern Pacific, until the U.P. finally controlled 46 per cent of the stock. Thus, by 1906 the Harriman lines consisted of about 25,000 miles of road.

Smallest of the seven rail groups were those headed by George Gould and William H. Moore. George, the son of Jay Gould, had inherited much of the $77,000,000 rail and telegraph fortune left by his tubercular father in 1892. He also inherited some ill-will. When George was feuding with the Pennsylvania Railroad in the late 'nineties that railroad retaliated by cutting down all the Western Union telegraph poles along hundreds of miles of its right-of-way. Western Union was a Gould property. George never had the flair for rail management his father possessed, but in 1906 the Gould roads still came to a total of perhaps 17,000 miles, including the Missouri Pacific and other southwestern rail properties. Judge William H. Moore was a railroad promoter and financial buccaneer whose operations might have excited the envy of the elder Gould. With financial pooling operations Moore had worked his financial magic upon the Diamond Match Company and also various cracker and biscuit companies in the late 'nineties. By 1901 he was ready for railroads, specifically the Chicago, Rock Island & Pacific Railway. Moore and his group managed with no more than $5,000,000 and the clever exchange of holding company securities eventually to control a rail system of 15,000 miles and with a capital structure which listed a par value of close to $1,500,000,000. Much of it of course was water. It had been Judge Moore who had said of common stock back in 1899: "Everybody knows what they are getting when they get common stock; they know they are not getting anything that represents assets."

But one aspect of rail development at the turn of the century was a very solid achievement. Many elaborate and luxurious union stations and terminals were completed in the twenty years prior to World War I. When the St. Louis Union Station was completed in 1894 it had the distinction for a brief time of being the "largest depot in the world." Its giant train shed covered several acres and boasted 42 stub tracks serving 18 different railroads. Boston's new South Station, opened in 1898, was almost as large. The classical and more beautiful Union Station in the nation's capital was finished in 1907. But New York City was the location of the two largest railroad terminals. During the presidency of Alexander Cassatt the Pennsylvania undertook a major improvement at the New Jersey end of their line by extending their track into New York City. The project entailed the purchase of 18 acres of high-value real estate in the heart of mid-town New York and of having tunnels dug under both the Hudson and the East rivers. The fabulous new Pennsylvania Station contained two immense halls, each as large as a normal trainshed. When the terminal was opened in 1910 it had cost well over $100,000,000 to complete. Rivaling this new terminal was the New York Central's new Grand Central Terminal, built a few blocks to the northeast, and opened in 1913. Both of the new mid-Manhattan rail terminals were served by electric locomotives. A generation earlier a trade journal had claimed: "Railway termini and hotels are to the nineteenth century what monasteries and cathedrals were to the thirteenth century." The costly and complex rail terminals being opened at the turn of the century clearly seemed to support this thesis.

But in the early years of the twentieth century the depot most Americans knew best was the small well-painted—boxcar red or brown or green according to company policy—structure down at the end of Main Street. Thousands of such depots served rural and small-town Americans, the warp and woof of society in the innocent generation before World War I. With its telegraph office, its mail and express service, and its full complement of daily passenger and freight trains, the local depot was the focal point of communication with the outside world. America in its pre-war years depended upon the train for the great bulk of its freight and passenger movement. In 1916 more than 77 per cent of the intercity freight traffic in the nation went by rail. In the same year—well before the appearance of the "family car"—98 per cent of all intercity commercial passenger movement was by rail. Traveling salesmen, families moving their furniture to a new home in a distant city, farmers sending their stock to market, merchants waiting for the consignment of groceries and notions from the big-city wholesale house—all were patrons of the railroad.

The half-century between the Civil War and 1916 had been, all things considered, good years for American railroads—years so good that the five decades could well be called the Golden

Age of American railroading. Railroads had given much to the changing economy, as America had evolved from an agrarian-oriented second-class industrial society into the major industrial power in the world. But the age was slipping away, as were the last of the nineteenth-century railroad builders. The desk in the cramped little New York office was closed for the last time when the thrifty hard-working Collis P. Huntington died in 1900. His successor in control of the Southern Pacific, Edward Harriman, died in 1909, and the elder Morgan, banker for dozens of railroads, passed on in 1913. And Jim Hill, the "Empire Builder" in the Northwest, died in 1916, the year the rail network reached an all-time high in mileage. The railroad barons were all gone. And new problems and challenges lay ahead in the twentieth century for American railroads.

4

A New Century– Years of Maturity

If the long generation after the Civil War was a "Golden Age" for American railroading, the first years of the new twentieth century were years of growing maturity and middle age. America too was growing up in these years. The last frontiers had been settled to a great extent by the end of the ninteenth century, and the superintendent of the Census for 1890 had in fact announced that no longer could a frontier line be easily traced in the American West. In 1907 (Oklahoma) and in 1912 (Arizona and New Mexico) the last three of the forty-eight states were admitted to the Union. In the late nineteenth century American population growth also slowed from the explosive increases typical before the Civil War. Each new decennial census in the half-century after that war showed a further slowing in the population expansion. Small wonder then that the earlier hectic pace of rail construction and expansion should also be slowed.

During the ten years following Appomattox, American rail mileage had nearly doubled, and in the decade of the 'eighties the network was again enlarged by about 75 per cent. The depression of 1893 definitely put the brakes on railroad building, which never regained its earlier pace, even with the return of prosperity following the Spanish American War. In the first decade of the new century slightly more than 47,000 miles of new track was laid in the nation for a 1910 total of 240,293 miles, and an increase for the ten years of not quite 25 per cent. The rate of railroad construction was very uneven from section to section during the decade. The older northern and eastern areas showed a much slower growth than the southern and western states. Four eastern states—Connecticut, Delaware, Massachusetts, and Rhode Island—either showed no mileage gain, or had a net mileage loss for the decade. Of the six New England states only Maine showed a construction gain of more than 100 miles in the ten-year period, and the total increase for the six-state region was only 400 miles. The mid-Atlantic region showed an increase of 1325 miles, and four of the five states had mileage gains, but construction was of major importance only in New York and Pennsylvania. The Keystone state added nearly 1000 miles of new line, but in 1910, with a total of 11,290 miles, still dropped to third place in the nation, behind Illinois and Texas.

Out in the Old Northwest, or the western half of the trunk-line territory, new rail construction was fairly even in each of the five states with the exception of Ohio. New mileage in the region came to a total of nearly 4000 miles for the decade. In the area south of the Ohio and Potomac and east of the Mississippi railroad building was more active still. In this eleven-state area stretching from Virginia and Kentucky to Florida and Louisiana almost 13,000 miles of new road were built in the first ten years of the new century. Every state except Kentucky added at least 600 miles, and Florida, Georgia, Louisiana, Mississippi, North Carolina, and West Virginia each constructed more than 1100 miles of new line in the period. Every southern state built more railroad mileage in these years than did all of New England; and three states, Georgia, Mississippi, and West Virginia, built even more rapidly than the entire region of the mid-Atlantic states. Obviously the South was still catching up after years of lagging construction during the wartime and the Reconstruction 'sixties and 'seventies.

But the great bulk of the construction in the new century was in the West. Well over 28,000 miles of the 47,000 miles of new road were built in the twenty-one states located west of the Mississippi River. The western states on the average added over

1300 miles each in the decade, while in the states east of the Mississippi average construction was well under 700 miles per state. Nineteen of the twenty-one western states built more miles than all six of the New England states during the ten years. The almost 4400 miles of new line built in Texas was a greater mileage than that built in the Old Northwest plus New England. It gave the Lone Star state a 1910 total of well over 14,000 miles, placing her easily in first place in rail mileage in the nation, and well ahead of both Illinois and Pennsylvania. Oklahoma, which had achieved statehood only in 1907, built almost as much new line as Texas, and two western territories, New Mexico and Arizona, had enough construction to give them a combined mileage of over 5100 miles in 1910, two years before they achieved statehood. The rate of new rail construction in the West was slowest in the two farming states of Kansas and Nebraska, a region already well served by railroads and one where the agricultural depression of the 'nineties had definitely retarded the pace of homesteading and farm settlement.

Much of the new rail mileage in the first years of the century consisted of branch lines or modest additions to existing routes. But in the first dozen years of the century at least four new major construction programs were pushed through to completion. Three of these were located in the Far West and one in Florida. Two of the three new lines in the West—the San Pedro, Los Angeles and Salt Lake Railroad, and the Western Pacific —were direct challenges to the growing rail empire of Edward H. Harriman. By 1901 this brilliant railroad operator and financier was in full control of a thoroughly rejuvenated Union Pacific as well as having become a dominant figure in the Illinois Central. Before the end of that year, Harriman's Union Pacific was also to own a controlling interest of the stock of the Southern Pacific, shares which had become available with the passing of Collis P. Huntington. The twin threats to Harriman's rail empire were located in the region to the west and south of Salt Lake City—threats to the very heart of his western rail system.

Harriman's first challenge in the Southwest came late in 1900 when the Montana copper magnate, William A. Clark, headed a group which announced its intention of building a line from Los Angeles to Salt Lake City. Clark was a small tight-fisted Scotch-Irishman who had gone west as a young man seeking gold. He arrived in Virginia City, Montana Territory, in 1863 and, although almost penniless, managed to set up a small store. Finding tobacco in short supply he located almost a ton of it in Idaho, mule-packed it back over the mountains to Montana, and sold it for a small fortune. Nine years later he was a leading banker and businessman in the Territory. Before he would invest much of his money in mining properties he decided he had to learn the best methods of metal extraction. He left Montana to spend a year in New York City, where he enrolled in the Columbia School of Mines. By the end of the century he had an interest in some two score copper and silver mines in the state and was the largest copper king in Montana. Like many wealthy men, his fancy now turned to politics. None of Clark's enemies had ever accused him of the common vices of harlotry, gambling, or drunkenness, but in the 'nineties he was frequently accused of open bribery in his efforts to obtain a seat in the United States Senate. By early 1901 he had finally been named, beyond dispute, to a seat in the Senate, and he was ready to try his hand at railroad building.

Harriman was alarmed at Clark's proposal to build a 775-mile line connecting Salt Lake City and Los Angeles. Such a new route would not only furnish unwelcome competition for Harriman's California traffic, but it might possibly help George Gould, son of Jay Gould, in his efforts to create a new transcontinental system from the Midwest to California. Harriman also had the suspicion that his northern rail rival, James J. Hill, who now controlled the Burlington route into Denver, might be interested in cooperating with Clark.

Harriman's efforts to stall the rail venture of Senator Clark were helped by the fact that a Union Pacific subsidiary had earlier built a branch road from Salt Lake City down into the southwestern corner of Utah. Some survey work and rough grading had even been extended on into Nevada into a long narrow canyon known as the Meadow Valley Wash. Harriman at once ordered this abandoned branch line extension to be reactivated. Soon the rival survey and grading crews of Clark's San Pedro, Los Angeles and Salt Lake Railroad and Harriman's Union Pacific were facing each other in the narrow and strategically located gorge of the Meadow Valley Wash. According to the federal law concerning the occupancy of gorges and canyons, neither company could exclude the other. Soon it appeared that the rival lines might cross each other more than twenty times in the narrow confines of the gorge. The rival work gangs hindered the opposition with fences of barbed wire and barricades of logs and tree stumps. Clark and Harriman both appealed to state and federal courts. The litigation was lengthy, and both parties soon realized that there was absolutely no economic justification for two parallel roads to Los Angeles. The new road for the greater part of the distance traversed an uninhabited desert which would furnish little or no local traffic. The Harriman and Clark parties entered into extended conferences during the winter of 1901 and the spring of 1902, and in July 1902 an agreement was reached whereby the two men would jointly control the complete San Pedro line. Construction on the 775-mile road now proceeded, and the line was finished without further delay, being opened in the spring of 1905. Mineral regions in the Southwest now had a new outlet, and the route also sped the fruit of California to eastern markets. Harriman had added an important new route to his Union Pacific, and in January 1906 recognized this fact with the inauguration of a new passenger train, the *Los Angeles Limited,* companion flyer to the *Overland Limited.* While Senator Clark did not have a line which he could call his alone, he did have some extra running trackage for his brand new private car, built in the summer of 1905, "No. 2001."

Harriman was much less successful in fighting off his second challenge in the West, the Western Pacific Railway, a line which was to connect Salt Lake City and Oakland. As indications of the new project first appeared, the president of the Union Pacific turned a wary eye toward both James J. Hill and George Gould. When George Gould in 1901 had added the Denver and Rio Grande to the other rail properties inherited from his father, he possessed a loose-jointed system that stretched from Buffalo, New York, to Ogden, Utah. He now sought a way to extend his lines to the Pacific coast. A second rail route across the California Sierras had been a dream of a young Scotch surveyor, Arthur W. Keddie, back in the 'sixties. In exploring for a new mountain wagon road up the valley of the Feather River— so named because of the numerous, floating feathers from wild pigeons—Keddie had found a possible rail route of low grade which crossed the mountains via Beckwourth Pass, a crossing more than 2000 feet lower than the famous Donner Pass to the south. Efforts to utilize the favorable route failed until the first years of the twentieth century largely because of the insistent opposition of the Central Pacific and Collis P. Huntington.

The aging Keddie eventually found financial support for his railroad scheme, and late in 1902 he incorporated a railroad in California which was projected to follow his original line of survey. Finding George Gould interested in such a western line, the Keddie group made a profitable capitulation to the larger financial interests, and on March 3, 1903, the new transcontinental line, the Western Pacific, was organized in San Francisco. Gould was the dominant figure in the new line, but managed to avoid any public connection with the venture until the spring of 1905. Surveyors and engineers from the Denver and Rio Grande quietly completed surveys and profiles for the new road, and some $50,000,000 in Western Pacific bonds was underwritten by the Rio Grande at the direction of Gould. Edward T. Jeffery, a confidant of Gould and head of the Denver and Rio Grande, became president of the Western Pacific in early summer 1905. The mountainous terrain in California and the desert conditions in Nevada confounded the problems of locating and constructing a line in a region already quite remote and inaccessible. But at the same time much of the line was constructed with equipment and machines far more efficient than the pick, shovel, and wheelbarrow methods of transcontinentals built in the 'sixties. Large steam shovels were extensively used in making cuts and fills, and much track was laid with the "Improved Harris Track-Layer."

Labor was often scarce in the remote area, even when top wages were offered, but after the depression of 1907 many more workers were available, and at lower wages. Trouble also came from the Union Pacific-Southern Pacific and Mr. Harriman. Harriman was a quiet man who rarely, if ever, accepted an invitation to make a public address. But Harriman did not intend to let George Gould built to the Pacific if he could prevent it. The Union Pacific charged unusually high rates for the delivery of ties and other necessary materials needed by the new road. While they never obtained firm evidence on the point, Western Pacific construction bosses suspected that Harriman agents were stirring up trouble among the W.P. workers. There were stories current to the effect that Harriman's road had hired away W.P. personnel with the promise of extra high wages only to haul them to distant points on the system where they were summarily discharged. At the same time an S.P. superintendent out in Ogden complained that he was losing his track men to Western Pacific hiring agents. Clearly, the Southern Pacific made every effort to keep the Western Pacific from obtaining a practical waterfront terminal on the San Francisco Bay at Oakland. Since the older California road had for years held a tight legal grip and control over all the Oakland waterfront, they felt quite secure against the newcomer. The S. P. forces were caught off guard early in January 1906, when 200 W. P. workers, supported by thirty guards carrying sawed-off shotguns and carbines, quickly proceeded to build a crude mile of track on top of a rock quay or training wall earlier constructed by the government to keep silt out of the inner harbor at Oakland. Despite the best legal efforts of Harriman and the Southern Pacific the coup of the Western Pacific prevailed. The people of Oakland

and California welcomed any successful challenge to the transport monopoly held so long by the Southern Pacific.

But the 927-mile Western Pacific was built in spite of all opposition, and was finished just a few weeks after the death of Harriman. The last spike was driven by a track foreman on November 1, 1909, as track gangs from east and west met on a steel bridge across Spanish Creek high in the mountains of California. Unlike another final spike ceremony forty years earlier, there were no cheering crowds, no engines pilot to pilot, and no magnums of champagne. The spectators who watched an Italian trackman drive home the last spike consisted of but a few local housewives and their children. The finished road, while 150 miles longer than the rival Southern Pacific route, crossed the Sierras at a much lower level, had few sharp curves, and boasted a maximum grade of not over one per cent. Freight traffic was started at once, and late in the summer of 1910 passenger service was begun on the line, much to the joy of the sixty-eight-year-old Arthur Keddie, who almost wept as he welcomed the first Western Pacific passenger train. But in its first years of service the W.P. never obtained the freight or passenger traffic which had been expected, and since the construction costs of the new road had been so high this lack of traffic soon hastened financial embarrassment for the Denver and Rio Grande and the rest of the rail empire of George Gould.

The last new major western route built in these years was never a threat to Harriman. Instead, when the Milwaukee decided to build an extension from South Dakota out to the Pacific Northwest one of the reasons for the decision to build west was the railroad war waged in 1901 between Harriman and James J. Hill, who controlled both the northern transcontinentals, the Northern Pacific and the Great Northern. When the Northern Securities Company was created in November 1901 as a peace pact between Harriman and Hill, it in effect created a giant rail combine which dominated the railroads of the entire Pacific Northwest. The two men plus J. Pierpont Morgan, Hill's financial backer, controlled the three major transcontinental lines in addition to Hill's recently acquired Burlington, a prosperous Granger road which gave the U.P., the Great Northern, and the Northern Pacific easy access to Chicago. Such a giant rail combination made the Milwaukee officials believe that their only chance for survival was an outlet of their own to the Pacific coast. The Milwaukee had always been a road willing to expand. It had been so back in the 'fifties when Byron Kilbourn, in his efforts to have the city of Milwaukee outstrip its rival Chicago, had convinced hundreds of Wisconsin farmers to mortgage their farms in order to help finance the railroad. And Alexander Mitchell, Scotch-born banker and insurance man in Milwaukee and perhaps the ablest of all early presidents of the railroad, had taken some chances as he extended his line northward to St. Paul and southward to Chicago in the years after the Civil War. By 1890 the Milwaukee, while not the most prosperous, was the longest of the Granger roads, with branches out to Omaha and into the Dakotas.

As the managers of the Milwaukee road decided in the first years of the new century that they should build to the Pacific, their line was directed by new leadership, Albert Earling having been elected president in 1899 after more than thirty years of service on the road. Earling completed plans for a 1385-mile extension running from Mobridge, South Dakota, via Butte, Montana, northern Idaho, and Spokane, Washington, to Seattle. During 1905 the Pacific Railroad Company was given incorporation papers in each of the four states, and the four new companies were soon drawing upon the Milwaukee for construction money. The best estimates of Earling and his staff of engineers placed the cost of the westward mainline extension at not more than $60,000,000. In 1905 the Milwaukee had a fairly moderate funded debt of $116,000,000, and had annual earnings which were easily three times the amount of the yearly interest charges. At the turn of the century the presence on the Milwaukee board of directors of such men as Philip D. Armour, Chicago meat packer, and William Rockefeller and Henry M. Flagler, both of Standard Oil, seemed to assure the financial stability of the road on the eve of its major expansion program. The project faced many of the same problems of remoteness and difficult terrain which had beset the Western Pacific, but modern equipment again hastened the project. Actual construction took less than three years, beginning in September 1906 and completed on May 14, 1909, with the final spike being driven at a location a few miles north of Butte, Montana. A number of branch line feeders were soon being built, or purchased, along the entire length of the 1385-mile new main line extension out to Seattle.

Shortly after the new route was put in operation a new director of the Milwaukee, John D. Ryan, convinced the company of the wisdom of electrifying the steepest mountain grades in western Montana and Idaho. Ryan, as president of the giant Anaconda Copper Mining Company and also one financially interested in water-power developments in Montana, was felt by some observers to have more than a casual concern in the proposed electrification program. But there were several solid arguments supporting such a move. Steam engine failures on steep grades in cold weather, the presence of cindery smoke in long mountain tunnels, and the delays caused by hot brake shoes and wheels on steep descents were problems which could be alleviated through electrification. Long-term contracts for power were let in 1912, work on the electric route was started in 1914, and by the end of 1916 the electrified tracks were in operation on 438 miles in Montana and Idaho. The Milwaukee had completed the first major long-distance electrification route in the country. But traffic and business on the western mileage never came up to the earlier expectations. The earlier lumber and building boom in the Pacific Northwest did not continue, the entire railroad rate structure became inadequate, and the business lost to the Panama Canal opened in 1914, aggravating even more a bad situation. The entire western extension had proven to be fantastically expensive. The building of many needed branches had been costly. Land needed in the extension had cost more than anticipated because of a "very vicious competition" with rival railroad interests. The electrification had cost about $23,000,000. All in all, the total cost of the western construction was $257,000,000, or several times the original estimates. Wages, interest charges (on the new bonds), and taxes all climbed. Revenues which had been three or four times the interest charges early in the century were soon down to only twice the interest charges, and the downward trend continued during the 'teens and the war years. In the early 'twenties the net railway operating income on the Milwaukee was no larger than it was fifteen years earlier, while the funded debt had increased more than threefold! Receivership for the Milwaukee was inevitable. It came in 1925.

The last of the four major railroad construction projects was in the opposite corner of the nation, down in Florida. Henry Morrison Flagler, an early partner of John D. Rockefeller and a prime mover in gaining lush railroad rebates for his company, had made so much money by middle life that he retired from an active interest in the Standard Oil Company. He turned increasingly to an interest in railroads. Long before he became a director of the Milwaukee, Flagler had embarked upon an engrossing project down in Florida. Charmed by the winter climate and the scenery, and appalled at the terrible railroad service and bad hotels, Flagler purchased a short narrow-gauge line in northern Florida in 1885. He purchased and built new lines and organized the Florida East Coast Railway, which soon connected Jacksonville, St. Augustine, and Palm Beach; and it was extended on to Miami by the spring of 1896. To gain traffic for his road he built giant resort hotels at Jacksonville, Palm Beach, and Miami, and ran luxury trains from the North each winter to fill them. He helped to finance new churches, schools, and hospitals, and his total investments and donations in the state finally were to reach a total of more than $40,000,000.

The aging and temperate Flagler began seriously to consider extending his Florida East Coast Railway on to Key West early in the new century. His railroad already hugged the eastern coast of the state from Jacksonville to Miami, some 347 miles, and he saw the 156-mile extension on to Key West as a grand climax to the Florida chapter of his crowded life. He felt that a railroad built to the southernmost city in the continental United States would be a good investment, especially since it should share in the expanding trade he foresaw with Cuba, only 90 miles distant. Flagler also believed that Key West, one of the largest cities in Florida in 1900, was destined to become an "American Gibraltar" once the federal government completed a canal across the Isthmus of Panama. As preliminary surveys and cost estimates were completed in 1904 and 1905, many of Flagler's friends and associates were frankly aghast at the risk and expense involved in the project. Many spoke of it as "Flagler's Folly." When Flagler told his aging clerical friend the Reverend George M. Ward of his decision, the good man exploded, "Flagler, you need a guardian." When Flagler advertised for construction bids in all the leading papers in the nation only one contractor responded, and he insisted on a cost-plus contract. The financier refused to agree to such a contract and decided to have his own staff tackle the difficult project.

The construction job, which took seven years to complete, employed as many as 4000 men. Even though the pay was excellent it was difficult to keep the labor force up to optimum size. The mosquitoes were vicious, the heat was oppressive, the work was dangerous, and Flagler's strict Presbyterian upbringing resulted in a rigorous rule against intoxicants in camp, a prohibition unpopular with many workmen. Water trains from the mainland brought fresh water each day to the work camp, strung along the keys, but any "boozeboat" that showed up was quickly driven off. The work was difficult because 75 miles of the 156-mile route was over either open water or marshland. Numerous bridges, usually constructed of concrete, carried the sea-going railroad from key to key. The weather in the keys also caused trouble. An October 1906 storm caused much destruction to the floating camps, houseboats, and equipment and resulted in a substantial loss of life. Flagler's engineers were better prepared for an even more severe hurricane in 1909. The problem of high winds on the completed railroad resulted in the establishment of a safety precaution: any recorded wind velocity of 50 miles per hour or more automatically set the block signals against any train movement. But all the difficulties were met, and the $20,000,000 project was finally finished just before the aging Flagler's 82nd birthday, January 2, 1912. A few days later, a giant three-day festival celebrated the arrival of the first passenger train in Key West and the completion of Henry Morrison Flagler's dream. The anticipated traffic never was realized on the 156-mile extension from Miami to Key West, but the line did remain in operation for twenty-three years until an unusually severe hurricane on Labor Day of 1935 washed away miles of railroad embankment and track. The ruined sea-going railroad was later replaced by the Over-seas Highway to Key West.

In contrast to the first decade of the new century the pace of rail construction during the teens was much slower. Only one year in the second decade had a rate of construction at all comparable to even the less productive years of the first decade. Between 1910 and 1916 the nation's rail network increased from 240,293 miles to an all-time record of 254,037 miles in 1916, after which some new mileage was built each year, but the mileage abandoned was always greater. By 1920 the total had dropped to 252,845 miles. The American preoccupation with war in the late 'teens of course accentuated this trend toward slower construction. Thousands of miles of new electric interurban line in the early years of the century had also been responsible for decreased construction of steam railways. Most of this new interurban service was located east of the Mississippi and north of the Ohio River, the very region where new steam rail construction was in decline. On a decennial basis fourteen states had already achieved their peak rail mileage in the period from 1890 to 1910. Eight of these states were in the northeastern part of the country. During the teens only ten states added 500 or more net miles of railroad. All ten of these were southern (Florida and North Carolina), Plains or Mountain (Idaho, Montana, North Dakota, Oklahoma, and Texas), or Pacific coastal (California, Oregon, and Washington) states. Clearly by World War I American railroads had achieved most of their physical growth.

In the years before World War I when the construction of new rail mileage was slowing, the same could not be said of governmental regulation. By the early twentieth century the failure of the Interstate Commerce Commission to regulate effectively the railroads of the nation was quite clear. Richard S. Olney, Boston corporation lawyer and the attorney general who helped Grover Cleveland break the Pullman strike in 1894, had earlier predicted failure for the new Commission. In 1892 he had written a railroad friend that the railway industry had little to fear from the new legislation, since it created regulation in which the "supervision is almost entirely nominal." Under the Act the five-man Commission could not fix rates, but rather could only declare, upon complaint, that certain railroad rates were not just and reasonable. The resulting lawsuits and appeals made necessary by the protesting railroads were apt to be complicated, quite technical, and very prolonged. The average length of such railroad litigation was four years, and many cases lasted even longer. And the railroads generally won, for they had excellent legal counsel, and often benefited from judges who had little sympathy with the objectives of the I.C.C. Between 1887 and 1905 sixteen such cases reached the Supreme Court. Fifteen were decided in favor of the carrier and against the Commission. In addition to its inability really to fix rates, the Commission had little power to control drawbacks, rebates, or other special rate concessions, all of which were commonplace throughout the industry.

The revival of the regulation of railroads accompanied the appearance of the Progressive Movement in America. Most Americans in the twentieth century felt that railroads needed more stringent public control. They did not like what they read and heard concerning the continuing manipulations of the big bankers like James Stillman, who headed a syndicate which financially ravished the Chicago and Alton, or William H. Moore's equally ruthless treatment of the Rock Island. The public was further angered when Governor Robert M. LaFollette's investigation of Wisconsin railroads showed extensive rate rebates in his state. LaFollette found that between 1897 and 1903 the unlawful rate discriminations in Wisconsin came to over $7,-000,000, with every major road in the state involved in such activity. Actually, the railroads themselves favored an end of rebating. They supported an amendment to the Act of 1887 introduced in 1903 by the Republican senator from West Virginia, Stephen B. Elkins. The Elkins Act, passed that year by Congress almost without opposition, was designed to end the practice of rebating, and it made both the railroads and the company receiving special rates liable to prosecution. There was general satisfaction with the new legislation, since it publicized and increased the stability of railroad rates.

Major changes in regulation came in the second term of the energetic President, Theodore Roosevelt. Roosevelt had earlier tangled with western railroad magnates when in 1901 he had directed Attorney General Philander C. Knox to start a suit, under the Sherman Act, against the Northern Securities Company, a giant holding company formed by Harriman and Hill. In 1904 the Supreme Court outlawed the company, and in November of the same year Roosevelt was elected in triumph over a conservative Democrat to a second full term. In December 1904 and the next year, Roosevelt asked Congress to increase the powers of the I.C.C. to establish reasonable freight rates, calling railroad legislation "a paramount issue." Such legislation was favored by men like Representative William P. Hepburn of Iowa, and Senators Robert M. LaFollette of Wisconsin and Jonathan Dolliver of Iowa. The Hepburn Act was approved in June 1906 with only three negative votes in the Senate and seven in the House. This legislation increased the size of the Commission to seven members and extended the authority of the body to additional common carriers, such as express, sleeping-car, and pipeline companies. The Act strengthened the prohibition against rebates and forbade the issuance of free passes, except to railroad employees, the clergy, and charity cases. But by far the most significant provision was the one which empowered the Commission to establish "just and reasonable" maximum rates. Many liberals were dissatisfied with the Hepburn Act because it permitted the railroads still to use court action to reverse, or at least delay, Commission orders. Also, Senator LaFollette was unhappy at the failure of the new law to authorize an appraisal of the value of railroad property, a step the progressive senator felt to be essential to the establishment of rates which would provide a fair rate of return to the carrier. Shippers were prompt to take advantage of the Hepburn Act. Within two years of its passage more rate complaints—some 1500—were made with the I.C.C. than had been filed in the two preceding decades.

Roosevelt's successor in the White House, William Howard Taft, had never shown any great sympathy for the railroad industry. He viewed the companies as monopolies run by a handful of men who were "exceedingly lawless in spirit." Since many progressives desired a more rigorous regulation than that provided by the Hepburn Act it was not too difficult to pass the Mann-Elkins Act in June 1910. The new legislation greatly strengthened the 1887 provision against long-and-short-hauls by deleting the phrase "under substantially similar circumstances and conditions." The Mann-Elkins Act also gave the Commission the power to change rail rates upon its own initiative, and to suspend new rates proposed by the carriers for as long as ten months. The burden of proof that the new carrier-proposed rates were reasonable, was also placed upon the railroads. In the last days of Taft's presidency Senator LaFollette finally obtained the legislation which he had been promoting since 1906. The Railroad Valuation Act of March 1, 1913 provided that the Interstate Commerce Commission should start to assess the true value of all the separate railroads in the nation. The I.C.C. was to consider the financial history of the respective carriers, including original cost, reproduction cost, depreciation, present value, and the value of all grants and gifts received by the railroad. The complexity and immensity of this task kept the employees and agents of the Commission busy for years, but never really resulted in a system of fair and equitable railway rates which the Wisconsin progressive had anticipated.

Thus by the eve of World War I the railroads of America had become increasingly regulated by a comprehensive system of governmental controls. Generation-long mismanagement, discrimination, and corruption from the days of Gould, Drew, and Vanderbilt had eventually resulted in Granger state regulation which had now been made much more stringent on a national level by the liberals and progressives in the first dozen years of the twentieth century. Much of the rail regulation set up in the forty years after the first feeble efforts of the distressed western Grangers was justified and overdue. But by the decade of the teens the maturing railroads were about to lose much of their long-held transportation monopoly. In 1914 one could travel all the way from Utica, New York, to Chicago and beyond, on the newly built interurbans. In the year war was declared on Germany more than 5,000,000 motor vehicles were registered in the United States, including nearly 400,000 trucks. And in 1918 airmail service was started between Washington, D.C., and New York City. Furthermore the federal regulation on the books by 1913–14 was largely negative in approach and character. The total regulation did not go very far toward assuring an adequate rail service, and there was often a great difference between the I.C.C.-directed rates and rates that would assure progressive management and channel a satisfactory supply of new capital into the rail industry.

The economic health of American railroads did suffer a decline in the early years of intensified governmental regulation. The general prosperity of the early twentieth century plus the increased cost of living brought about a substantial increase in wage rates for railroad labor. Between 1900 and 1915 the total number of railroad workers increased a bit more than one half, while the total compensation paid more than doubled, the average annual wage of $567 in 1900 climbing to $825 by 1915. Total labor costs which had been but 39 per cent of total railroad operating revenue in 1900 had jumped to 43 per cent by 1915. Railroad taxes also rose. Tax accruals more than tripled in the first fifteen years of the new century, while gross revenue only doubled in the same years. Fuel costs and other operating expenses also were up.

An excellent way of judging the financial health of our nation's railways is to examine the "operating ratio" of the entire industry. The experience during the nineteenth century had indicated that an operating ratio of 65 per cent to 68 per cent revealed a fair degree of prosperity. In the 'nineties and the first decade of the twentieth century the ratio remained within these limits, climbing above 70 per cent only once, in 1908. But in the 'teens, prior to our involvement in war, the ratio was generally about 70 per cent. Another weakness in financial structure was evident in the same years with a growing industrial reliance on borrowed money rather than risk capital. In 1900 the total outstanding railroad stock (common and preferred) slightly exceeded the total funded debt. But most of the new capital needed in the next decade and a half was borrowed money, and in 1917 the unmatured funded debt (nearly $10 billion) was almost two-thirds of the capital outstanding. As a consequence of these several factors the financial condition of several systems, such as the Frisco, the Rock Island, the New Haven, and the Wabash was quite desperate by the middle 'teens. In 1916 more than 37,000 miles of line, nearly one-sixth of the national total, was being operated by trustees or receivers.

Certainly by 1910 the railroads of the nation were deserving of rate increases. Both passenger and freight rates, after a long period of consistent decline in the late 1800's, had leveled off at the turn of the century. Between 1900 and 1910 the total average freight rates remained virtually unchanged at .75 cents a ton-mile. In the same years passenger rates were at a fairly constant two cents a passenger-mile. But an increase in freight

rates was of greater priority, since freight accounted for between three-fourths and four-fifths of the total rail revenue. In
1910 the railroads filed new freight rate schedules with increases
of from 8 to 20 per cent. The new federal regulation had transferred the burden of proof to the railroads in such rate cases,
and the I.C.C. suspended the increase while conducting an investigation. Public opposition to the railroads had been building
up for decades and the rail industry received slight sympathy
from either the I.C.C. or the general public as it now asked for
higher rate schedules. After long hearings the I.C.C. unani-
mously refused the rate increase request early in 1911. During
1911 and 1912 the industry's operating ratio increased, general
prices continued to inch upward, and railroad labor made new
demands for higher pay. A second request made in 1913 to the
I.C.C. for increased freight schedules eventually resulted in a
modest 5 per cent hike in rates. The I.C.C. again was slow in its
deliberations, and when the moderate increase was authorized it
was clearly inadequate. In the decade and a half after 1900 the
general price level in the nation had climbed almost 30 per cent,
while rail rates had stayed practically motionless. Average railroad freight rates in 1916 were actually a shade below those of
1900. Clearly American railroads were ill-prepared in a fiscal
and financial way for the challenge of war which lay ahead.

The outbreak of war in Europe in 1914 had a rather quick effect upon all American labor, including railroad workers. As
America began to supply munitions to the warring nations
across the Atlantic the supply of labor became short in factory
after factory. Increased production created new traffic for the
railroads, and soon the extra-boards were short of names. Railroaders who had retired came back to pound telegraph keys,
punch tickets, or swing the brakeman's lantern. Clearly, 1916
found railroad labor in a strong bargaining position, and the operating brotherhoods (engineers, firemen, conductors, and trainmen) did not propose to let the opportunity for action be lost.
During the 'teens much of American labor was anxious for the

full acceptance of the eight-hour day. Early in 1916 the four operating brotherhoods demanded an eight-hour work day to replace the ten-hour day then in effect. They also asked for time and a half for all overtime work. The hours of train service could not easily be shortened, and the demand by the brotherhoods was actually a request for a major boost in wages. These demands were rejected by the nation's railroad managers, and subsequent efforts at arbitration and mediation failed to bring any agreement. Feeling their strength, the four railroad unions voted overwhelmingly for a nation-wide strike.

In mid-August 1916 President Woodrow Wilson summoned the brotherhood chiefs and the railroad managers to a White House conference and reminded them of the catastrophic effects that would result from a general railroad strike. When neither side would budge Wilson proceeded to set forth his own settlement: the workers should have their eight-hour day, but they should abandon their request for extra overtime pay rates, and a special commission should survey the entire issue of railroad labor. The union leaders accepted Wilson's proposal, but the railroad managers quickly rejected it. Wilson at once invited the presidents of the major lines to a special conference in Washington, and uged Congressional leaders to work on possible special railroad labor legislation, should it be required. Still more railroad presidents were called to Washington, and about forty top rail executives met with Wilson in the White House on August 21. The rail executives were not in a happy mood, for they felt as if they had been summoned to a public reprimand by a tough-minded schoolmaster. It was a sweltering summer day—about 100 degrees—and as one railway executive noted the shaded quiet of the East Room he said to a fellow president, "Now we should sing, *Lead Kindly Light.*" For hours Wilson pleaded with the group, in the name of humanity, to accept his compromise. But to no avail. Some of the railroad presidents may have welcomed the prospect of a long general strike, thinking that it might result in the destruction of the brotherhoods.

Finally, in exhaustion and bitterness, President Wilson threw up his hands and exclaimed, as he left the room, "I pray God to forgive you, I never can."

The brotherhood leaders at once called for a nation-wide strike for Labor Day, September 4, 1916. Wilson addressed a joint session of Congress on August 29, asking for legislation which would provide the eight-hour day. William C. Adamson, Georgia Democrat, chairman of the House Interstate Commerce Committee, and a long-time friend of labor, sponsored the Adamson Act, which was passed by Congress on September 2. Wilson signed the bill in his private car in the Union Station the next morning, one day before the strike deadline. The legislation gave the operating brotherhoods the eight-hour day, effective on January 1, 1917, but without extra pay for overtime. Since there was to be no reduction in wage rates the effect of the law was to give the operators a major boost in pay. The Adamson Act prevented the strike but did not really solve the problem, for the railways refused to obey the law. They contended that the act was unconstitutional and carried their case into the federal courts. The eight-hour-day soon became an issue in the hot 1916 presidential campaign in which Charles Evans Hughes challenged Wilson's record. Hughes picked up much support from business as he accused Wilson of knuckling under to the railroad brotherhoods. He called Wilson's action "the most shameful proceeding that has come to my attention since I have observed public life." When the railroads refused to abide by the Adamson Act after January 1, 1917, railroad labor naturally felt cheated out of a victory. Early in March 1917 American involvement in the World War seemed very close, and the operating brotherhoods, noting the slow action in the Supreme Court, grew fearful that the emergency of war might prevent or delay the eight-hour-day law from going into effect. On March 15 the brotherhood leaders voted for a second general strike to take effect on Saturday, March 17.

With the nation near a transportation crisis Daniel Willard, the able president of the Baltimore & Ohio Railroad, assumed a major role in avoiding the nation-wide strike. Willard, whose broad railroad experiences had ranged from brakeman to general manager in the years before becoming the B & O president in 1910, had always been able to see the railroad man's point of view. In October 1916 Wilson had appointed Willard to the newly formed Advisory Commission of the Council of National Defense. As chairman of a Commission committee on transportation and communication it was natural that he should be asked to make a final effort at arbitration between the railroad executives and the brotherhoods. When these efforts failed in New York City on the night of Friday, March 16, Willard made a quick trip down to Washington to confer with Franklin K. Lane, secretary of interior and a member of the Council of National Defense. With the strike deadline only a few hours away, Willard and Lane early on Saturday morning decided upon one final effort. Lane asked and received word from a member of the Supreme Court that on the following Monday, March 19, the high court would deliver its irrevocable decision on the eight-hour law. Willard, now certain that a final decision was close at hand, hurried by fast train back to New York City where a last-minute conference with the labor leaders resulted in a forty-eight-hour postponement of the strike. Telegrams ordering the strike delay were sent to the brotherhoods throughout the country. Two days later, Monday at noon, the Supreme Court, in a five to four decision, upheld the constitutionality of the Adamson Act. The brotherhoods had gained their eight-hour day. With this decision, in the case of *Wilson* v. *New,* the Court had clearly affirmed the absolute control which Congress held over the interstate operations of American railroads.

But the pre-war years, while years of increased pressure from railroad labor, were also years in which the railroads of the country clearly furnished the vast preponderance of all commercial carriage of both freight and passengers. The Interstate Commerce Commission reported in 1916 that the railways of the nation, both steam and electric, were moving more than 77 per cent of all the intercity freight traffic. Most of the nonrailroad traffic was either on the Great Lakes or by pipeline rather than on canals and rivers. Passenger traffic was even more heavily a railroad monopoly. In 1916 railroad passenger traffic amounted to 98 per cent of the total intercity passenger business. The dependence of the national economy upon the railroad was overwhelming as the nation drew closer and closer to full participation in World War I. In 1916 private automobiles, buses, trucks, and airplanes were all in operation, but they furnished an extremely small share of the commercial intercity movement of goods and people. In the pre-war years (1912–16) the gross national product of the United States averaged about forty billion dollars a year. Annual railroad revenues in these same years averaged a bit over three billion dollars, or nearly 8 per cent of the total gross national product. Railroad labor was also an important fraction of the total labor force. Railroad workers in 1916 numbered 1,700,000, or roughly 4 per cent of the nation's gainfully employed.

Half a century ago when an American thought of his transportation he thought of railroads, their cheap and dependable freight service, the fine new depots and terminals being opened in major cities, and the passenger trains that crowded those stations at almost every hour of the day. In the pre-war 'teens one of the best of these passenger trains was the *Twentieth Century Limited,* a New York Central deluxe all Pullman flyer which had made its first run on June 15, 1902. George H. Daniels, the ingenious passenger agent and top-flight public relations man of the Central, claimed that the new train, pulled by powerful new "Atlantic" locomotives, could easily make the announced twenty-hour schedule between New York City and Chicago. English newspapermen were skeptical and predicted that the high cost and wear and tear on rails, coaches, and engines would soon cause an abandonment of the fast schedule. But the New York Central officials gave the new flyer running rights over all other trains, and often had relief engines, with steam up and a crew nearby, ready to speed the train on should any delay develop. The extra fare *Century* was an on-time train, and for years its passengers were paid a refund of a dollar per hour if the train was late. The movement of first-class mail was sped by the new train, and it was possible after its appearance to mail a letter in New York one afternoon and to expect delivery in Chicago the next afternoon. On the first run of the train into New York City one of the passengers was "Bet-a-Million" John W. Gates, the daring Wall Street operator and early promoter and manufacturer of barbed wire. Upon arriving at the Grand Central Station he told reporters that the new train made "Chicago a suburb of New York." There were reports that on his return trip several Chicago newspapermen were informed by Gates that the de luxe flyer made "New York a suburb of Chicago."

The *Twentieth Century Limited* was indeed a de luxe train. The New York Central had standing orders with Pullman for the very latest passenger equipment for its name train. The *Century* in its early years served a one dollar meal in its richly appointed diner, and the opulence and variety of food available in the car was a constant surprise to visitors from Europe. Daniels supplied the original train with a valet, maids, stenographic service, a barber shop, and electric lights with the current supplied from the car axle. Other extras were added down through the years, including a red carpet, 6 feet wide and 260 feet long, which was unrolled each afternoon on the station platform of the Grand Central in midtown New York. The company was proud of its top-name train, and each morning a report on the train's gross revenue, on-time performance, and occupied space (including celebrities on board) was placed on the desk of Alfred H. Smith, president of the Central in the late 'teens and early 'twenties. The only important rival of the *Century* among the name trains of the nation was the *Broadway Limited,* which was introduced by the Pennsylvania also in the late spring of 1902. For years the two trains kept almost identical schedules for their New York to Chicago runs. The two rivals were quite evenly matched, and created a running feud between the regular travelers of each: the *Century* claimed the smoother water-level route, while the Pennsylvania had shorter and more direct mileage. West of Chicago travelers could take the *Overland Limited,* a train of almost equal prestige which rode the rails of the Chicago & North Western, the Union Pacific, and the Southern Pacific from Lake Michigan out to San Francisco and the Golden Gate.

The half-century since 1916 has largely been a time of relative decline for American railroads. In 1966 the total railroad freight traffic, in ton-miles, was roughly twice the 1916 figure, but it had dropped from 77 per cent to less than 43 per cent of the total intercity freight movement. The river and canal barge, the pipeline, and especially the intercity truck, had all expanded their traffic much more rapidly than had the fading red railroad freight car. But the collapse of the railroad passenger traffic in the half-century was even greater. While the nation's population had nearly doubled, from 100 million to 197 million in the five decades, rail passenger traffic had been cut in half. The 1916 figure of 35 billion passenger-miles had dropped to 17 billion passenger-miles by 1966. By that year passenger trains were running on only about one-third of the total rail network. By the 'sixties the intercity bus, the swift airliner, and especially the private automobile had combined almost to relegate the aging railroad passenger coach to the museum. In the middle 'sixties it was estimated that the total outlay for all types of private and commercial passenger and freight transportation in America was costing $150 billion a year or 20 per cent of the $750 billion gross national product. The current railroad revenues of about $10 billion a year are but a small part of the total national transport bill, and constitute less than 1.5 per cent of the gross national product of the middle 'sixties. The same decline can be seen in railroad employment. Railroad workers in 1966 numbered no more than 630,000, a figure not much over a third of the earlier 1916 total, and well under one per cent of today's total labor force in the nation.

One clear symptom of the aging and decline of American railroads in the middle decades of the present century can be seen in the passing of the passenger service. As passenger trains and runs were eliminated, railroad timetables grew thin, terminal and depot lights were dimmed, and the railroad restaurant quit trying to emulate the Harvey House of an earlier day. Even the name trains were less numerous by the 'fifties. In 1957 the *Twentieth Century Limited* suffered the downgrading of having ordinary daycoaches added to its consist. Faced with such ignominy the *Century* could hardly continue the boast of being "the greatest train in the world," and the resulting relative upgrading of the *Broadway Limited* warmed the hearts of those who rode the Tuscan red Pullmans of the Pennsylvania train. Ten years later the end came for the *Century*. She made her last New York to Chicago run on December 2–3, 1967, being replaced by a train with just a number—coaches, Pullmans, and a diner— and no observation car or red-carpet treatment. Unfriendly railroad critics were quick to note that the last *Century* arrived in the Chicago LaSalle Station some nine hours late, because of a freight derailment up ahead. But the real reason for the death of the train was the simple fact that thousands of her one-time passengers simply preferred the jet-age speed of the airlines to the 15-hour 40-minute schedule of the *Century*. On the same page of *The New York Times* that reported the passing of the famous 65-year-old train there was a notice announcing four new American Airlines' nonstop jet flights between New York City and Chicago.

As railroads went into decline in the twentieth century, the airplane was easily the most dramatic challenger of the iron horse. Few people listened to or believed the words of Colonel John Jacob Astor when in 1903 he predicted that before long the gasoline engine would permit an age of air travel. Nor was there any great excitement later that year, on December 17, when the Wright brothers made four powered flights with their "flying machine" down at Kitty Hawk, North Carolina. The flights were short, lasting from twelve seconds to a minute, and the longest flight, of 582 feet, was hardly longer than the typical local passenger train then familiar to every small town in America. But two world wars and several decades of aviation engineering progress made the Astor prediction a fact long before mid-century. The speed of air travel is amazing. When President Lyndon B. Johnson made his 1967 pre-Christmas air trip to honor the memory of the Australian Prime Minister, Harold Holt, and to meet with Pope Paul VI in Rome, he was out of the country only five days. The Presidential jet was in the air not much over sixty hours for the 27,600 mile globe-circling journey. The President's total air-borne hours were not many more than the time required for the cross-country schedules of the few remaining transcontinental trains which today serve Chicago and the Pacific coast. And the speed of Johnson's trip in the blue and silver jet *Air Force One* is not unique. In 1967 Pan American World Airways was scheduling daily Boeing 707 jets out of San Francisco flying westward 19,894 miles to New York City. The time was less than 58 hours, and 75 per cent of the trips were completed within ten minutes of the printed schedule.

But the magic and glamour of today's air service are but symptomatic of an entire spectrum of new transportation facilities and modes that in the twentieth century have increasingly challenged American railroads. In recent decades the mature and middle-aged railroad industry has frequently been slow in facing and meeting such challenges.

5

The New Competition

In the half-century of maturity and decline which American railroads have experienced since their record high mileage in 1916 the industry has successively faced challenges from a broad variety of new modes of transport. In turn the railroads have had to compete with the electric interurban, thousands and soon millions of private cars, intercity buses, larger and larger trucks, airplanes which crowd the skyways, and a growing network of pipelines of greater size and capacity. In addition the century saw improved and more efficient transport appear on the nation's lakes, canals, and rivers. Some of this competition has been transitory in nature, but much of it has been stubbornly permanent. These new facilities are in a way reminiscent of an earlier day, an era of internal improvements when the turnpike, the canal, and the river steamboat stirred the imagination and energies of a younger America. In those antebellum years the Conestoga wagon, the Concord coach, the canal packet boat, the stern-wheeler, and side-wheeler had each in turn given way to the next succeeding mode of transportation. In the years after the Civil War only the railroad—the lines of Vanderbilt and Tom Scott, of Jay Gould and C. P. Huntington, or of Jim Hill and E. H. Harriman—had seemed to have any permanence.

Now in the twentieth century, this golden age of railroad monopoly was to be rudely challenged by a flood of unique and varied facilities. The railroad has not totally succumbed to the new competition, but the losses have been substantial. The family automobile, the economical Greyhound bus, and the high-flying jet airliner had combined, by the 'sixties, to make the market and demand for new railroad passenger cars practically nonexistent. Farm and commercial trucks were so efficient in carrying cattle, hogs, and sheep to the packing plants that between 1922 and 1966 the number of railroad stock cars declined from 80,000 to less than 20,000. Long-haul furniture vans soon made boxcar movement of household furnishings a thing of the past, and the increased use of intercity trucking caused a reduction of less-than-car-load lot freight from 51,000,000 tons in 1919 to 1,000,000 tons in 1966. The railroad industry was in trouble.

The first new mode of transport to challenge the steam railroad in America was the electric interurban, which appeared rather suddenly in the first decade of the new century. This challenge to the American railroad's long-held monopoly of intercity passenger transport was to prove of rather short duration. But use of the interurban became a kind of transition step to the almost complete dependence the traveling public was to have upon the automobile by the middle decades of the century. The development of the interurban in America can easily be traced back to changes which were occurring in urban transport in the 1880's and 1890's. In the mid-'eighties horse drawn stages and omnibuses had been carrying passengers in American cities for half a century. More than 400 different street railway companies employed some 35,000 men on 18,000 cars using nearly 100,000 horses and mules. The horsecars were small, slow in speed, and becoming quite inadequate for the mushrooming American cities. Modest experiments using electricity to power the cars had been made earlier in Cleveland, Ohio, and in Montgomery, Alabama, but the first practical electric railway system was probably the one opened in Richmond, Virginia, in 1888.

The man who gave Richmond its electric street railway system was a young engineer and former United States Navy officer, Frank J. Sprague. While on Navy duty in England in 1882, Sprague became aware of the health hazards present in London's smoky and dingy underground railway, a system that used steam locomotives for power. Sprague soon became convinced that the answer to urban transportation, both underground and surface, lay in electrification. He soon resigned from the Navy and for a short time became a technical assistant to Thomas A. Edison in New York City. In 1884 Sprague left Edison and set up his own business, the Sprague Electric Railway & Motor Company. His first opportunity came with a contract to provide electric power for forty street cars in Richmond. Sprague himself was at the controls of an electrically driven car when it first successfully climbed the steep grade of the Franklin Street hill on election night 1887. The entire line was opened for service on February 2, 1888. In the following decade the transition from the mule and horse car to the electric trolley was indeed rapid. Between 1890 and 1902 the street railway trackage using animal power declined from 5661 miles to 259 miles, while that operated by electricity jumped from 1262 miles to 21,902 miles during those years.

With the coming of the electric trolley car in the late nineteenth century, several traction financiers came to the fore such as Thomas Fortune Ryan and August Belmont in New York City, Henry M. Whitney in Boston, Charles T. Yerkes in Chicago, and Peter A. B. Widener in Philadelphia. Fortunes were to be made, and were made, in this traction business. Often the street car tycoons were as adept at playing politics as they were careless with the needs or rights of the urban traveling public. It was Yerkes who was reported to have said: "It's the strap-hanger who pays the dividends." This same Chicago businessman once admitted that the key to his success was: "to buy old junk, fix it up a little, and unload it on the other fellows." The Philadelphia traction king Widener, former butcher and meat provisioner to the Union army, was equally callous concerning the rights of the little man. Once he brushed aside the opposition of some minority stockholders by declaring firmly: "You can vote first and discuss afterward."

The shift to electric interurban service came quite early after the turn of the century. Expanding street railways for some time had been opening up new suburbs and bringing them within commuting range of downtown centers. By 1902 the long-distance transmission of power was so much improved that electric railway service covering longer and longer distances was feasible. Soon the intercity equipment was both heavier and faster than the ordinary urban streetcars. Interurbans normally operated on city streets near their terminals, but shifted their tracks to the sides of roads or private rights of way once the open country had been reached. Americans in the first years of this century witnessed the arrival of both the automobile and the electric interurban, but the more enthusiastic reception was clearly given to the interurban. A major investment boom in the interurban industry came in the very years in which many bankers were turning deaf ears to the financial requests of such automobile men as W. C. Durant and Henry Ford.

Between 1901 and 1908 more than 9000 miles of interurban lines were built in the country, and hundreds of individual local companies were dreaming of constructing routes which would steal local passenger traffic away from the railroads. Soon some new lines were also carrying modest amounts of baggage, mail, express, and freight. The greater frequency of service, and often a higher average speed, gave the electric interurban a real advantage over much of the local passenger or branch line railroad service. Since the interurbans had a faster rate of acceleration it was easier for them to have more frequent scheduled stops than was true of the steam railroad. The top year for electric interurban mileage was 1916 (the same year that steam railroad mileage was at its height) when 15,580 miles were in operation. By 1914 it was claimed that a combination of interurban and city street railway trackage could make possible a trip from Chicago to New York or from New York to Portland, Maine. In fact, in March 1912 a party of street railway officials made such a trip in the private car "Huguenot" from Park Square in Boston down to New York City. The trip took twenty hours and used the tracks of at least a dozen different traction or interurban companies. With perhaps less speed, and certainly less comfort, any hardy and persistent private citizen could have made the same trip by spending $2.40 in nickels and fare tokens.

Two-thirds of the total mileage was located in the six northern and eastern states of Illinois, Indiana, Ohio, Michigan, Pennsylvania, and New York. Ohio, with 2798 miles of route, was easily first in interurban mileage. Although a poor second with 1825 miles, Indiana boasted a network which made it the most thoroughly covered of any state. More than twenty different companies gave service to every corner of Indiana, with thirteen different routes radiating out of Indianapolis. All Hoosier towns of over 5000 people were served by the interurban except for three—Bloomington, Madison, and Vincennes.

Many of the projected Indiana interurbans succeeded in completing a line which fairly resembled the original projected company objective. Other companies showed a great contrast between intention and achievement. Perhaps the classic example of such a failure would be the ambitious project, the Chicago-New York Electric Air Line Railroad. This company proposed to build a double track 742-mile straight-line route between Chicago and New York City having no grade crossings, no grades of above 0.5 per cent, and curves so slight that they would permit operation at 90 miles per hour. Ten-hour service at a flat $10 fare was to be offered. The Air Line route, which would be 150 miles shorter than any existing trunk line's steam railroad, was the dream of Alexander C. Miller, a midwestern railroad man with twenty years of operating experience. Miller was said to have first thought of the Air Line route while traveling on a passenger train. Possibly he was on a New York Central train to Chicago, where three hours fast travel north out from New York City found the train at Albany, almost more air miles away from its destination than when the trip started. Miller's dream line never got out of the Hoosier state. His insistence on low grades helped bring financial disaster to the company when it planned and built a colossal fill in crossing Coffey Creek a few miles east of Gary. Hundreds of tons of dirt and thousands of dollars went into the two-mile fill which was 180 feet wide at the base. In 1909 the short completed mileage had cost more than $300,000 a mile to construct, and the gross revenues per mile of road were under $1000.

But hundreds of lines with less stringent engineering standards were soon in operation across the nation. Passenger traffic on many interurban lines was fairly brisk but the hoped-for prosperity and profits generally remained illusive. Even during the best years the rate of return in the industry was barely 3 per cent, a figure perhaps two-thirds that of steam railroads. By World War I the automobile was taking away some business, although a few brave prophets still refused to take the automobile seriously. The pioneer Hoosier interurban promoter, Charles L. Henry, saw the car as a passing fad and in a 1916 speech claimed: "The fad feature of automobile riding will gradually wear off, and the time will soon be here when a very large part of the people will cease to think of automobile rides. . . ." But another Henry, with the mass production of his Model T, was to prove the Hoosier interurban enthusiast very wrong.

Increasing private auto use and new intercity bus routes in the 'twenties definitely caused higher operating ratios and frequent deficits for many interurban companies. More than 4000 miles of line were abandoned by 1929, and another 5000 miles had been given up by 1934. One Indiana interurban in the depression 'thirties was reduced to paying its workers partly with fare tokens. Interurban trackage continued to be abandoned even in the years of economic recovery, and by Pearl Harbor less than 3000 miles remained. Little interurban passenger service was found in the United States by 1960, but the Chicago South Shore and South Bend was still furnishing a substantial suburban service south of Chicago with some trains going as far as South Bend, Indiana. Rather surprisingly, in the early 'sixties about 2000 miles of interurban line was still providing some freight service. But the interurban as such was dead. The passenger traffic which the interurban for a few years had taken over from the steam railroads had in turn been largely lost to the private automobile.

The automobile in its various forms has clearly been the most important of the several challenges to American railroads in the twentieth century. In the last half-century, the family car and to a lesser degree the intercity bus have brought about a great decline in the railroad passenger business. The volume of motor truck freight in the years since World War II has grown to at least half the rail freight traffic, and truck dollar revenue is several times that of the railroad freight revenue. Few Americans in the first years of the new century could foresee the social revolution that would come with the automobile—the decline in rural isolation, the explosive growth of Suburbia, the expensive and expansive new highway programs, and the complications of an economy based on the assembly line. The livery stable owner, the harness maker, and the proprietor of the wagon factory in the America of 1910 certainly could not foresee the day, a half-century later, when the total automotive industry would employ (directly and indirectly) one worker in seven of the nation's gainfully employed. And the railroads thought it a preposterous notion that a few self-propelled contraptions on the streets of pre-war America could ever become a serious threat to their long-held monopoly of transportation.

Only four automobiles were built in the United States in 1895. The new words "garage," "chauffeur," and "chassis" would correctly suggest that the automobile had its origins in France. But before 1895 American-built horseless carriages had been constructed by Charles Duryea in Springfield, Massachusetts, Henry Ford in Detroit, and Elwood Haynes in Kokomo, Indiana. These first vehicles were little more than ruggedly built buggies with hard rubber tires, and small gasoline engines giving power to the back axle via a belt or bicycle chain. Until 1900 there were probably as many cars run by electricity as were run by gasoline engines, but the internal combustion engine was soon to be triumphant. Ransom E. Olds, one of the earliest advocates of mass production, built 4000 of his "curved dash" Oldsmobiles during 1903. Two years later, one of these cars, steered by a tiller as were many early models, was driven in a transcontinental race from New York City to the Lewis and Clark Exposition out in Portland, Oregon, in the winning time of 44 days. But changes in design and construction soon appeared. Pneumatic tires and improved springs soon smoothed the ride over the rough roads of pre-war America. The early "one lung" gasoline engine soon gave way to a more powerful motor with four, or even six cylinders. Cadillac was building an eight-cylinder engine in 1914, and the next year Packard introduced a twelve-cylinder model. Earlier, in 1913, Charles F. Kettering, an electrical engineering genius, had perfected an electrical starter which gave the internal combustion engine certain victory over steam or electric-driven models. In eliminating the crank, the self-starter not only reduced the incidence of sprained wrists and broken arms, but also did much to put the woman driver behind the steering wheel. The automobile had definitely achieved most of the basic structural and mechanical form by 1929, the year in which a record-breaking five million cars were built.

While high-priced models and a reluctance to desert the horse kept many Americans from buying a car, a major obstacle was the condition of the roads in the nation. The two million miles of country and rural roads in America were often almost impassable because of mud, ruts, and pot-holes. The road improvement efforts of thousands of bicycle riders, working through their League of American Wheelmen, had brought but modest results during the 1890's. Farmers were generally reluctant to tax themselves to improve roads which they felt were already adequate for their slow-moving wagons and buggies. The maintenance of highways was a function of local government, and in nearly every state it was possible for local citizens, it they so desired, to pay off their road taxes with their own personal labor. Such road work efforts were normally almost worthless, especially when directed by amateur "commissioners of highways." In the decade before World War I highway engineers with any degree of training and skill were quite rare. The automobile owners who ventured out on the pre-war American roads went outfitted with goggles and linen dusters, and were resigned to slow speeds with frequent punctures and tire trouble. In 1903, when more than thirty cars started on the first Glidden Tour, designed to test the reliability and endurance of the early automobile, it took eight days to reach Pittsburgh from New York City.

In the first years of the twentieth century many Americans viewed the horseless carriage as a rich man's toy. Many put motoring in about the same far-out category as playing golf or wearing a wrist watch. The energetic President Theodore Roosevelt wrote in 1905 that his two "auto rides" were all that he desired. Roosevelt's attitude may have been influenced by the fact that his second ride had resulted in unfavorable publicity when his chauffeur had been stopped for speeding. In 1907 Woodrow Wilson, then president of Princeton University, cautioned his students against the snobbery of motoring, saying: "Nothing has spread socialistic feelings in this country more than the automobile . . ."

The answer to the unsympathetic views of Roosevelt and Wilson came in 1908, when Henry Ford brought out his first Model T, a rugged all-purpose car which sold, in the roadster model, for as little as $825. The "flivver" or "tin lizzie," as Americans were soon calling it, was being produced by assembly line methods by 1914, and two years later Ford was selling 500,000 cars a year. The price of the roadster by 1925 had declined to $260, f.o.b. Detroit. Fifteen million Fords, black and ungainly but very durable, had been sold when the model finally went out of production in 1927. Everybody bought a Ford. It often provided the urban worker with transportation to a job that might be some miles away. The farmer used the Ford to haul light produce to market, to do light chores around the farmyard with the power from a jacked-up rear wheel, or to take a brief family vacation after the harvest was in. In the 'twenties, most new automobiles were open cars, but by 1929 the great majority were closed models. The average family purchased its first automobile during the 'twenties, and by 1930 there were 23,000,000 passenger cars registered in the nation, or an average of one car for every five to six Americans.

A major development accompanying America's acceptance of the automobile has been the increasing attention given to the planning, construction, and maintenance of highways. There had been a time before World War I when the typical motorist, especially in the northern states, had put his car up on blocks during the winter months, going back to the reliable horse. All of this was changed as the family car became commonplace. The demand for "good roads" became overpowering when millions of car owners joined the earlier tens of thousands of bicycle riders in such requests. As a consequence of these demands, Congress in 1916 established the first federal highway program. The legislation matched federal with state money and provided for through roads and major highways. A registration fee for automobiles had first been introduced in New York in 1904, and in 1919 Oregon introduced a novel, and very useful, tax on gasoline. By the 'twenties every state was providing more and more money for new and improved roads. In the following decades it was a race between highway building and the rush of millions of new cars coming out of Detroit. Muddy country roads and wagon tracks went through grading, gravelling, straightening, and paving to become the highways we use today.

More than one-fourth of the 3,000,000 miles of road in rural America are under either state or federal control, being designated as state or national highways. The toll roads built by several states in the 'forties and 'fifties have in the 'sixties been rapidly augmented by the projected, and partially completed, interstate system of over 40,000 miles of superhighway. This road building has been expensive. Between 1921 and 1965 the federal government spent more than $43 billion on highways. In the same 45 years, the state and local governments of the nation spent another $173 billion on roads and highways. User charges, chiefly state and federal gasoline taxes, have furnished only about 60 per cent of this $216 billion. In other words, something more than $80 billion of public tax money, beyond user charges, have been expended on the nation's highways in the last half-century. Most of these highway expenditures must be charged off to the travel benefits enjoyed by the general public and their more than 80,000,000 family cars. But a considerable fraction of the $80 billion of tax money clearly has provided a *public* route for the more than 16,000,000 buses and trucks which crowd our highways today. Most of these buses and trucks are in commercial operations, and compete for business with railroads: companies which have provided their own privately built and maintained tracks and right of way. A public that can never forget the government's largess in the nineteenth century railroad land grants should remember that in the twentieth century governmental aid to the commercial bus and truck industries has been even more generous.

Most of today's highway traffic, however, consists of private automobiles. While the Republicans in 1928, in the glow of Coolidge prosperity, had talked of "two cars in every garage," any substantial development of this sort was delayed until after World War II. By 1963 one family in five of all car-owning families owned two or more vehicles. The typical American in the prosperous mid-twentieth century was a car owner living in Suburbia. He used his car to go to work, and with it increasingly patronized the new spacious shopping centers, numerous drive-in banks, theaters, and restaurants. For years the summer vacation, when the car was driven as much in three weeks as it had been in the last six months, has been an annual family event. In the 'twenties the private automobile had ruined the passenger traffic of many interurban lines, and began to threaten the passenger traffic of the steam railroad. Railroad passenger traffic declined steadily during the 'twenties, and in 1930 was only three-fifths of the volume at the start of the decade. During the 1920's private intercity automobile traffic (in total passenger miles) soon surpassed traffic by rail, and by 1930 was six times as extensive. The depression 'thirties slowed the increase in automotive traffic only briefly, and the total traffic increased by only one-half during the decade. Even during the gas and tire-rationing days of World War II, the volume of private vehicular intercity traffic was larger than the combined commercial operation of railroads, buses, and air carriers. By 1965, with over 70,000,000 family cars on American roads, the volume of automotive intercity traffic was eight times that of all commercial traffic. In 1967, intercity auto traffic pushed to an all-time high of 937 billion passenger-miles, a figure roughly sixty times the volume of railroad passenger traffic.

In the post-war 'twenties many Americans became aware of the convenience, cleanliness, and especially the novelty of the few buses which were available for short intercity trips. The first motor buses had been little more than elongated passenger cars with a stronger chassis and extra seats. Within a few years two brothers, Frank and William Fageol, had designed a new type of bus which would revolutionize bus transportation. The Fageol bus was built close to the ground with a low entrance step and a low center of gravity. A later model placed the engine underneath the floor so that the entire body space was available for a passenger payload. Hundreds of small bus companies competed for the patronage of the early bus traveler. The reaction of railroad officials to this new competition was to view the bus as only a minor irritant, but some companies did set up subsidiary bus lines of their own. In the 'twenties and early 'thirties the Burlington, the Union Pacific, the Great Northern, the New York Central, and the Pennsylvania all either set up bus lines of their own, or acquired stock in the new Greyhound System which had been established in 1929. By 1930 enough highways had been improved for intercity bus service to have achieved a certain respectability. In that year, almost one-fifth of all intercity commercial travel was by bus.

The very first buses offered the obvious advantages of extensibility, economy, and convenience, and in recent years both the speed and the safety of bus travel have become competitive with the railroad. The 3,000,000 miles of highways and roads in America gave both the bus and the truck a flexibility of service which the railroad industry has never been able to provide.

Hundreds of villages and small communities have never seen or heard their first locomotive. A recent study of towns and villages in Virginia has revealed that in that state alone there are some 300 towns and hamlets (with a total population of nearly 300,000) where the sole commercial passenger service is that provided by the bus. By the 'sixties the mileage of highway bus routes was easily three times that of railroad passenger route mileage. As improved roads, new turnpikes, and through express highways appeared after World War II, bus companies have been able to substantially speed up their schedules. The New York City to Washington bus trip which took 7 hours and 30 minutes in 1947 was reduced to 4 hours and 10 minutes by 1965. The longer trip from New York City to Chicago had taken almost 28 hours on express runs in 1947. By 1965 this had been reduced to 16 hours and 20 minutes, a time almost as fast as that of the crack New York Central's *Twentieth Century Limited* back in its best days.

The smaller seating capacity of the bus, as compared with the typical railroad passenger car, also allowed a greater flexibility in schedules as compared with railroad service. In 1965 there were two and one-half times as many intercity buses in operation as there were railway passenger carrying cars. By the 'sixties most buses were air-conditioned, many were equipped with washrooms, and some even had snack bars. Bus travel has always been a bit cheaper than railroad coach accommodations. In the late 'fifties and 'sixties bus tickets ranged between 2½ and 2¾ cents a passenger mile, or about 10 per cent below railroad fares.

In recent years the accident or safety record of bus travel has been excellent. Bus travel in the last decade has been approximately twenty times safer than travel in a private automobile. It is as safe as train travel, and in most years has been considerably safer than travel by air. The safety, economy, and convenience of bus travel paid off in increased business. By 1962 the total intercity bus traffic, in terms of passenger miles, for the first time exceeded the volume of rail passenger business. Since

World War II, in spite of a rapidly growing use of the family car and the airliner, bus traffic in America has generally held rather steady at between twenty and twenty-four billion passenger-miles per year. The average bus trip is somewhat shorter than the normal railroad journey, and only a small fraction of the average trip by air. In the middle 'sixties the total number of individual bus tickets sold annually was slightly larger than the combined rail and air ticket sales. Clearly the advertising slogan, "and leave the driving to us" has appealed to the public.

Unlike today's railroads, which often seem to wish to divest themselves of their passenger traffic, the revenue of the typical bus lines is mainly derived from passenger business. But since World War II there has been a marked increase in the transportation of package express by bus. By 1965 this was up to $61,-000,000 annually, or 10 per cent of the total operating revenue for the industry. No doubt some of the financial well-being of the bus industry today can be attributed to the efficiency and courtesy which the traveling public generally associates with the typical bus driver. While few of the 25,000 bus drivers in the country have the sex appeal of the pert airline hostess, or the glamour of the airline pilot, they generally present an image more favorable to the public than the aging, and often grouchy, railroad passenger conductor. Certainly the average bus driver, who in a typical year drives his bus more than 50,000 miles, is not guilty of the featherbedding or short work-day practices so common with railroad passenger personnel today.

Truck traffic has also grown very rapidly in the twentieth century. Almost as soon as the first automobiles were built, light-weight trucks were beginning to compete with the horse-drawn dray and delivery wagon on the city streets of America. In 1899 the Post Office Department began modest experiments with the truck delivery of mail in some American cities. In 1904 there were still only 700 trucks sold in America, but the number grew as many manufacturers added a truck line to their regular passenger car production. Over half a million trucks were in use by 1918, and those that were sent overseas to serve with the fighting doughboys in France made at least a modest contribution to the final victory of the Allies. The number of trucks in America grew rapidly during the post-war 'twenties. The three million trucks in the nation at the end of the decade were already providing almost 4 per cent of the total intercity freight ton-mileage. Most of such traffic consisted of light loads moving rather short distances.

The trucking industry was one segment of the economy that expanded even during the depression 'thirties. The four and one-half million trucks in America in 1940 represented one-seventh of the total vehicle registration. In these years America easily led the world in truck production, and until the early 'fifties more than half the trucks in the world were running on American highways. Back in the 'thirties many unemployed truck drivers managed to buy a truck on credit in order to establish a little "fly-by-night" intercity trucking business. These small operators knew little of sound business practice, and were only trying to get sufficient business to buy gas and oil, meet the monthly truck payments, and have a few remaining dollars upon which to live. A large damage claim or a big truck repair bill could force such an operator out of business, but others quickly seemed to take his place. The aggregate of such operations grew, and the railroads began to feel the competition.

Truck operators were unregulated by the federal government prior to 1935 and, like the bus companies, they were aided by a right of way that reached into every corner of every state. Today twenty-nine states have one or more counties that lack any railroad service. There are seventeen such counties in Virginia, fourteen in Texas, and six in Nebraska. Furthermore, these truck routes (as compared with the railroads) are virtually free. Furniture, animals and animal products, poultry, dairy products, fruits and vegetables, and less-than-carload freight all tended to be shifted from the freight car to the highway truck. From 1935 until the early 'sixties from 50 to 90 per cent of all motor vehicles were shipped from the factory via the highway. By 1940, on the eve of Pearl Harbor, intercity truck freight had climbed to 62 billion ton-miles a year, or one-tenth of the total freight traffic in the nation.

During World War II American trucks continued to be manufactured, even though the production of passenger cars stopped. A large part of the two and a half million trucks produced were of course for military use. The role of trucks in the military effort was greater than in World War I, a signal contribution to allied victory being the "Red Ball Express," which by truck supplied the Allied armies in France in the weeks after the Normandy beachhead. Truck production boomed in the early post-war years, and in 1950 more than one-sixth of all motor vehicles registered in America were trucks. Improvements soon appeared in both the size and power of the post-war trucks. The cab-over-engine truck appeared, and diesel power was used increasingly for the larger trucks. Soon the larger trucks could carry loads of twenty tons or more, powered by engines that might have as many as sixteen different gear ratios. The tractor-trailer combination, in which a detachable trailer was pulled by a motive power unit, became popular and more than a million such units were in operation by 1960. A leading manufacturer of many of these innovations was the White Motor Company of Cleveland, Ohio, whose president for twenty years was Robert F. Black. Black, who had spent his entire life in the trucking industry, was so successful in revitalizing his company, that in the industry it was often claimed that "Black took White out of the red."

Trucks, large or small, offered the American shipping public the same flexibility of service that the bus did. The post-World War II highway improvement programs accelerated the trend of transporting more freight by highway. Between 1950 and 1966 the volume of highway freight more than doubled. In 1966 the nearly 15,000,000 trucks in the country carried a volume of 396 billion ton-miles, almost one-fourth of the total intercity freight movement. In that year the volume of freight traffic moving via rubber and concrete was over one-half as large as that moved by rail. The average cost per ton-mile for highway freight, since it consisted so largely of finished goods or freight of relatively high value, was several times the ton-mile rate by railroad. Thus, the gross freight revenues of the total trucking industry is higher than that of the railroads. As trucks successfully competed with the older railroad industry, they also had the advantage of being less rigorously regulated by the state and federal governments. In the 1840's and 1850's the traveling and shipping public in the United States was deserting the Concord stagecoach and the Conestoga wagon for the early railroad. In turn a century later the Greyhound bus and the cross country truck were increasingly appealing to the American public. The combination of the internal combustion engine plus improved highways was proving to be a serious challenge to the iron horse.

In the early twentieth century, American interest in aviation developed in a somewhat slower fashion. The economic life of the country was certainly not significantly changed by aviation until the 1920's. Suggesting in 1900 that someday a man might travel through the air in a machine heavier than air itself was viewed by most people as a preposterous idea. Americans were shocked in 1898 when they read that Congress had actually voted $100,000 for the financing of a crazy experiment to see if an engine-powered flying machine could carry a man. And they laughed out loud when John Jacob Astor, great grandson of the fur-trading Astor and an inventor in his own right, predicted in 1903 that an age of air travel would soon be possible through the use of a lightweight gasoline engine. Astor did not live to see his prophecy proven correct, for he was lost in the *Titanic* disaster in 1912.

In the same year of the Astor prediction, a pair of brothers, Orville and Wilbur Wright, made their first powered flights. The two brothers owned a bicycle business in Dayton, Ohio, but their first love was clearly aviation. They read everything they could find on the subject, and spent their spare time in designing and flying both model and man-carrying gliders. Finally they built their own flying machine, powered by a home-made 12-horse power, 200-pound gasoline engine. It was this airplane which made history at Kitty Hawk in 1903. The American public was not very excited over this event, and it was several years before the importance of the historic flight by the Wright brothers was generally recognized. People who saw the Wright brothers fly their plane around Dayton, Ohio, in 1905 still seemed to think it was some kind of trickery. But aviators on both sides of the Atlantic coaxed their clumsy and fragile crafts to fly longer and longer distances in the dozen years after 1903.

As an increasingly curious public finally became aware that a new air age had arrived, it became apparent that air transportation was significantly different from earlier transport facilities in at least two ways. Unlike all other modes or forms of transport, the route or way for air travel and service was quite unlimited and relatively free. There were very few restrictions upon the expansion and extension of new air routes once a fairly dependable aircraft was generally available. This point is well illustrated by the marked extension of new airmail routes in the United States in the years just after the 1927 crossing of the Atlantic by Charles A. Lindbergh. Airlines have also been fortunate in the extent to which the government has largely provided increasingly sophisticated weather and navigational services so necessary to air transport. Since 1925 the federal government has paid out several billion dollars for airway facilities and the building of a number of civil airports. The second unique feature in air transportation development has been the degree to which the air industry has been aided by the needs and developments of national security and defense. By 1908 Orville Wright had convinced the U.S. Army of the military possibilities of the airplane, and six years later the U.S. Navy set up a training school for aviators at Pensacola, Florida. In World War I American pilots, led by such aces as Captain Eddie Rickenbacker, shot down almost three enemy planes for every American plane lost, though nearly all the planes they flew were of British or French manufacture. Nevertheless, the lessons learned in both World Wars were of immense value in the expansion of commercial air transport that followed each war.

Certainly in the years of peace the defense and security needs of the country have helped to justify numerous governmental subsidies in the support of extended and improved air service.

In the early post-war years the civilian population continued to applaud the efforts of "barn-storming" aviators at numerous county fairs. A U.S. Navy crew captured the headlines in 1919 when they flew a flying boat across the Atlantic, and in 1923 a pair of Army lieutenants made a twenty-seven-hour nonstop flight in a Fokker monoplane from Long Island to San Diego. Earlier on May 15, 1918, the first regular airmail service had been inaugurated when two Army pilots had flown a Curtiss "Jenny" from Washington, D.C., to New York City. Later civilian pilots took over the service, and airmail was established between New York City and San Francisco in the fall of 1920 with the mail being transferred at night to fast passenger trains. Once the airways were lighted, night airmail service followed in 1923.

In Europe a passenger carrying airline had been established across the English Channel as early as 1919, but in the United States air travel was slower to be accepted. Even with the relative lack of public interest in commercial aviation, several aircraft designers and builders such as Glenn Curtiss, Glenn Martin, William Boeing, and Donald Douglas remained active throughout the 'twenties. In 1927 scheduled air passenger service in the United States was begun with flights between New York City and Boston. Interest in all facets of air service increased markedly after Lindbergh's flight to Paris in the spring of 1927. Very soon a combined air-rail passenger service was available on a route provided by the Pennsylvania Railroad, Transcontinental Air Transport, and the Santa Fe Railway. Going by rail at night and flying during daylight hours allowed such passengers to cross the country in 48 hours. By 1929 three major airlines—American, Trans-World, and United—had all been organized. An all-air passenger service soon appeared. Some 73,000,000 passenger-miles were flown in 1930, the year in which the first airline hostess appeared to serve airline passengers. In the late 'twenties dozens of new airmail routes were opened across the nation. Pan American Airways was flying mail down to Cuba by 1927, and by 1930 had such service into much of Latin America.

Aviation was one form of transport generally unaffected by the depression in the 'thirties. Dozens of small and large companies with hundreds of planes flew more and more passengers and carried increasing loads of mail and air express during the decade. Between 1930 and 1940 air passenger traffic increased more than a dozenfold to just over a billion passenger-miles in 1940, and air-freight traffic more than tripled in volume. In 1936, for the first time, more than a million airline tickets were sold in a single year. It was in that same year that the Douglas DC-3, a plane that many have called "the Model T of aircraft," was first introduced. Donald Douglas in 1932 had sold T.W.A. several planes of an earlier model, the DC-2. After 1936 the new all-metal DC-3 quickly became the most popular type on all major airlines. Maximum economy, safety, and speed were admirably combined in this durable craft which had a payload of twenty-one passengers and was powered by two 900 horsepower Wright cyclone motors. The DC-3 was the first plane which could make a profit by carrying passengers without the benefit of an airmail route subsidy. More than 10,000 of these rugged planes were to be produced between 1936 and the end of World War II. In the middle and late 'thirties Juan Trippe, president of Pan American, was establishing new air routes for his Martin-built flying boats across both the Atlantic and the Pacific. In these early years transoceanic flight was an adventurous and experimental thing. Hardly a dozen years later—certainly by mid-century—when someone said he was leaving for Europe the first question he might be asked was, "Are you going by air or by boat?"

The Second World War made such extraordinary demands upon the designers and manufacturers of aircraft that soon air travel became a normal mode of transportation. In the fifteen years after Pearl Harbor the airports in the nation tripled in number, and the number of qualified pilots increased sixfold. In the two decades after 1941 the number of privately owned aircraft more than tripled reaching a total of 84,000 in 1962. The private plane never challenged the railroad as did the family automobile, but the growth of commercial air travel was indeed sensational. Faster and larger civilian planes built by Donald Douglas and William Boeing, the builder of the World War II Flying Fortress (B-17), flew over extended and new routes. Domestic air passenger travel increased tenfold during the decade of the 'forties. Overseas air travel also expanded rapidly as the monopoly of transoceanic service held by Juan Trippe's Pan American in the 'thirties was shared by several other airlines after the war. The flying boats and seaplanes of the late 'thirties and war years were soon replaced by the faster jet-propelled land planes. Since the transoceanic craft soon were crossing the water in as many hours as a ship takes days, the new fast jets soon were capturing the cream of the overseas passenger traffic. The same year, 1967, which saw the disappearance of the *Twentieth Century Limited* from the tracks of the New York Central, also saw the last voyage of the Cunard liner, the *Queen Mary*. The fast new jet airliner was responsible for the demise of both the famous train and the luxury liner.

Domestic air travel continued to boom in the sixties. Commercial air travel in the United States in 1963 was as extensive (in passenger-miles) as the combined total of railroad and bus passenger business. In the quarter of a century after 1940 commercial air travel had grown more than fiftyfold to a total of 58 billion passenger-miles in 1965. During the same twenty-five years travel by private automobile had more than tripled and bus passenger traffic had slightly more than doubled in amount. And railroad passenger traffic had declined by one-fourth in the same period. Today the airliner dominates commercial passenger traffic, in total passenger-miles traveled, with about three-fifths of the total commercial movement. At the same time the typical American still does not fly. In 1965 less than one-fourth of all intercity passenger tickets sold were airline tickets (84 million air, 106 million rail, and 193 million bus, for a total of 383 million tickets). One of the reasons, of course, is that the usual air trip generally taken by a businessman is a much longer trip than that taken by the average citizen, who is more likely to travel by bus or train.

Since World War II, air freight has also grown rapidly. In many segments of the American economy the rapid delivery of valuable freight, by air, has become quite common. In 1968 the total air freight and cargo flown in the nation was about 3.1 billion ton-miles. Nevertheless, in the total volume of intercity freight traffic, the portion moving by air is still very small (about one-fifth of one per cent) when compared with the freight traffic of rail, truck, waterway, or pipeline facilities.

Improving air safety has certainly helped commercial air travel develop in recent years. While air accidents still occur, they have relatively declined as air travel has graphically increased during the last decade. In the late 'fifties air travel was three or four times more dangerous than travel by train or bus, but less than one-fourth as dangerous as highway travel in the family automobile. The airline fatal accident rate (per 100,000,-000 passenger-miles) was cut in half by the middle 'sixties. For the years 1963 through 1965 there was only one airline death for every 435,000,000 passenger-miles flown.

But another facet of commercial aviation, that of noise, promises to be increasingly troublesome in the years ahead. Millions of Americans who live near large city airports are increasingly tormented by the noise from hundreds of jet engines. People living near O'Hare airport in Chicago—reported to be the busiest airfield in the world—have to put up with a jet aircraft landing or taking off on the average of one every forty seconds. The victim of such noise can complain and he can sue. Recent estimates suggest that presently there are some $200,000,000 in jet noise lawsuits pending—very few have much chance of success. The average American is not as fortunate as the President of the United States. No aircraft, either prop or jet, is allowed to fly over or near the White House. Nor can the average citizen shut

"The Iron Horse Comes to Frederick, Maryland." This painting by
H. D. Stitt shows the arrival of a Baltimore & Ohio train in the mid-
1830s. Horses were still being used when the sixty-one-mile line out of
Baltimore was opened in December 1831.

(Courtesy, Baltimore & Ohio Railroad)

"Sacramento Railroad Station" by William Hahn shows the bustle associated with rail travel on the Central Pacific in the 1870s.

(Courtesy M. H. de Young Memorial Museum, San Francisco)

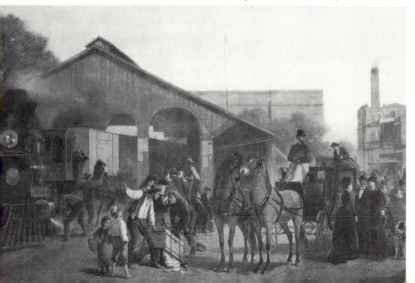

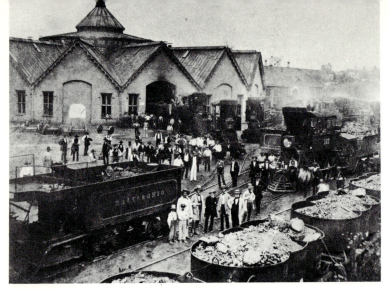

Baltimore & Ohio shops at Martinsburg, West Virginia, during the Civil War. As the most exposed of the northern trunk lines to the West the B.&O. suffered severely from Confederate raids during the war. In the summer of 1861 Stonewall Jackson made off with fourteen locomotives from this terminal. *(Courtesy, Baltimore & Ohio Railroad)*

Remains of a roundhouse in Atlanta in the fall of 1864. The railroads of Georgia and South Carolina received very rough treatment as General William T. Sherman moved into the heart of the Confederacy.
(Courtesy, Association of American Railroads)

Recent newcomers waiting to board an immigrant train for the West. Photograph taken in the 1880s at a B. & O. Locust Point pier in Baltimore.
(Courtesy, Baltimore & Ohio Railroad)

Homesteaders crowd a train as they await the signal opening the Cherokee Strip, Indiana Territory, in September 1893.
(Courtesy, Chicago, Rock Island & Pacific Railroad)

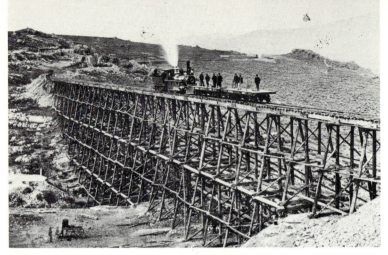

This A. J. Russell photo of 1869 shows the Union Pacific engine No. 119, with a full head of steam, on the "big trestle" just a few miles east of Promontory, Utah. A few days later this 4-4-0 engine faced the Central Pacific's *Jupiter* in the golden spike ceremony of May 10, 1869.

(Courtesy, Union Pacific Railroad)

In 1969, the centennial year of transcontinental railroading, the Union Pacific ordered a number of new "centennial" diesels. The 6900 series units each have a length of nearly 100 feet and are rated at a record 6600 horsepower. *(Courtesy, Union Pacific Railroad)*

The *Pioneer Zephyr* nears Chicago on May 26, 1934 as it completes its 785-minute nonstop trip from Denver to Chicago, a distance of 1015 miles. *(Courtesy, Chicago, Burlington & Quincy Railroad)*

The *Turbotrain* entered high speed service between New York and Boston on April 8, 1969, joining the earlier *Metroliner* which gives fast passenger service between New York and Washington. On a special test track the *Turbotrain* has reached a speed of 170 miles per hour.

(Courtesy, Sikorsky Aircraft)

Chicago & North Western suburban train runs parallel to expressway serving Chicago commuters. Most experts agree that rapid transit railroads can serve the commuter needs of large cities much better than highways. *(Courtesy, Chicago & North Western Railway)*

Automatic fare collection gates on the Illinois Central. In 1966 this Chicago commuter line introduced a new automatic suburban revenue collection system in which riders use magnetic tickets to activate station ticket gates. *(Courtesy, Illinois Central Railroad)*

A variety of new automatic track maintenance machines contribute to the efficiency of railway track crews.

(Courtesy, Association of American Railroads)

Auto rack cars being unloaded at Little Ferry, New Jersey. One bright spot in railroad freight traffic is the recent graphic increase in the low-rate high speed delivery of new automobiles.

(Courtesy, Association of American Railroads)

An all piggyback Illinois Central "Fastback" train arrives in Chicago from Memphis. Piggyback traffic has grown sixfold in the last dozen years, and in 1968 accounted for almost 5 per cent of all freight car-loadings. *(Courtesy, Illinois Central Railroad)*

A new 50,000-gallon tank car being loaded with liquid chemicals. Such cars, often called "Pregnant Whales," have a capacity several times that of the older tank car shown on the left.

(Courtesy, Association of American Railroads)

off the noise, as President Lyndon Johnson did at the Lincoln Memorial. Realizing that the noise of aircraft landing at the nearby National Airport was going to spoil his eulogy of Carl Sandburg, the President asked the Secret Service to have planes temporarily rerouted. They were.

In the 'fifties and 'sixties the dramatic growth of air travel has clearly been the greatest challenge to railroad passenger service. In the same years rail freight traffic has had to face new competition from transport facilities established at a much earlier time. Pipeline traffic has grown so extensively in the past century that today it ranks just behind the highway truck in its challenge to railroad freight. In 1859 the area around Titusville in Western Pennsylvania experienced the oil boom. During the Civil War the transportation of the crude oil to the nearest refinery proved difficult and expensive: haulage costs per barrel, by wagon over rutted roads and by barge in streams that always seemed short of water, averaged about $3. A Titusville businessman, Samuel Van Syckel, thought he had a solution to the problem—a pipeline constructed of two-inch wrought iron pipe with four steam pumps located at strategic spots to supply pressure. Van Syckel was laughed at as a crazy visionary, and irate teamsters seeing a threat to their jobs took up rifles, feuded with the pipe-layers, and even tore up pipe and burned storage tanks. But this first crude five-mile line was finished by Van Syckel in the fall of 1865. Since the line soon started to pump 1000 barrels of oil a day, haulage costs of the dark green liquid quickly dropped to a dollar a barrel. In 1867 William Hawkins Abbott, merchant, builder of plank roads and an early oil refiner of Titusville, formed the first consolidation of pipelines by establishing the Pennsylvania Transportation Company. In the same years in which the oil magnate, John D. Rockefeller, was asking and getting rebates from railways for his oil shipments, he was also constructing and buying up long-distance oil pipelines. Rockefeller controlled a pipeline network of perhaps 40,000 miles by the turn of the century.

The twentieth century brought increased oil production with

the appearance of the automobile, and pipelines continued to expand. By 1916 pipelines were carrying 21 billion ton-miles of liquid freight, or 4.4 per cent of the total intercity freight movement in the nation. The age of the automobile caused still more pipeline to be constructed, and by 1939 petroleum pipeline mileage reached a total of 122,000 miles, with many of the lines running from Texas or Oklahoma toward population centers north of the Ohio and east of the Mississippi rivers. Pipelines could move oil at an average cost of about three mills a ton-mile, a rate only half the rail rate, but still well above that of the ocean-going tanker. This economy of pipeline transportation became the greater with the use of improved steel and alloy pipes, the electric welding of joints, and the introduction of more powerful pumping engines. During World War II the submarine threat and the shortage of tankers led to the diversion of some of the tanker traffic to the railroads, but the federal government in the same years sponsored and largely financed the construction of the "Big Inch" and the "Little Inch" lines. The network of pipelines in the nation had grown to 150,000 miles by 1947, and more than one-sixth (236 billion ton-miles) of all intercity freight was carried by pipeline by 1957. The shipment of crude and refined petroleum products via railroad had declined from 24 per cent of total oil production in 1929 to only 6 per cent in 1953. The pipeline share of all intercity freight traffic has continued to grow in recent years. By 1968 21 per cent (397 billion ton-miles) of all intercity freight was moving by pipeline. The traffic loss of the railroads of the nation was the greater as an increasing number of factory and industrial plants shifted their basic fuel from coal, long a major item of railroad freight, to natural gas or fuel oil.

While pipeline traffic has grown rapidly in recent years, the nature of the largely underground freight movement has left the general public remarkably uninformed. The man in the street is more likely to be aware of water transport, which is one of the oldest but least threatening of the competitors of American railways. Passenger traffic, generally slower and more indirect than rail, in recent decades has never been of any significant size. In the last half-century it has rarely risen above 3 or 4 per cent of the total commercial intercity traffic. Water-borne freight, because of its substantially lower rates, has always been more important. In the half-century since the middle 'teens the freight movement on the nation's inland waterways has generally ranged from 15 to 18 per cent of the total ton-mileage.

In recent years this inland water freight has expanded much more rapidly on the rivers and canals than it has on the Great Lakes. In the 'twenties the large vessels on the lakes along the Canadian-American border carried cargoes of iron ore, coal, grain, and other bulky staples in an amount six times the traffic upon rivers and canals. In 1930 the freight moving on the Great Lakes was one-seventh of the national total. But this lake-freight tonnage has grown very slowly in the last generation, and in the middle 'sixties, while a quarter larger than earlier, it constituted no more than 7 per cent of all intercity commercial freight. Though the traffic on the St. Lawrence Seaway in the mid-'sixties has not met the expectations of earlier predictions, it is entirely possible that this foreign traffic will help reverse the current trend of domestic freight movement on the Great Lakes.

Since the 'thirties the railroad industry has had a much more serious threat from the growing barge and tow-freight traffic on the canals and rivers of the country. On the Mississippi, Ohio, and Missouri Rivers the white-hulled side-wheelers and stern-wheelers of Mark Twain's day have long been gone. While these interior rivers may still be haunted by the stately steamers of an earlier era, the work has been taken over by some 4000 diesel towboats and more than 16,000 barges. These huge carriers have a capacity and an efficiency undreamed of by the old steamboat men. The earlier technique of river depth measurement—"mark twain"—which helped name the onetime river pilot from Hannibal, Missouri, has given way to the fathometer, a gadget far faster and more accurate than any hand-thrown lead line. Radar installed in the tow boats—so accurate that often a barge captain can spot ducks as they take off from the water—allows the long strings of barges to operate easily at night and even in fog. These innovations have sped up the barge traffic, so much so that a tow of five or six barges can often make the downstream run of 1400 miles from Cincinnati to New Orleans in no more than six days.

The renaissance in river traffic in a sense can be traced back to the winter of 1917–18 when the combination of bad winter weather and the massive freight of war brought a staggering railroad industry to its knees. Uncle Sam turned again to river traffic, and Congress from 1922 on appropriated tens of millions of dollars to canalize the Ohio and upper Mississippi rivers. By 1929 a series of forty-six dams and locks had been completed between Cairo and Pittsburgh, and a decade later more than a score of dams had been constructed on the upper Mississippi. Federal money poured into river and harbor improvements between 1922 and 1953 amounted to more than $3.5 billion. Currently a giant program of further improving the Ohio traffic by replacing the 46 steps with only 19 high-lift dams is well under way. By the early 'sixties the traffic on the Ohio was already twice the volume of the Panama Canal and three times the volume of the St. Lawrence Seaway.

Passenger traffic on the Ohio and Mississippi has so completely vanished that today there is only one overnight passenger boat left on the entire river system, the *Delta Queen*, operated by the Greene Line out of Cincinnati. But the freight traffic is heavy. Coal, grain, iron and steel products, sulfur, limestone, and oil products all move in massive amounts up and down the river system. Venezuela crude oil moves up the entire lengths of the Mississippi and Ohio Rivers to Cincinnati and above. South of Cairo no dams obstruct the big river as it flows south to the Gulf. While there are no dams on the lower Mississippi the Army Engineers have for years been busy with their efforts to control and restrain the ancient river. Oxbows and great loops in the channel have been replaced with enough cutoffs to shorten the river's length by about 150 miles. Dikes, wing dams, stone levees, and retaining walls have been constructed up and down the length of the lower Mississippi. The danger of flooding has been at least in part reduced by numerous new floodways and reservoirs along the lower valley of the river. All the improvements have paid off in cheaper water freight rates, rates that recaptured much north and southbound railroad traffic. Grain from central Illinois can be shipped by boat to New Orleans for only 9½ cents a bushel, a rate so low that millions of tons of grain now move by river barge. By the middle 'fifties the freight (in ton-miles) moving yearly on the canals and rivers of the nation was over ten times the volume for the late 'twenties. By 1960 it was larger than the domestic freight of the Great Lakes and by 1966 was about 40 per cent more than the Lake's traffic. In the latter year canal and river traffic, at 158 billion ton-miles, was well over one-fifth of the volume of railroad freight.

Clearly in the last half-century the river barges, the ore and grain boats on the Great Lakes, the unseen but highly efficient pipeline, the airliner jet, the intercity truck and bus, and the ubiquitous family car, all had combined to take much traffic away from American railroads. As earlier noted, the last half-century has seen a precipitous decline of the rail industry's share of the gross national product and total national employment. Today the industry's fraction of the total national transportation bill is but a minor one, with less than half of the country's freight moving by rail. The passenger picture is even more bleak. Intercity passenger trains, which numbered close to twenty thousand in 1929, had declined to less than a thousand in number by the end of 1967, and every month brought new railroad requests for additional cuts in passenger service.

Naturally the new competition has also caused substantial abandonment of railroad mileage. From a record high of over 254,000 miles of line in 1916, the American rail network had dropped to an estimated 211,500 miles in 1966, or a decline of almost 17 per cent in the half-century. The extent of railroad abandonment can be seen in the following table.

As can be seen in these figures, the great majority of rail mi-

GROWTH AND DECLINE OF RAILROAD MILEAGE, BY STATES

	1840	1870	1900	1920	1940	1955	1968
Alabama	46	1,157	4,226	5,378	4,996	4,668	4,579
Arizona	—	—	1,512	2,478	2,228	2,179	2,052
Arkansas	—	256	3,360	5,052	4,482	4,001	3,611
California	—	925	5,751	8,356	7,947	7,531	7,485
Colorado	—	157	4,587	5,519	4,552	3,866	3,746
Connecticut	102	742	1,024	1,001	887	831	734
Delaware	39	197	347	335	295	293	292
Florida	—	446	3,299	5,212	5,218	4,691	4,469
Georgia	185	1,845	5,652	7,326	6,334	5,945	5,474
Idaho	—	—	1,261	2,877	2,746	2,691	2,668
Illinois	—	4,823	11,003	12,188	11,949	11,384	10,928
Indiana	—	3,177	6,471	7,426	6,889	6,614	6,488
Iowa	—	2,683	9,185	9,808	8,904	8,542	8,291
Kansas	—	1,501	8,719	9,388	8,564	8,416	7,871
Kentucky	28	1,017	3,060	3,929	3,691	3,558	3,529
Louisiana	40	450	2,824	5,223	4,357	4,025	3,807
Maine	11	786	1,915	2,295	1,882	1,794	1,679
Maryland (and D.C.)	213	671	1,408	1,472	1,402	1,308	1,159
Massachusetts	301	1,480	2,119	2,106	1,793	1,693	1,520
Michigan	59	1,638	8,195	8,734	7,303	6,680	6,372
Minnesota	—	1,092	6,943	9,114	8,421	8,303	7,990
Mississippi	—	990	2,920	4,369	3,919	3,741	3,653
Missouri	—	2,000	6,875	8,117	7,042	6,714	6,414
Montana	—	—	3,010	5,072	5,149	5,029	4,937
Nebraska	—	705	5,685	6,166	6,044	5,748	5,498
Nevada	—	593	909	2,160	1,941	1,649	1,635
New Hampshire	53	736	1,239	1,252	1,002	871	815
New Jersey	186	1,125	2,259	2,352	2,108	1,971	1,789
New Mexico	—	—	1,753	2,972	2,812	2,475	2,225
New York	374	3,928	8,121	8,390	7,739	7,291	5,689
North Carolina	53	1,178	3,831	5,522	4,668	4,325	4,222
North Dakota	—	—	2,731	5,311	5,266	5,257	5,165
Ohio	30	3,538	8,807	9,002	8,501	8,377	8,031
Oklahoma	—	—	2,151	6,572	6,302	5,957	5,506
Oregon	—	159	1,724	3,305	3,385	3,232	3,091

	1840	1870	1900	1920	1940	1955	1968
Pennsylvania	754	4,656	10,331	11,551	10,328	9,305	8,477
Rhode Island	50	136	212	211	194	181	155
South Carolina	137	1,139	2,818	3,814	3,466	3,194	3,140
South Dakota	—	65	2,850	4,276	4,006	3,916	3,818
Tennessee	—	1,492	3,137	4,078	3,573	3,431	3,285
Texas	—	711	9,886	16,125	16,356	15,441	14,051
Utah	—	257	1,547	2,161	2,082	1,731	1,771
Vermont	—	614	1,012	1,077	919	860	770
Virginia	147	1,486	3,779	4,703	4,261	4,128	4,025
Washington	—	—	2,914	5,587	5,243	4,983	4,943
West Virginia	—	387	2,228	3,996	3,831	3,710	3,569
Wisconsin	—	1,525	6,531	7,554	6,639	6,257	6,006
Wyoming	—	459	1,229	1,931	2,008	1,883	1,848

GROWTH AND DECLINE OF TOTAL RAILROAD MILEAGE IN
THE UNITED STATES

Year	Mileage	Year	Mileage
1830	23	1925	249,398
1840	2,808	1930	249,052
1850	9,021	1935	241,822
1860	30,626	1940	233,670
1870	52,922	1945	226,696
1880	93,267	1950	223,779
1890	163,597	1955	220,670
1900	193,346	1960	217,552
1910	240,439	1965	211,107
1916	254,037	1968	209,000
1920	252,845		

leage loss occurred during the depression 'thirties or later. Less
than 5000 miles of line were abandoned in the late 'teens and
prosperous 'twenties, and the rail network still stood at 249,000
miles in 1930. Some new mileage was built each year during the

'twenties, but except for two years the mileage given up exceeded the new construction. At the end of the decade, the downward trend was reversed, both 1928 and 1929 showing slight increases in total rail mileage for the nation. During the twenties fifteen states, most of them west of the Mississippi, actually increased their rail mileage totals. Also during the decade the construction of multiple main tracks, sidings, and terminal trackage continued to increase and this total climbed some 23,000 miles to a record high of 429,883 miles in 1930.

The rate of rail abandonment quickened during the depression, and the 'thirties saw the usage of more than 15,000 miles of main line discontinued. Every state, save little Rhode Island (which for some reason added three miles of new track), shared in the decline. At least 1200 miles of road were abandoned each year from 1932 through 1943. More than 2000 miles were given up in 1935, and in 1942 the decline was even greater. After 1943 the transportation war needs and gas rationing combined to definitely slow the rate of abandonment. Even so, almost 10,000 of line was given up during the 'forties. Abandonments have been slower since 1950, but more than 14,000 miles of line have been lost since that date.

Every state in the union has lost mileage in the years since World War I, but the rate of total abandonment has varied greatly, ranging from a low of 2 per cent for North Dakota, to a high of over 33 per cent for New Hampshire. Texas, in losing 3018 miles since 1930, has had the highest total reduction in mileage, but the Lone Star state still remains first for total mileage (14,051 miles) in the nation by a wide margin. The greatest rate of rail mileage loss has been among the northeastern states. Every one of the six New England states has lost one-fourth or more of the railroad mileage it once had. All but three of the fourteen states east of the Mississippi and north of the Ohio and the Mason-Dixon line have lost 20 per cent or more of their rail mileage. Those three states, Ohio, Indiana, and Illinois, have had a less than normal trackage loss because of their strategic location in the trunk-line region east of Chicago. West of the

Mississippi River the rate of rail abandonment has generally been slower. Each of the seven states (Nebraska, South Dakota, North Dakota, Wyoming, Montana, Idaho, and Oregon) with a trackage loss of not more than 10 per cent is located either in the Missouri Valley or in the Pacific Northwest. Several states west of the Mississippi, such as Louisiana, Arkansas, Nevada, and Colorado have had rail abandonment well above the national average.

Colorado, which has lost more than 1700 miles of railroad in the last half-century, has given up a major portion of its once extensive narrow-gauge network in the mountains and mining regions west and south of Denver. Another state which has lost most of its narrow-gauge mileage is Kentucky. A major portion of the nearly 1000 miles of railroad which have been abandoned in Kentucky since 1900 were narrow-gauge roads. As in Colorado most of these short roads were built to serve mining or lumber and timber operations. When these natural resources neared exhaustion or depletion the little Kentucky railroads became ghost lines. But much mileage in Kentucky, in Colorado, and in the other states across the nation, was abandoned simply because of the new competitive modes of transport. If our rail network seems a little emaciated today, it is because of the success of the new transportation facilities which are increasingly using the highways, the airways, the pipelines, and the waterways of America.

6

The Iron Horse Goes to War

Even though the railroad industry in the twentieth century was facing new competitive challenges, it still possessed sufficient strength to serve a nation in two wars. When the world went to war in the fall of 1914 an increasing traffic soon appeared on the rail lines of the country, even though America was a neutral nation thousands of miles distant from the muddy trenches of France. This war freight caused a flood of new railroad traffic by 1917, as our domestic economy started to prepare for what seemed to be a total conflict.

The problem of railroad freight was made the greater because Americans had forgotten a lesson taught the nation in a simpler war half a century before, by that tough old Civil War general William Tecumseh Sherman. The public remembered Sherman's troopers as hardy tough foot soldiers who had made Confederate rail destruction an art as they pushed through Georgia and the Carolinas in the last year of the war. They forgot that it had also been Sherman who in 1864, in his approach to Atlanta, had insisted that railroad box cars should never be used for storage. The Union commander had made certain that every one of the 160 freight cars which daily arrived from Chattanooga was unloaded on arrival so that it could be returned to the North at once.

The traffic situation grew so bad by Christmas time, 1917, that Woodrow Wilson placed the nation's railroads under the Railroad Administration headed by William G. McAdoo. The twenty-six months of federal control (until March 1, 1920) were so distasteful to the railroad managers and owners that they firmly resolved to avoid such government direction should war ever again face the nation. (Twenty years later, after Pearl Harbor, the railways recalled their earlier resolve and the lessons learned in World War I. During the early 'forties a rather substantial co-operation within the rail industry was formed under the leadership of such men as Ralph Budd and Joseph B. Eastman. American railroads managed to meet the tremendous transport requirements of World War II without having to endure any substantial measure of governmental direction.)

As war came to Europe in late summer 1914, and indirectly to America, the rail lines of the nation were not well prepared for the transportation requirements which they would soon face. Public ill-will against the railroads had been building up for decades, and the rail industry had received scant sympathy from either the public or the Interstate Commerce Commission in connection with its earlier request for rate increases in 1910 and again in 1913. Between 1900 and 1915 the general cost of living had climbed by nearly one-third, and many railroad costs had climbed even more. This was especially true of the railroad taxes and wage scales. In the same years average railroad passenger fares and freight rates had declined slightly. We have already noted the increase in number of miles of railroad in receivership at this time.

These years of American wartime neutrality, were also years of a labor crisis for American railroads. As America shifted from a stance of neutrality in 1915-16 toward full involvement in the conflict in the spring of 1917, the increase in rail traffic became pronounced. A Europe at total war was seeking more and more military supplies and foodstuffs from a productive America. The 1916 rail ton-mileage was up 30 per cent over the 1914-15 figure, and the traffic climbed another 43 per cent in 1917.

As the flood of war freight grew, the railroads of America had few precedents upon which to build a coordinated system of war transport. The nation had forgotten the earlier lessons of the Civil War, but it did recall the unhappy experience of the Spanish-American War. In 1898 the war effort had clearly suffered from a decentralized program in which co-operation with, and among, the railroads had been totally absent. As Woodrow Wilson faced troubles on the Mexican border, the War Department in the fall of 1915 suggested that the American Railway Association, composed of the managers of the various railways, be asked to create a special committee on military transportation. The committee was appointed and plans for co-operation between the War Department and the nation's railroads were established. These plans went into effect with the mobilization of the National Guard in June 1916. The movement of thousands of troops to the Mexican border in the following weeks was handled efficiently. Through an arrangement worked out between the Master Car Builders' Association and the War Department's quartermaster-general, car-load shipments of government freight had a special priority as they moved toward the southwestern border. The success of these modest cooperative efforts between the railroads and the federal government gave the railroads a certain confidence as they faced the problems of a larger European conflict.

On August 29, 1916, the Army Appropriation Act was passed including a provision which established the Council of National Defense "for the coordination of industries and resources for the national security and welfare." The idea had been suggested by Secretary Newton D. Baker of the War Department, and President Wilson quickly endorsed the proposal. The council was to consist of six cabinet officers, but it was early decided that the real work of the body should be performed by an Advisory Commission composed of industrial leaders of the nation. The transportation member of the Advisory Commission was Daniel Willard, president of the Baltimore & Ohio Railroad. Willard had been president of the B. & O. only since 1910, but in those half-dozen years he had managed to greatly improve the efficiency and property of his line. The B. & O. president was a

patriotic American who believed in a strong national defense
and he cheerfully accepted the Wilson appointment. He obtained living quarters in the Willard Hotel in Washington, and
spent far more time with his new job than he did in the direct
day-to-day direction of his own railroad. Willard and his fellow
members of the Advisory Commission considered such diverse
subjects as the organization of industry in the event of war, the
fixing of prices, conscription, wartime food control, daylight-sav-
ing, possible shortages of raw materials, and a more efficient
railroad service. Willard's specific duty as a transportation expert was to review the railroads of the country "with reference
to the frontier of the United States so as to render possible ex-
peditious concentration of troops and supplies to points of defense." Commissioner Willard was taking steps and making recommendations which would make easier the work of the Railroad Administration a year later.

In February 1917 the American Railroad Association expanded the earlier committee of five railroad officials who had
served at the time of the Mexican difficulties. This enlarged
committee of eighteen men worked under the chairmanship of
President Fairfax Harrison of the Southern Railway. The Harrison committee sought to find new ways of enlisting co-operation between the rail industry and the national government during the last few weeks of American neutrality. When war was
declared against Germany on April 6, 1917, Daniel Willard, now
chairman of the Advisory Commission, asked the top railroad
managers of the nation to come to Washington, D.C. Every one
of the fifty-one railway presidents, representing perhaps 90 per
cent of the rail mileage in the nation, accepted Williard's invitation. They, and their numerous subordinates, met at the Willard
Hotel on April 11, 1917, and approved and signed a resolution
to aid the war effort by operating their several lines as if they
were "a continental railway system." To co-ordinate these efforts the group of railroad leaders created an executive Committee, thereafter known as the Railroads' War Board. The new
five-man board was chaired by the scholarly Fairfax Harrison

the other members being Howard Elliott, president of the New Haven; Julius Kruttschnitt, chairman of the board of the Southern Pacific; Hale Holden, president of the Burlington; and Samuel Rea, president of the Pennsylvania. Ex-officio members of the board were Daniel Willard and Edgar E. Clark of the Interstate Commerce Commission. The new agency had an extensive staff in its Washington headquarters, with branch offices in several other railroad centers across the country. Under the aggressive direction of Harrison, the Railroads' War Board urged heavier loading of freight cars, suggested the reduction of duplicate passenger service, and organized freight car pools to relieve the troublesome car shortages. In the months of May and June 1917 some thirty orders were sent out providing for the movement of over 100,000 empty box cars into areas of the most acute shortages.

Certainly by 1917 the railroads of the nation needed all the assistance available. The greatest problem was the shortage of cars. Back in 1914 and 1915, when the railroads had been seeking more traffic, there often had been a surplus of box cars. The net surplus of freight cars in the early months of 1915 exceeded 300,000 cars, or nearly one-seventh of the total in the nation. But 1916 saw the freight traffic climb some 14 per cent higher than any previous year on record, and car shortages quickly appeared. Early in March 1916 there was a shortage of 19,000 cars, and by November the shortage had reached 115,000. Such figures are easier to visualize if one imagines a solid train of 115,000 freight cars, each forty feet in length. Such a train would stretch out for more than 850 miles, and would extend the entire length of the Pennsylvania main line from Philadelphia to St. Louis. The rail traffic continued to grow in 1917—12 per cent more passenger business and a 9 per cent increase in freight—and the car shortages also grew. The shortage was 145,000 cars on March 31, 1917, and 158,000 cars on November 1 of that year.

The traffic jam was compounded by under maintenance on many lines, and other shortages of motive power, terminal trackage, and yard facilities. Many locomotives which the companies had ordered for 1917 delivery were delayed because of a higher priority given to the building and shipping of engines needed by the Allies in Europe. This was true of many of the 3400 engines which the industry had expected to obtain in 1917, and American railroads actually owned fewer locomotives in 1917 than in 1914. The railroads also owned 20,000 fewer freight cars at the beginning of 1917 than they had in 1914. Railroad shops and roundhouses were often inadequate. In some railroad centers roundhouses twenty-five or thirty years old could not take care of locomotives nearly twice the size of those for which the original engine stalls had been built. When running engine repairs had to be made out-of-doors in severe winter weather a frequent result was the freezing and bursting of air pumps or steam pipes. Freight cars which deserved shop work were patched up in a makeshift fashion, a practice which constantly increased the number of defective cars in service.

During 1917 there was a growing unrest within the ranks of railroad labor. The train and engine men, who had just gained the eight-hour day in the spring of 1917, constituted the only major group in the industry which was thoroughly organized. In many railroad shops and in most section work gangs the nine or ten-hour work day was still standard. It was easy for a railroad worker to have low morale as he saw the cost of living in 1917 climb faster than his wages. Most railroads faced problems of a constant labor turnover as many workers were drafted, or attracted by the high wages paid in war plants and war-stimulated industries.

Since the Sherman Antitrust Act of 1890 made any real unification difficult, the railroad managers and executives found it hard to run their lines as the "continental" rail system which Harrison's Railroads' War Board advocated. Every railroad was naturally prone to keep and use any strategic or geographic traffic advantage it might have. This was especially true since there were no means available to compensate a particular line where a rational or "continental" method of operation might suggest a diversion or redirection of traffic. Thus, in spite of the best efforts of Daniel Willard and Fairfax Harrison and their respective co-ordinating boards, a highly competitive individualism continued to exist among the railroads of wartime America.

Even as the railroads sought to meet the growing transport crisis the government had, by legislation, taken out something of an insurance policy against the future. The Federal Possession and Control Act, a portion of the Army Appropriation Act of August 29, 1916, permitted the President to take over any system of transportation should a wartime emergency require such action. The Esch Car Service Act, passed late in May and several weeks after the declaration of war against Germany, gave full authority to the Interstate Commerce Commission to set up rules governing the operation and movement of all railroad cars. The I.C.C. was quite slow in exercising any real authority under this legislation. Very early in the war, officials of the Army, the Navy, and the United States Shipping Board, under the authority of the Federal Possession and Control Act, started to issue priority orders for rail freight shipments. Bundles of "preference tags" were given to thousands of government agents throughout the country, and soon the bulk of all railroad shipments seemed to be moving as priority freight.

Most shipments were moving toward the eastern ports, where the congestion soon became acute. The Pennsylvania Railroad declared late in 1917 that probably 85 per cent of all the freight traveling over its Pittsburgh division were war goods moving as priority traffic. It was approaching terminals many of which were ill-prepared for the crush of business. President Samuel Rea of the Pennsylvania had testified before the I.C.C. in the spring of 1917 that most of the major eastern terminal facilities on his railroad were inadequately prepared for the war traffic. Sometimes the total lack of over-all planning was unbelievable. As the Hog Island shipyard was started on a salt swamp near Philadelphia, thousands of freight cars loaded with building materials were rushed into the area under priority orders some weeks before there were any available unloading facilities. Soon sidings and terminal tracks throughout much of eastern Pennsylvania became jammed with unloaded box cars. The government belatedly tried to bring some order to the confusion of priority orders when on August 10, 1917, it passed the Priority Law. President Wilson at once appointed Judge Robert S. Lovett of the Union Pacific to be director of priority. Lovett evidently did not believe that the legislation gave him the power to cancel any existing priority orders, but at least he granted very few new priorities.

In the weeks before Christmas 1917 an unusually severe winter set in, and the railroad crisis grew worse. President Frederick D. Underwood of the Erie Railroad admitted that service on his railroad was breaking down. By December, New England was threatened with a lack of coal. Railroad operating efficiency further declined with the cold weather. The average freight car moved only 21 miles a day as compared with 26 miles in November and 28 miles the preceding summer. The prices paid by the railroads for everything—ties, coal, or engine oil—climbed while the Interstate Commerce Commission permitted only a token increase in freight rates. Finally the Commission recommended that the government take over the railroads. On the day after Christmas 1917, under the authority of the Federal Possession and Control Act, President Wilson issued a proclamation providing for government operation, as of noon December 28. When he spoke to Congress on the subject early in January 1918 the President recognized the valiant efforts of the railroad leaders: "If I have taken the task out of their hands, it has not been because of any dereliction or failure on their part, but only because there were some things which the government can do and private management cannot." The government take-over was necessary and inevitable, given the existing conditions in December 1917. It should be noted that the United States was the last of the warring nations to take such action. In England, where private railroad ownership also prevailed, government control had come on the same day that war was declared.

The property rights of the railroad owners were to be protected under government control, and the details were spelled out in the Railroad Control Act passed by Congress on March 21, 1918. This legislation provided that the individual railroad companies should receive an annual compensation from the government equal to the average net railway operating income for the three years ending June 30, 1917. Most owners of railroad securities would have preferred a rental based on the more prosperous returns of 1916 or 1917. The three-year base period which the government specified included the lean year 1914–15 when traffic had been light and earnings low. The act of Congress also provided for repairs and maintenance during the period of federal operation and promised each line that at the end of the war the property would be "returned to it in substantially as good repair and in substantially as complete equipment as it was in at the beginning of Federal Control . . ." This last clause was to result in many disputes when the lines were returned to private ownership. The law provided for the return of the lines within twenty-one months after the ratification of the treaty concluding the conflict. Congress also set up a revolving fund of $500,000,000 to provide for the expenses of federal operation and control.

William G. McAdoo was appointed director general of railroads by Wilson in his proclamation of December 26. McAdoo, a Georgian, had moved to New York City as a young man in the early 'nineties to practice law and sell railroad securities. Early in the century he had become interested in the completion of railroad tunnels under the Hudson River connecting New Jersey with lower Manhattan. McAdoo had tackled the tough financial and engineering task, and he eventually succeeded in completing a system of several Hudson tunnels by 1909. In the process he had met and received the financial support or co-operation of such men as Walter G. Oakman, president of the Guarantee Trust Company; Pliny Fisk; Alexander J. Cassatt, president of the Pennsylvania Railroad; and J. P. Morgan. McAdoo's financial skill was soon shown to be matched by his expertise in public relations. A generation which remembered the gross efforts of the Vanderbilts in this field was pleased when in 1909 McAdoo coined the phrase "The Public Be Pleased" for his Hudson and Manhattan Railroad Company. McAdoo had helped to manage President Wilson's 1912 campaign, and as the secretary of the treasury was clearly one of the ablest members of the new cabinet. As the war emergency worsened President Wilson found more and more jobs to give the competent McAdoo. The secretary of the treasury was soon wearing many hats. Among other jobs he was director of Liberty Loans, manager of the U.S. Soldier Insurance Company, and director of the U.S. Farm Loan Bank. McAdoo's numerous positions soon inspired the pun, "McAdoo's work is never McAdone." Fairfax Harrison grumbled a bit, and Dan Willard was not too happy with McAdoo's appointment to run the railroads of the country. But in general the nation applauded the selection of McAdoo, noting his general knowledge of the railroads, his proven administrative skill, and his extensive financial experience.

When McAdoo took over control of the nation's railways in 1917 they had an annual gross revenue of just over $4 billion. More than 70 per cent of this was from freight traffic, with the rest coming from passenger business including supplementary revenue from mail and express. As he viewed the complexities of the giant industry, McAdoo decided that three elements were of first importance: rates, wages, and equipment. The new Director General of Railroads thought to himself: "If we can get these three things fixed right, we shall solve at least 90 per cent of the problems facing the railroads." Almost immediately after his appointment McAdoo sought the advice of Alfred Holland Smith, longtime friend and president of the New York Central. Smith had a wealth of rail experience, having worked his way up through the ranks at the Central from the lowly position of track hand on a section gang. The New York Central official became a temporary assistant to McAdoo. Smith argued that after relieving the problem of congestion in the East the next most important problem was the raising of railroad wages. McAdoo was soon to agree with this advice.

Especially in the first days of the Railroad Administration, McAdoo retained intact the operating organizations of the nation's individual railways. Federal managers replaced railroad presidents of a number of lines as the war months passed, especially in those cases where full government-industry cooperation proved difficult. One of the railroad executives that McAdoo found difficult to work with was Julius Kruttschnitt, chairman of the Southern Pacific. Kruttschnitt had worked his way to the top in the S.P. under the not too gentle tutelage of Collis P. Huntington and Edward H. Harriman. On one occasion when Kruttschnitt had finally convinced his boss of the wisdom of a major $18,000,000 improvement program, Harriman dismissed his lieutenant with the order, "Spend it in a week, if you can."

The final word of course remained with McAdoo and the staff of the Railroad Administration in Washington which was to supervise the creation of a single great national rail network. Most of McAdoo's staff in Washington were active railroaders. He appointed Walker D. Hines, chairman of the board of the Santa Fe, to be assistant director general. Others on McAdoo's immediate staff or "cabinet" included Carl R. Gray, who became president of the Union Pacific after the war; William S. Carter, president of the Brotherhood of Locomotive Firemen and Enginemen; and John Skelton Williams, first president of the Seaboard Airline and later assistant secretary of the treasury under McAdoo.

Quite early in 1918 McAdoo divided the railways of the country into three regions, each under a regional director: the Eastern (north of the Potomac and Ohio rivers and east of Chicago and the Mississippi), the Southern (east of the Mississipppi and south of the Eastern Region), and the Western (west of Chicago and the Mississippi). Alfred H. Smith of the New York Central was put in charge of the Eastern Region, clearly the location of the worst jam and congestion of rail traffic. The Pennsylvania Railroad managers resented Smith's previous position with the rival New York Central, and claims were that Smith intentionally diverted traffic away from the Pennsylvania road.

Clearly, in the winter of 1917–18 the Pennsylvania was the most congested of the major eastern lines. The road's congestion was compounded by shortages of equipment and a general run-down condition, facts which Samuel Rea, the line's chief executive, had admitted to the I.C.C. in the spring of 1917.

But in the interests of a co-ordinated and more efficient wartime rail service the Pennsylvania, along with all the other roads, had to become resigned to a number of changes in railroad operation. Throughout the country stringent controls were placed on railroad freight. McAdoo insisted that all rail freight, if at all possible, should be sent via the shortest route. Earlier it had been common practice to carry goods hundreds of miles out of the way simply to keep the freight moving over a single railway. Also terminal managers at the more important shipping points tried to have new shipments accepted only if it seemed probable that prompt delivery at the destination point was possible. These procedures of planned traffic control resulted in the increased use of lines previously carrying far less than their capacity. At the same time relief was generally given to the more congested trackage. Over-all efficiency of operation was also achieved by diligence in the movement and return of empty cars from the Atlantic seaboard. During 1918 more than 850,000 empties were moved from congested areas to locations where essential traffic was originating.

The Railroad Administration also achieved certain economies through the use of standardized procedures in repair work and in the insistence on standard specifications for new equipment. Such expenditures were naturally heaviest on those high traffic lines also suffering from inadequate equipment and maintenance. The maintenance and betterment expense of the Pennsylvania was just over $160,000,000—about one-fifth of the total of such expenditures by the Railroad Administration. The McAdoo staff ordered 1930 locomotives and 100,000 freight cars—all built to standard specifications—for the rail industry. This expenditure of $380,000,000 used up a large part of the original revolving fund set up by Congress. The new freight controls plus the new cars resulted in the virtual ending of freight car shortages by the spring of 1918. The new locomotives ordered were built to standards set by a committee of representatives from the major locomotive builders: American, Baldwin, and Lima. A number of the new locomotives, known as USRA engines, were switchers, but nearly half of the total were Mikado freight locomotives (2-8-2).

Many changes were also made in the nation's railroad passenger service during 1918. Naturally, the highest priority in passenger movement went to the operation of troop trains. From the beginning of federal control until the Armistice—a bit over ten months—the railroads carried 6,496,000 men, or an average of over 20,000 men per day. Unnecessary civilian travel was discouraged, and much duplicate passenger train service was eliminated. Duplicate and competing trains serving such midwestern cities as St. Louis, St. Paul, and Chicago were cut out, and the remaining trains rescheduled to improve the total service. Trains that carried few passengers were discontinued, and a number of limited or through trains were obliged to lengthen their schedules so as to provide local service. Timetables were consolidated, city ticket offices combined, and passenger tickets were made good on alternative trains and routes. The number of dining cars was reduced without any reduction in the total food service. Much of this was possible by abolishing "à la carte" service, a change which reduced wastage of food and gladdened the heart of Herbert Hoover, the wartime food administrator. Many Pullman cars were taken off trains as sleeping car and parlor service was curtailed. A total reduction of 67,000,000 passenger-train miles was made during 1918, according to McAdoo's estimate. This amounted to more than one-tenth of all passenger service in 1917. Walker D. Hines figured that annual savings of $95,000,000 were made by eliminating trains and consolidating ticket offices and terminal facilities. In spite of all these reductions and economies, the hardworking American railroads handled 8 per cent more passenger traffic in 1918 than in 1917.

The problem of railroad labor was given high priority by McAdoo. Following the advice of his friend Alfred H. Smith, McAdoo on January 18, 1918, had created a Railroad Wage Commission to study railroad working conditions and the need for wage increases. Any wage increases to be granted were to be retroactive to January 1, 1918. Attention to wage increases was imperative, since railroad workers were generally restive as the government took over the railroads of the nation. Living costs were increasing almost daily, and high-pay war-industry jobs were attracting many railroad workers. On December 1, 1917, two of the operating brotherhoods had presented demands asking for a wage boost of about 40 per cent. Other railroad unions were considering comparable demands during the last weeks of private railroad operation. Substantial wage increases were clearly justified, for McAdoo's Wage Commission soon discovered that the cost of living had climbed about 40 per cent between December 1915 and December 1917. Average annual compensation per railroad worker, which had been $828 in 1915, had climbed only to $1004 per year by the end of 1917.

In its report on April 30, 1918, the Railroad Wage Commission pointed out that in December 1917, 51 per cent of all rail workers were making $75 per month or less, and 80 per cent were making no more than $100 per month. At the end of 1915 railroad section men were averaging under $38 a month, section foremen were making only $64 a month, and passenger train brakemen were being paid $85 a month. The engineer in a passenger train locomotive, on the other hand, was getting an average monthly pay of $178. In recommending pay increases, the Commission decided to grant increases on a sliding scale, and to base them upon wage rates in existence as of December 1915. The sliding scale naturally favored the workers with lower pay. All workers making under $46 a month received a flat increase of $20, an increase of at least 43 per cent. The $85 a month worker received a pay boost of 40 per cent ($34), while the $100 a month man went up 31 per cent and the $150 a month worker's pay rose by 16 per cent. Railroad workers making as much as $250 a month—there were only a handful of these fifty years ago—received no wage boost at all.

The new rates went into effect on May 25, 1918, with the pay increases for the 1,800,000 railroad employees retroactive to New Year's Day 1918. At the same time McAdoo directed that all women employees, when their work was identical with that of men, should receive equal pay. The same directive also ended the long-standing wage discrimination against Negro switchmen, trainmen, and firemen. Later in 1918 McAdoo also extended the eight-hour work day to all rail employees, with extra pay for extra work. Some of the new work rules and rates of pay violated wage differentials that had existed for years in the industry. Many railroad jobs were also classified with such detail by the McAdoo Wage Board that railroad economy and efficiency of operation were imperiled in future years. Thus many of McAdoo's new work rules were to be the basis for later featherbedding.

The total wage boosts of 1918 were substantial, with the annual railroad labor bill climbing from $1,782,000,000 in 1917 to $2,665,000,000 in 1918. The new work rules caused the roster of employees to climb from, 1,732,000 in 1917 to 1,841,000 in 1918, and to over 2,000,000 by 1920. Additional wage increases came after the war. The yearly average wages climbed from $1004 in 1917; to $1419 in 1918; $1485 in 1919; and $1820 in 1920. Thus the part of the railroad revenue dollar going to the working man climbed from only 40 cents in 1917 to 55 cents in 1920, the year in which the federal government gave the railroads back to their owners. The railroad presidents and managers were bitter about the high costs of labor they inherited after years of government direction. They pointed out that in 1917 the average railroad worker was being paid 27 per cent more than the average worker engaged in manufacturing. In 1920 rail wages were 33 per cent above those in manufacturing.

During the war years all railroad expenses and costs, like those of labor, climbed rapidly. Between 1916 and 1918 the average maintenance cost per locomotive more than doubled, and the charges for maintaining passenger and freight cars rose almost as steeply. The total expenditures for locomotive fuel doubled between 1916 and 1918, while the total volume of revenue freight (in ton-miles) climbed only 12 per cent. Because of these heavy operating expenses McAdoo was forced to raise both passenger fares and freight rates, as of June 25, 1918. Passenger fares were boosted 18 per cent, while the average freight rates went up 28 per cent. These increases, unlike the wage hikes, could not be made retroactive, and thus during 1918 operating costs climbed much faster than revenues.

After the end of the war this trend did not change. The national railroad operating ratio which had been 70.4 per cent in 1917, climbed to 81.5 per cent in 1918, 85.5 per cent in 1919, and 94.3 per cent in 1920! From the standpoint of helping to win the war the McAdoo Railroad Administration had clearly been necessary. From any pure dollars and cents point of view the financial results presented a very different picture. The official report of the Railroad Administration admitted that the total operating expenses (plus rentals paid to the individual railroad companies) exceeded total revenues for the twenty-six months of federal operation (January 1, 1918, to March 1, 1920) by just over $900,000,000. Nor does the figure include the final settlements of over $200,000,000 which were paid to the several companies for their claims of under-maintenance during the federal operation.

The long years of public service in Washington had been hard on the personal finances of McAdoo, and shortly after the Armistice he sent Wilson a letter resigning from his many governmental offices. Learning of McAdoo's personal financial reasons for leaving government service, the nearly 2,000,000 railroad employees in the nation started a campaign to keep McAdoo on the job by having each rail worker contribute a dollar. McAdoo refused the generous offer, left the Railroad Administration, and was succeeded early in January 1919 by Walker D. Hines, his assistant director.

With the war crises past, Hines had the thankless chore of running the lines in the face of a rapid decline in traffic. By March 1919 there was an unprecedented surplus of almost half a million cars. Freight traffic continued to decline in the fall of 1919 partly because of a coal strike that was nation-wide. While operating expenses continued to climb, Hines did not believe the national economy should be burdened with an additional hike in rates. The monthly deficits grew and grew. Clearly, most of the total financial deficit associated with the twenty-six-months of federal operation came in the sixteen months between the Armistice and the return of the lines to private control on March 1, 1920.

But it was, and is, difficult to assess definitively the total amount of those deficits. Throughout 1919 Hines intentionally followed a policy of limiting and restricting improvements and betterments on the rail network. As a consequence by March 1, 1920, the nation's railroads had been under-maintained for some months. Thus in 1920 most railroads filed claims against the federal government for alleged under-maintenance, defective equipment, breakage, wear and tear, the loss and damage of tools, and hundreds of other items. Many of the claims were extravagant and some were close to barefaced fraud. The railroad company claims and the counter claims by the government were often miles apart. The Erie Railroad alleged losses of more than $10,000,000, but in the final settlement the road paid Uncle Sam $3,250,000 for net improvements gained during the period of government direction. The Wabash asked for $13,694,000, but finally settled for a mere $1,500,000. The Pullman Company asked for more than $24,000,000, including $256,000 for pillow cases and $114,000 for porters' coats, but eventually settled for about 30 per cent of the original claim. In total, the nation's rail lines asked Uncle Sam for more than $677,000,000 for losses, damage, and under-maintenance. After years of expert surveys and investigation these claims were settled for $222,000,000.

But the success or failure of the wartime governmental management cannot be judged by financial standards alone. The management of McAdoo and Hines was certainly not designed to make money. The poor condition of the rail lines in 1917 was no doubt partly the result of earlier excessive or mistaken regulation, but the rail transport crisis existing by Christmas 1917 was a fact Wilson could not possibly ignore. The war clearly demanded a more effective movement of both troops and war material. The Railroad Administration did make a significant contribution to America's war effort and final victory.

With the end of the war there was a rather wide-spread belief in the country that in some way the pre-war climate of government-railroad relations should be improved. In a message to Congress made by the President on December 2, 1918, Wilson urged the Congress to give a high priority to the total railroad problem. A month later the retiring McAdoo suggested that federal control should be continued for another five years. Hines, the new director general, felt that such an extension of control was logical unless it was decided to return the lines to their owners promptly. The most extreme proposal was probably that of Glen E. Plumb, the legal counsel for the four major railroad operating unions. Under the Plumb Plan the federal government would buy up the nation's railways with bonds, and let a fifteen-man board, composed of railroad labor, railroad managers, and the government, run the total national rail network. Having fared so well under the wartime federal control, railroad workers and organized labor generally endorsed the Plumb Plan. The American public was not so enthusiastic, however, and the railroad managers and owners were downright hostile to the proposal. Daniel Willard, of the B. & O., and Howard Elliott, of the New Haven, strongly urged a return to private ownership, and also asked for an improved pattern of federal regulation. Woodrow Wilson in general favored this approach, and during the year 1919 Congress worked long and hard on new regulatory legislation.

The rival efforts of Senator Albert Cummins and Congressman John Esch were merged in the Esch-Cummins Act, or Transportation Act of 1920, which was signed by President Wilson only a day before the railroads were returned to private control on March 1, 1920. The new regulatory act gave both greater scope and power to the Interstate Commerce Commission, now increased in size from nine to eleven members. For the first time the Commission could set minimun as well as maximum rates, a feature intended to avoid serious losses to carriers which might result from unrestrained rate reductions. The approved rates were supposed to assure a "fair rate of return" on the total railroad investment. This rate of return was originally set at 5.5 per cent, with the added feature that one-half of any income in excess of 6 per cent would be subject to recovery by the federal government. Since the post-war federal operation was so much in the red, and since there was little chance of the railroad's immediately being able to set their financial houses in order, the Transportation Act offered any interested railroad a guarantee of the federal rental rate for the first six months of private control (i.e. to September 1, 1920). Most of the lines accepted this offer, but some three dozen Class I roads (lines then having a yearly operating revenue of $1,000,000 or more) declined with thanks, preferring to take their own gamble on profit or loss. The great majority of the companies needed such financial help, and the guaranty period cost Uncle Sam and his treasury another $500,000,000. At the end of the six-month period a general increase in freight rates, ranging from 40 per cent in the East to 25 per cent in the South and the Far West, was put into effect. Passenger fares were also substantially increased.

A major change in regulation appeared in the new law with the provision which anticipated the merger of numerous lines into a relatively few giant systems. The I.C.C. could not impose a master merger plan upon the nation, but it did quickly employ a transportation expert to suggest such a master plan of major consolidation. Professor William Z. Ripley of Harvard, an expert on American railroading, in 1921 proposed a merger plan calling for nineteen great systems. Included in the plan was the combination of the Northern Pacific and the Burlington, a merger the Supreme Court had expressly frowned upon half a generation earlier at the time of the Northern Securities case. In the years between World War I and Pearl Harbor no important mergers based upon the proposals of Professor Ripley were ever achieved. In addition to mergers, the Transportation Act of 1920 also granted the I.C.C. extensive new powers over new railroad security issues, new construction, and the abandonment of existing trackage. Finally the legislation created a new nine-man Railroad Labor Board, with railroad owners, railroad workers, and the general public equally represented.

The owners and managers of American railroads were not too happy as they resumed the direction and operation of their lines in the spring of 1920. The new Railroad Labor Board ended another labor dispute in the summer of 1920 by ordering a general wage boost, averaging 22 per cent, effective as of May 1, 1920. Fuel, taxes, and general operating costs were all high. The general bleakness for 1920 could be measured by the record high operating ratio of 94 per cent for the entire year. But the year 1921 saw considerable improvement, even though the general downturn in business during the year caused a 10 per cent drop in total railroad revenues. Railroad employment was sharply reduced during the year, and wage reductions, averaging 12 per cent, made possible a major cutback in operating expenses. The operating ratio dropped to 82 per cent in 1921, and fell below 80 per cent the following year. During the rest of the 'twenties the operating ratio averaged no higher than 75 per cent, and a return of general prosperity by 1923 gave the nation's railroads annual operating revenues which averaged a bit over $6 billion a year.

Few railroads were faced with the problem of returning any excess income to the government beyond the 6 per cent figure mentioned in the legislation of 1920, but the industry as a whole was certainly in fair financial health. For the decade of the 'twenties American railroads had an average rate of return on their net property of about 4½ per cent, and went above 5 per cent four years of the ten. But at the same time the freight and passenger traffic moving by rail did not keep pace with the general growth of business activity. Freight shipments grew very slowly, and the total passenger traffic actually fell off long before the stock market crash of 1929. The new competition provided by Henry Ford's Model T and the other automotive products coming out of Detroit was making itself felt in the railroad annual reports by the mid-'twenties. The early trucks, intercity buses, and new pipelines which soon followed were all starting to eat into the traditional railroad traffic monopoly. By the late 'twenties the new air age, foretold by the hero worship accorded Charles Lindbergh, indicated the early arrival of still other forces hostile to the railroads of the nation.

The fair financial health of the railroads during the 'twenties changed very quickly after the stock market crash in the fall of 1929. Total operating revenues dropped about a billion dollars a year in 1930, 1931, and 1932. By 1933 they stood at just over three billion dollars, or less than half the 1929 figure. The drop in freight revenue in the four years was steep, but it did not match the collapse of the passenger business, which in dollar volume in 1933 was only 40 per cent of the 1929 revenue. After the low point of 1933 a modest recovery in rail traffic did develop. Nevertheless the depression years were hard ones for the total industry. Railroad freight traffic, in ton-miles on an average yearly basis, was down by one-fourth from the 'twenties. Modest reductions in freight rates and larger cuts in passenger fares resulted in average yearly revenues for the decade of under four billion dollars, a figure which was more than one-third below comparable averages for the previous decade. The railroads sharply reduced the number of their employees and also cut wages slightly in 1932 and 1933. Other operating costs were also reduced. But these reductions did not fully compensate for the lost traffic, and many lines were soon in serious financial trouble. The total industry suffered deficits in net income for the years 1932, 1933, 1934, and 1938, and for the entire decade the average rate of return on the net property of the entire rail industry was only 2.25 per cent, or only half of the average yearly return in the 'twenties.

During the prosperous 'twenties dozens of railroads in the country had embarked upon multimillion dollar programs for major capital improvements. By 1930 more than 15,000 new steam locomotives, costing $765,000,000, had been installed on American lines. Between 1923 and 1930 more than $1,700,000,000 of new capital was spent on some 850,000 new freight cars. Comparable new money was also invested in new passenger equipment and for improvements in roadway and track. Much additional double trackage, as well as many new passing sidings, were constructed in these years. Heavier rail was used in much of the construction, an improvement which permitted heavier, longer, and faster trains. Naturally, a great portion of the resulting increases in operating efficiency came during the 'twenties, when most of the capital improvement programs occurred. But a great deal of the increased efficiency came during the 'thirties.

During the depression the necessity of cutting costs, reducing wages, and even laying off unneeded personnel resulted in savings in the total railroads operation. All railroads had to follow such cost-saving programs. The prosperous Granger road, the Burlington, was typical. The new president of the Burlington, Frederick E. Williamson, insisted that only "the most important and necessary" improvements of plant and equipment should be urged. Nevertheless the Burlington, along with most other progressive lines, managed to markedly improve its operating efficiency even during the 'thirties. The daily ton-mileage performed by each serviceable freight car actually increased more rapidly during the 'thirties than during the preceding decade. While freight trains were not much longer in the 'thirties, the average speed of freight trains was pushed up almost 20 per cent during that period. Thus in many ways the hard-pressed railways were toughened during the 1930's and prepared for the arduous wartime challenges which they were to face in the early 'forties.

The economic health of American railroads did improve as Europe drew closer and closer to war. The trend toward higher revenues and lower operating ratios which had appeared in 1936 and 1937 was reversed in the recession of 1938, but business improved again in 1939. Many railroads experienced an upswing in traffic during the summer of 1939 when Hitler's legions started World War II. American defense preparations at home helped create the new boost in rail traffic. On the Illinois Central, the line which likes to think of itself as "the main line of mid-America," freight tonnage increased 59 per cent between June and October 1939. Business was even better for nearly all lines the next year. American railways in 1940 had higher revenues ($4,296,000,000) than for any year since 1930, and could claim an operating ratio (72 per cent) lower than any year in the 'thirties. The nation's lines were eager for all the traffic they could get.

John Lansing ("Jack") Beven, president of the Illinois Central and a man who had helped that line weather the long depression, spoke for the industry as well as his own road in the early summer of 1940. Remembering the lean days of the depression he said: "Throughout these years of hardship, they [the railroads] have sacrificed nonessentials and even at times have neglected appearances in order to concentrate upon the things that really mattered—safety, speed, comfort, strength, adequacy, and efficiency." During the next year, 1941, the railroad freight traffic reached 475 billion ton-miles, 6 per cent higher than the previous record year of 1929, and 17 per cent higher than the peak World War I year of 1918. The national operating ratio in 1941 dropped below 69 per cent, the lowest since 1916 and several points below the average of the 'thirties. The rate of return rose to 4.28 per cent for the year, the first time the figure had been above 4 per cent in a dozen years. The return of rail prosperity was a welcome change.

In the weeks and months after Hitler's troops stormed into Poland, the top executives of American railroads did everything possible to avoid the ordeal of government management and operation which they had endured twenty years earlier. The railroad presidents believed that converting a rail network from a peacetime to a wartime footing should not be as difficult as the conversion necessary in an industry where a whole new line of war products was required. The railroads existed to carry people and freight, the very demands which an all-out war effort would create. At the same time the managers realized that the experience of World War I had definitely shown the need for some measure of over-all control and co-ordination of the complex transportation system in wartime. Luckily for the industry the man in the White House was a friend of the railroads.

Franklin D. Roosevelt, in his twelve years in the White House, traveled nearly a quarter of a million miles by railroad, more than any other President. During World War I, as assistant secretary of the navy, Roosevelt had seen the obvious need for federal operation of the railroads. As World War II was starting, the President was well aware of the great improvements in operating efficiency that had been made by the nation's rail lines.

Shortly after the invasion of Poland, Roosevelt called to the White House a railroad leader who had helped shape some of those improvements. Ralph Budd, president of the Burlington Railroad and an early promoter of diesel-engine streamlined passenger trains, urged Roosevelt to leave the railroads under private direction. Budd also recommended that a fully coordinated wartime transport service could be achieved by working through such agencies as the Shippers' Advisory Boards, the Interstate Commerce Commission, and the Association of American Railroads. Roosevelt agreed with Budd's proposals.

When the European war broke into flames in May 1940 Roosevelt at once asked Congress for huge increases in defense expenditure. Later that same month the President set up the Council of National Defense and an Advisory Commission to the Council composed of seven experts. Ralph Budd was appointed Commissioner of Transportation for the group, and charged with the coordination of truck, bus, air, and pipeline transport, as well as that of railroads. When he set up his new office in Washington Budd's first objective was to establish realistic estimates of transportation needs as much in advance as was possible. The range of his duties was wide. He urged the construction of new access highways to improve truck transport, he helped set up additional ice-breaking services which allowed the 1941 Great Lakes navigation season to be of record length, and he so motivated his fellow rail executives that by November 1941 the bad-order freight car ratio (the percentage of freight cars out of service for repair work) was at an all-time low. Though Budd had few mandatory powers, he had managed through a combination of consultation and broad co-operation to avoid many of the problems that bothered the transportation systems that had served during World War I. Ralph Budd continued as an adviser to Roosevelt on transportation matters until the end of 1941.

Shortly after Pearl Harbor President Roosevelt established the Office of Defense Transportation (O.D.T.) to continue and expand the direction of wartime transport. As Director of the new agency Roosevelt selected Joseph B. Eastman, former member of the I.C.C. and federal co-ordinator of transportation from 1933 to 1936. Eastman's agency was specifically charged with the co-ordination of the various transport facilities, the direction of domestic traffic so that port congestion would be avoided, the full utilization of existing ocean shipping, and the estimation of the volume of present and future war traffic.

Eastman relied fully upon the earlier work and planning of Budd. In one area the O.D.T. was hardly any more successful than Budd, since its efforts to obtain fully adequate amounts of railroad equipment and supplies were invariably cut back and trimmed by the ever-watchful War Production Board. Eastman was permitted only 40 per cent of the 300,000 new freight cars he requested, and only about 60 per cent of the more than 4000 locomotives he asked for. But the individual railroads strained in every way to substitute co-operation for compulsion, and to avoid the confusion and errors of the earlier war. Out in Nebraska, Budd's Burlington line illustrated the extent of imaginative improvisation used by the industry. The Burlington leased a large chicken ranch near Lincoln which produced 30,000 birds a year. The Burlington wished to make certain that the wartime meat rationing did not result in any injury to the line's reputation for fine food on its dining cars. The all-out efforts by the industry for co-operation succeeded so well that the federal government took over the nation's railways only during very brief labor difficulties in December 1943 and January 1944.

One of Eastman's most pressing problems was the substantial decline in equipment and personnel which had developed in the years since World War I. As compared with 1917, the rail industry in 1942 had 31 per cent fewer locomotives, 24 per cent fewer freight cars, and 35 per cent fewer passenger cars. The number of railroad workers had declined nearly 27 per cent in the same twenty-five years. But the smaller roster of employees in 1942 was running heavier engines which produced a greater average tractive effort permitting longer, heavier, and faster trains. The capacity of the average freight car had been increased so greatly in the quarter of a century, from forty-one to fifty tons, that the 1,745,000 freight cars in 1942 had an aggregate capacity not noticeably less than all the cars carrying the war traffic of 1917. And the 42,000 locomotives which moved World War II troops and war material had a total tractive effort roughly as great as the more numerous steamers of the 'teens.

The railroad traffic during the years of World War II (1942–45) naturally far exceeded the traffic of 1917 and 1918. The freight ton-mileage in each of the four years 1942 through 1945 was far more than 50 per cent greater than the peak World War I year of 1918. The most hectic year, 1944, actually saw a total freight movement which was 82 per cent above 1918. The increase in passenger traffic was even greater. The passenger-mileage of 1942 was 25 per cent greater than in 1918, and each of the next three years created a passenger traffic (in passenger-miles) which more than doubled the 1918 figure. The great press of passenger traffic is the more amazing when compared with the lean years of the depression. The wartime 95 billion passenger-miles of 1944 were actually greater than the grand total of the years 1931 through 1935. During the war American railways carried some 43,000,000 members of the armed forces in 114,000 special troop trains, or an average of nearly a million men a month. Railroads provided 97 per cent of the organized movement of the armed forces of the United States during the forty-five months of the war.

During the same period heavy freight trains carried more than 90 per cent of all military and defense freight. Gas rationing and rubber shortages resulted in a 30 per cent decline in truck traffic between 1941 and 1944. German U-boats in the Atlantic drove coastal tankers from the open sea and caused a cut of more than 70 per cent in the traffic of coastal and intercoastal shipping in the same year. The railroads were called upon to handle the great majority of new passenger and freight traffic generated by the war. At the peak of their war effort the railroads were carrying more than 72 per cent of the commercial freight traffic and more than 74 per cent of the intercity commercial passenger traffic in the nation.

Even with the record flow of wartime traffic American railroads in the early 'forties managed to present a picture of marked operating efficiency. Twenty-five years before, in 1917, the railways had been faced with average daily car shortages of 113,000 cars. Under McAdoo's federal operation in 1918 the figure had only dropped to an average daily shortage of 52,000 cars. During the four years of World War II the car shortages never became acute, and the worst year, 1945, saw shortages which averaged only 10,000 cars a day.

One of the major factors contributing to the new operating efficiency was the growing use of Centralized Traffic Control, a new control method whereby a single operator-dispatcher sitting at a control panel sets switches and trackside signals for the movement of all trains over distances ranging from a few miles to as much as 400 miles. Since this new control method permitted trains to meet in the most efficient way, the savings in time were quite considerable. In 1929 only 341 miles of Centralized Traffic Control had been installed. This figure had grown to

2163 miles of road by 1941, reducing the congestion on many heavily used routes. During the war much western and southern trackage was converted to such control, and by 1945 Centralized Traffic Control was in use on 6495 miles of line.

Another factor in the record amount of railroad transportation achieved during 1942 to 1945 was the simple fact that World War II was a two-front conflict with huge war shipments headed both to the Atlantic and Pacific coasts. In contrast, World War I required nearly all movement to be directed to the east, which resulted in great amounts of empty or return car-mileage to western points. Not only did World War II permit the more efficient use of the railroad plant, but the vast rail traffic across the plains and mountains of the West provided another difference between the two war efforts. The length of haul, both for passengers and freight was appreciably longer in the 'forties than it had been in the late 'teens. In 1917 and 1918 the average trip per passenger was only 38 miles. During the Second World War it was 97 miles. While the total passenger-mileage was thus much greater in the early 'forties, the number of passengers actually carried was greater in the First World War. In both 1917 and 1918 just over a billion passengers traveled by rail. This was almost one-fifth more than the 910,000,000 passengers of 1944, the busiest passenger year of World War II. Passenger traffic was growing faster than freight traffic and soon reversed the passenger deficits typical of the 'thirties. The passenger business was in the black in 1942, and averaged almost a quarter of a billion dollars of net passenger-railway operating income for each of the years 1943, 1944, and 1945.

The story was rather similar for freight. The total freight carried in 1944, again the busiest war year, was 1,491,000,000 tons, or 18 per cent greater than the record for 1918, the busiest year of World War I. But since the freight cars were of smaller capacity half a century ago, the 44,592,000 cars of revenue freight loaded in 1918 were about 3 per cent greater than the 43,-408,000 cars loaded in 1944. Thus the larger freight car, the longer average haul, and the longer average trip, all typical of the wartime traffic of the early 'forties, go far to explain the operational success of American railroads in the Second World War. This operating efficiency plus the bulk of the war business also assured the nation's railways of an increasingly profitable war service.

Railroad labor was a problem in the early 'forties, just as it had been in the late 'teens. The crush of the war business naturally increased the labor force even with competition from the draft. Between 1941 and 1945 the average roster of rail workers increased by one-fourth to 1,420,000 by V-J Day. During the same years some 350,000 workers were giving up their blue work clothes of the railroad for the uniform of some branch of military service. On the Illinois Central only one-sixth of the work roster had gone off to war in 1917 and 1918. But in World War II the road lost more than 10,000 workers, or one-fourth of its total work force, to the military. The labor shortage on the Illinois Central was so bad by early 1943 that the company embarked upon a "teen-age" program of hiring and training boys of sixteen or seventeen to become brakemen, firemen, switchmen, and flagmen. Assistant General Manager Wayne A. Johnston, who later became general manager and then president of the road, directed the youth recruitment and training program. Between spring 1943 and late summer 1945 the four railroad training schools located at Chicago, Carbondale, Illinois, Louisville, and Memphis graduated more than 4000 youngsters who joined older workers in train service, yards, or general offices. Many of the energetic and alert youngsters stayed with the company after the war emergency was past.

More than 43,000 of the 351,000 railroad workers who put on uniforms in World War II were members of railway battalions or other units of the Military Railway Service. This organization carried on the heritage of the earlier work of General Daniel C. McCallum, director of the United States Military Railroads during the Civil War; and of General William W. Atterbury, who had left a vice presidency of the Pennsylvania Railroad to be the director general of the Military Railway Service in

France during World War I. In the Second World War the director general of the organization was Major General Carl R. Gray, Jr., a vice president of the Chicago, St. Paul, Minneapolis and Omaha Railway before his war service, and like most of his staff, able to bring years of previous railroad experience to his new position. The Military Railway Service operated extensive rail mileage for American troops in North Africa, Sicily, Italy, England, France, Germany, Austria, Alaska, Australia, New Caledonia, the Philippines, Iran, India, and Japan.

The railroad workers who remained on the job at home in the early war months were faced with the continual climb of the cost of living. Prices climbed 5 per cent during 1941 and another 10 per cent in 1942. Although the inflation was not as steep as it was during 1917–18 the railroad workers were soon restive. By the summer of 1941 nearly all the brotherhoods, operating and nonoperating alike, were agitating both for paid vacations and for increases in pay. When negotiations with the carriers broke down in the early fall, President Roosevelt appointed an Emergency Mediation Board under the chairmanship of Wayne L. Morse, dean of the University of Oregon Law School. The workers were not satisfied with the recommendations of the Morse board and called a strike for Sunday, December 7, 1941. Late in November, President Roosevelt reconvened the Emergency Board to hear further argument on the case, and on December 2 announced a settlement after the carriers had made concessions on every major issue. The workers were granted a program of short paid vacations and a new wage-scale somewhat above the original Morse proposals. Average annual compensation rose from $2045 in 1941 to $2307 in 1942.

In the months after Pearl Harbor the general wage hikes in war plants, the continued inflation, and the growing prosperity of the entire industry soon created a desire in the ranks of railroad labor for a second boost in pay. In late 1942 and early 1943 a whole new group of wage demands were made of the nation's railways. During 1943 a series of emergency boards successively failed to satisfy railroad labor. The problem was further complicated by the reluctance of the Office of Economic Stabilization, headed by Frederick M. Vinson, to approve any wage boost which would tend to break national wage stabilization policy.

When their wage demands were not satisfied, the railroad unions voted for a nation-wide rail strike for December 30, 1943. President Roosevelt personally intervened and called for a series of White House conferences between the contending parties. Requiring time for these arrangements to be carried out, the President took over the nation's railroads on December 27, 1943. The strike was called off, and the War Department formally took possession of the railroads, retaining control until January 18, 1944. Government control was rather nominal, since actual rail operations during the three weeks remained in the hands of railroad management. During the interval the unions finally accepted Roosevelt's offer of wage increases of from four to ten cents an hour, effective retroactive to February 1, 1943. Once again the American railroad workers had proven that by exerting political pressure upon the White House they could obtain wage increases above and beyond those available through the normal channels of the Railway Labor Act. Average annual wages for railroad workers during the war were $2598 in 1943, $2726 in 1944, and $2720 in 1945.

Between 1941 and 1945 consumer prices rose about 19 per cent. In the same years railroad wages climbed 33 per cent. But railroad freight rates and passenger fares were allowed to rise only slightly during the war years. The Interstate Commerce Commission and the Office of Price Administration proved to be much tougher on the subject of rates and fares than Franklin D. Roosevelt and his Office of Economic Stabilization had been on railroad wages. The average 1945 freight rate of .96 cents per ton-mile was less than 3 per cent higher than that of 1941, and was actually a bit lower than the rates of the mid-depression 'thirties. The average passenger-mile fare in 1945, of 1.92 cents, was about 3 per cent above that of 1941, and well below the fares of the early 'thirties.

The flood of wartime rail traffic brought a return of prosperity to the entire industry. Company after company that had faced or experienced receivership or default in the 'thirties was able to put its financial house in order in the 'forties The rate of return on the net property investment of the industry for the years 1941–45 averaged just under 5 per cent, better than for any comparable period since 1920. In 1942 the rate of return for the entire rail industry hit 6.3 per cent, the only time the American railroads had passed the 6 per cent figure since the First World War. Very wisely most railroads spent their new income less for dividends than for debt retirement. Actually, the dividend rate for the five years was appreciably below the level of the 'teens and the 'twenties.

During the first half of the decade the industry retired nearly $2 billion of bonds, or about one-fifth of its funded debt. The Burlington paid off $45,000,000 in long-term debt, while the Illinois Central reduced its debt $134,000,000 in the years 1942 to 1948. With such action the two lines and others like them not only reduced their annual fixed charges but also improved their credit rating for the challenging post-war years. Even though wages and expenses continued to climb, the railroads of the nation had so much traffic that the national operating ratio reached record levels. It averaged under 68 per cent for the war years, lower than for any comparable five-year period after 1905. Total taxes paid by the ralroads, on the other hand, reached record highs, being above a billion dollars annually in 1942, 1943, and 1944. The railroads paid more taxes in the years 1941 through 1945 than they had paid in the preceding eighteen years.

In the years since V-J Day the public relations men of the industry, especially the Association of American Railroads, have made much of the contrasting tax picture of the railroads at war in 1917–18, and twenty-five years later in 1942–45. The government control and operation under McAdoo in the First World War cost the American taxpayers roughly $2,000,000 every day.

In contrast, during the Second World War the federal income taxes paid by the railroad industry came very close to $3,000,000 a day. Critics of the rail industry were not able to refute these figures, and American railroads came out of the war years with an increased prestige. There was little talk in the post-war 'forties of governmental ownership or operation.

Several factors contributed to the performance of American railroads during World War II. Of greatest importance was the unshakeable determination of the entire industry to avoid any repetition of the federal direction it had experienced during the First World War. Thus the railroads of the country not only remembered the lessons learned in an earlier war, but also under the direction of Ralph Budd and Joseph Eastman learned to co-operate in an unstinting fashion. Of course the statistics of 737 billion ton-miles and 95 billion passenger-miles in 1944— seem the larger simply because of the very low level of railroad operations during the 'thirties. The longer average trip and the longer average freight haul, both characteristic of the Second World War, naturally made easier the achievement of the record high traffic marked up during the conflict. The excess, or surplus, of facilities available at the start of the war was of course important, but of far greater significance was the varied improvements in equipment, motive power, trackage, and signaling which had been achieved between the two wars.

America was valiantly served in both World Wars by the railroads of the nation. Half a century ago, faced with the perplexing transport problem in the deepening winter of 1917, the federal operation of our railroads was both necessary and inevitable. Twenty-five years later it was just as natural and appropriate for American railroads to face the challenge of war under private management and direction. In the years since V-J Day American railroads have continued to serve in the defense of the nation. General James A. Van Fleet, who commanded the 8th Army in Korea in the early 'fifties, commended rail transport for its flexible and economical logistical support of American forces in the Korean War. Since then, railroads were ready at the time of the partial mobilization during the Cuban missile crisis of 1962, and also during the long and frustrating fighting in Vietnam. Today American railways continue to play a vital role in our national security.

7

The Problem of
the Vanishing Day Coach

Back in 1958 most people laughed in disbelief when they heard Howard Hosmer, an I.C.C. hearings examiner, predict that the railroad passenger coach in a decade or so might ". . . take its place in the transportation museum along with the stagecoach, the sidewheeler, and the steam locomotive." Few people gave much credence to Hosmer's prophecy, based upon traffic trends and statistics, that Pullman service might disappear by 1965 followed by the end of coach traffic by 1970. But in the decade after 1958 the Interstate Commerce Commission approved the discontinuance of nearly a thousand passenger trains. In the late 'sixties so many railroads offered no passenger service at all that Mr. Hosmer's rating as a prophet had considerably improved. The first secretary of transportation, Alan S. Boyd, in commenting on the rapid passenger train loss, remarked: "Andrew Jackson was the first President to ride a train. We think one of our responsibilities at the Department of Transportation is to see that President Johnson is not the last." In June 1968 the National Railway Publication Company, in connection with its 100th anniversary of *The Official Guide of the Railways*, reissued the *Travelers Official Railway Guide* for June 1868. For many cities the railroad passenger service available in 1968 was more limited than that of a century before. Lafayette, Indiana, a small city of 12,000 or 13,000 in 1868, was served by fourteen daily trains of three different railroads. A century later the same city claimed a permanent population of perhaps 65,000 plus another 23,000 students at Purdue University. It still had three rail lines, but the Monon had become a "freight-only" line and the remaining roads ran a total of only four daily passenger trains. This was well under a quarter of the rail passenger service that served the community in the years just after World War II. But Lafayette was much better off than many other American cities which had seen their last remaining passenger trains disappear in the 'fifties and 'sixties.

The years since World War II have indeed been bleak years for the American who wishes to travel by rail. So many millions of Americans have been lured away from the downtown rail depot by the speed of the jetliner or the convenience of the private car that the railroad industry has consistently lost money on its passenger traffic. Almost every year since V-J Day has seen railroad passenger service deficits (according to the accounting rules or formula laid down by the I.C.C.) of close to half a billion dollars a year. While Americans are still buying about 300,000,000 railroad tickets each year, their average trips are short, and the aggregate passenger-miles are but a fraction of those of the competition. In 1968 the slightly over 13 billion passenger-miles of rail travel were only a half of the volume of bus travel, and less than one-seventh of the total air carrier traffic. The rail traffic constituted less than one-tenth of the total commercial intercity traffic, and was under 1.4 per cent of the total private automobile travel.

The year before, 1967, was a bad year for rail passenger service. Many name passenger trains were discontinued or reduced in status, and some lines cut out all remaining passenger business. The Kansas City Southern, which had long been a loyal supporter of passenger business, suddenly reduced its service to two trains serving the area between Kansas City and New Orleans. The nearby Frisco, with 4600 miles of road, became the longest freight-only line in the nation. The *Panama Limited,* long the pride of the Illinois Central, added some coaches and thus lost its rank as an all-Pullman train. The same thing happened when the Pennsylvania added coaches to its top train, the

American Rail Network Today

While the mileage of the late 'sixties had declined nearly one-fifth from the record mileage of 1916, railroads today still serve nearly all Americans. Few areas in the nation are more than twenty-five miles from a railroad, and these are regions of sparse population.

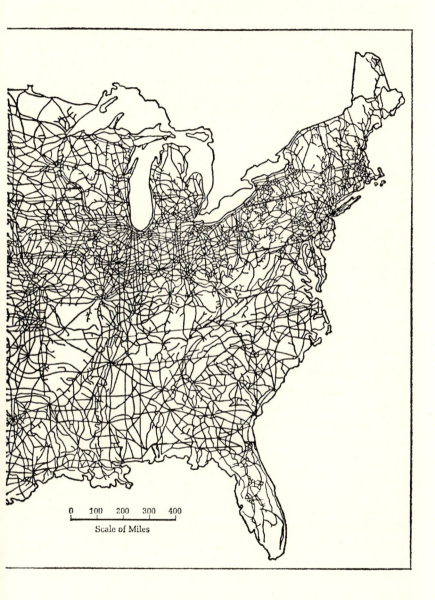

0   100   200   300   400

Scale of Miles

Broadway Limited, and dropped off the observation car. The Western Pacific tried again to give up its share of the *California Zephyr,* and the New York Central succeeded in dropping the famous *Twentieth Century Limited.* Even the Santa Fe management was heard to grumble about the cost of doing passenger business.

And 1967 was the year that the Erie Lackawanna cut their *Phoebe Snow* on the Hoboken to Chicago run. Sixty years ago the dainty young lady in white, Phoebe Snow, was created by the copywriters of the Lackawanna to publicize the fact that their engines burnt anthracite, instead of the softer and more grimy bituminous. For years Phoebe in picture and jingle— "Phoebe Snow, dressed in white, rides the road of anthracite" —helped convince the traveling public that travel on the Lackawanna was luxuriously spotless. In the same year that the *Phoebe Snow* was discontinued, the girl who had modeled for the original Phoebe died in New York at the age of 85.

There has been no general agreement as to who should be primarily blamed for the precipitous decline of the railroad passenger business in recent years. Those still addicted to rail travel like to blame the railroads for the reduced service. The railroads counter with statements that the general public abandoned the depot and the passenger coach long before the rail lines discontinued any significant number of passenger trains. The riding public in turn has become skeptical about the good faith of the rail industry in possible efforts to modernize, update, or improve passenger service. They read of recent Japanese or Canadian rail passenger efforts, and find the American performance inferior.

The railroads reply by pointing an accusing finger at the Post Office Department, which has removed so many mail cars from passenger trains that annual mail revenues paid the railways have dropped $80,000,000 in a five-year period. Nearly everybody—everyone but those from the ranks of organized labor, that is—does seem to agree that a major cause of the rail passenger deficits are the high wage costs of the passenger train crews. Engineers, firemen, conductors, and trainmen all work under obsolete basic-day rules unchanged since 1919, which are based on a mileage rather than an hourly basis. The result is that train crews work far shorter work weeks than Greyhound Bus drivers, and train crews chalk up only a small fraction of the passenger-miles every airliner crew can claim. Today the decline of passenger traffic is the most obvious aspect of the general decline of the railroad industry. Not many Americans in the mid-twentieth century would seem to agree with that nineteenth-century traveler who was quoted in an early Lucius Beebe volume as saying: "Bless me, this is pleasant, riding on the rail."

In the golden age of railroading, which probably ended in the middle 'teens just before World War I, there were few who would question either the pleasure or the necessity of travel by rail. The railroad had appeared when we were a nation of vast distances, small towns, and few dependable roads. The America at the turn of the century was not much different, and not many people listened to the few critics who sounded off against the steam cars. People only smiled when they heard James J. Hill, of the Great Northern and the Northern Pacific, compare passenger trains to the male teat—"neither useful nor ornamental." Not many railroad presidents agreed with Hill, or with Milton Hannibal Smith of the Louisville and Nashville, a rail executive who liked fast horses, brass work on locomotives, and freight traffic, but hated passenger traffic, "You can't make a g— d— cent out of it."

In the early twentieth century there were hundreds of name or express trains, and thousands of locals running over virtually every mile of railroad line in the country. The New York Central and the Pennsylvania had dozens of name flyers in addition to the *Century* and the *Broadway Limited*. Perhaps the best known of the de luxe trains to Florida was the *Florida Special*, which ran over the Atlantic Coast Line and the Florida East Coast Railway down to the private car house tracks near Henry Flagler's immense Royal Poinciana Hotel at Palm Beach. Many of the steam-powered all-Pullman name trains provided a quality and diversity of service which rivaled the finest hotels. When the Santa Fe in 1911 established their new once-a-week *de Luxe* flyer between Chicago and California, the fancy new train consisted of only six Pullman cars with accommodations for no more than sixty travelers. The train's crew included a valet, lady's maid, barman, librarian, manicurist, and barber, service which helped to justify the extra fare of $25. Gold-embossed pigskin wallets were given to all the gentlemen passengers, and as the train reached California all the ladies aboard were presented with orchid corsages.

But the bulk of the passengers in pre-war America rode the red plush or yellow straw seats in the day coaches and smoking cars of the common and nameless local trains. Traveling salesmen and drummers, families moving to new homes, college students going to school, and children on the way to visit grandparents or a favorite aunt, all crowded the cars in the years before most American families had purchased their first automobile. The thick timetables of every railroad company were crowded with the schedules of daily locals and tri-weekly mixed or combination trains. It was the rare feeder route that did not have one or more such trains giving daily service to every depot or station on the branch line. The importance of the railroad passenger service of that day could be seen in the ubiquitous station or depot found in almost every village, town, and city in the nation.

The depot, while not always in the best of repair, was open, active, and busy, for in those horse and buggy days the railroad station was the connecting link for commerce, communication, and travel with the outside world. Every passenger train dropped off and picked up mail, and the telegraph service of the Western Union was so important that stations of any size were often kept open continuously through the use of several shifts of telegraphers. Probably no single community agency or facility in urban America today provides the variety of important services associated with the railroad depot of yesterday.

Passenger traffic for the typical nineteenth-century line had always furnished an important fraction of company income. Before the Civil War passenger train revenue provided between one-fourth and one-third of the total company revenue, and the passenger share of total traffic did not materially decline in the last decades of the century. Until 1916, the year of top rail mileage in the nation, passenger traffic continued to produce nearly one-fourth of all railroad revenue. Even on the L. & N., where the passenger-hating Milton H. Smith allowed his coaches to become antiques, the passenger business was producing one dollar in five at the turn of the century. In the half-century after the Civil War railroad travel increased some sevenfold, increasing about twice as rapidly as the population growth. In the early 'eighties the average citizen purchased five or six railroad tickets a year. By 1916 he was riding the train ten times a year. Today, half a century later, the typical American buys only one and a half tickets a year, and many of the younger generation have yet to take their first train ride. There are few Americans today who remember an earlier era, when the average railroader was proud of his job, his train, and his company; when you could set your watch by the passenger flyer; when the whole business of railroad travel on most lines was a "spit and polish" operation.

In retrospect the decline in railroad passenger traffic probably began in the middle 'teens. The high point of the industry's golden age was clearly in 1916, the year of peak mileage. But that same year Congress provided new financial grants-in-aid for highways—highways which in a few decades would parallel almost every major rail line in the country. By 1917 there were almost 5,000,000 cars running around America, most of them fairly reliable, and some of them selling for as little as $345, f.o.b. Detroit. In 1918 the Post Office Department started a Washington, D.C., to New York City airmail route. The crew forgot to fill the plane's gas tank, the pilot got lost, the mail eventually reached New York in a railroad mail car, but the event marked the beginning of substantial federal support for a transport facility that today produces passenger-miles of traffic more than seven times as great as those of the railroad. And in 1919, at a time when passenger trains were averaging little more than twenty miles an hour, the train and engine crews of passenger trains obtained wage rules for a basic days' work which remain unchanged half a century later.

Thus by 1920 all the basic ingredients were present which could result in a serious decline in railroad passenger traffic. Growing federal subsidies have immensely aided both highway and air travel in the last half-century, years which have seen fantastic technological advances in both new transport facilities. At the same time the governmental regulation of railways has remained, while the competition is often unregulated. Finally, the successful insistence by the railroad brotherhoods on keeping an outdated set of work rules has resulted in an artificially high cost of railroad passenger traffic.

All of these factors made themselves felt during the decade of the 'twenties. Railroad passenger traffic stopped growing, and went into a decline which was to be really reversed only by the war transport needs of the early 'forties. By 1930 less than one-sixth of railroad revenue was earned from passenger traffic. During the 'twenties the American population grew by 13.5 per cent, but total railroad passenger-mileage dropped by about 43 per cent. Railroad tickets sold declined in the ten years by 44 per cent, and the drop in rail passenger revenue was 42 per cent.

Before World War I there had been little difference between the operating ratio of passenger service and freight service. Because of higher operating expenses (especially labor costs) associated with the wartime federal operation, both operating ratios were higher in the 'twenties. But the loss of passengers soon raised the passenger service operating ratio, and a gap between the two ratios soon developed. By 1924 the 84 per cent passenger ratio was 10 points above the freight figure, and by 1929 the passenger operating ratio of 90 per cent was 23 points above the freight ratio. During the 'twenties passenger service remained profitable, but just barely so. The net revenue earned in 1929 by passenger trains was only a tiny fraction of the total net income earned that year. Ticket sales dropped 10 per cent during 1930 and the year showed a deficit for the first time, a pattern which continued until 1942 and the heavy traffic of the Second World War.

As the stock market crash of 1929 was followed by receivership, sagging industrial production, and growing unemployment, all railroad traffic, both passenger and freight, sharply declined. Freight ton-miles and passenger-miles for 1932 were hardly more than half of the 1929 figures, and total railroad revenue dropped more than 50 per cent in the three-year period. Traveling salesmen in the early 'thirties and in fact the entire traveling public curtailed their travel to what was absolutely necessary. Ticket sales dropped as did average trip lengths. The decline in rail travel was caused not only by the depression but by the continuing and growing appeal of a competing form of transport, the automobile. Airline travel was in its infancy, and took few passengers away from the railroad. The same could not be said for the private family car and the intercity bus. The crash caused a serious drop in automobile production and sales, but only a slight dip in total registrations. Older cars, which in more normal times would have been junked, were continued in more or less active use though many drivers were among the unemployed. Many families on a meager W. P. A. budget managed to find a few dollars each month for gasoline and car up-keep. One recalls the story of the Hoosier housewife in the mid-'thirties who was asked by a visitor why the family had a car but no bathtub. The housewife very forthrightly replied: "But you can't go to town in a bathtub." During the 'thirties passenger automobile registrations increased by 20 per cent and annual car mileage climbed by 50 per cent, while total train travel dropped more than 10 per cent. In 1929 rail travel in passenger-miles was almost one-fifth that of the family car. By 1940 the private auto was producing almost twelve times the transportation furnished by the railroad.

Urged on by the president of the line, William W. Atterbury, the Pennsylvania had spent over $300,000 for Greyhound stock by 1930. Atterbury had worked all his life on the railroad, starting work as an apprentice mechanic in the Altoona shops at a nickel an hour in 1886. But by the 'thirties he was willing to have the Pennsylvania make trial investments in competing transportation facilities. Thus the Pennsylvania soon had money invested in airlines and trucking concerns as well as in the Greyhound system. In the same years the Burlington decided to establish a subsidiary, the Burlington Transportation Company, which soon set up bus routes to serve Chicago, Omaha, Kansas City, Denver, and Billings. Burlington bus service had a deficit of $58,000 in 1934, but company officials felt it was more than offset by the annual saving of $175,000 made possible by replacing poorly patronized local trains with buses. Burlington bus operations by the eve of World War II were serving more than 8000 route-miles, and in 1941 actually produced a small profit. In 1935 a truck division was added to the Burlington Transportation Company, and this service was modestly expanded during the late 'thirties.

But most intercity bus service during the decade was not operated by the railroads. The registration of buses climbed more than 80 per cent during the decade, and the intercity bus passenger-mileage also climbed quite rapidly. In 1930 the bus was providing slightly more than 25 per cent as much intercity traffic as the railroad. By 1940 the figure was above 40 per cent. During the 'thirties the bus ticket was generally about 10 per cent cheaper than a comparable railroad ticket, and this no doubt contributed to the rather sharp reduction in rail fares which occurred in the decade.

The railroads in general did not run away from the new competition which was eroding portions of their passenger business. Not many trains were discontinued and the numerous remaining through and local trains seemed very adequate during the depression years. Some trackage was abandoned and some branch lines became freight only, but the vast bulk of the rail network still retained passenger traffic. Timetables or schedule books were still fat, and all towns and cities in the late 'thirties still had very adequate railroad passenger service. In 1940 passenger trains were still running on about three-quarters of the 233,000-mile national network, and railroads were still carrying 65 per cent of all commercial intercity passenger traffic.

In fact the railroads staged something of a renaissance in passenger service during the 'thirties. Improvements or innovations in air-conditioning, safety, speed, and passenger comfort all appeared. Even earlier the rail industry had experiments on the air-conditioning of passenger equipment. The Pullman Company tried out air-conditioning sleeping cars in 1927, and Dan Willard's B. & O. was making tests with passenger coaches by 1929. In 1930 the B. & O. put into operation the first mechanically air-conditioned coach and a year later started regular operation of the first completely air-conditioned train. Air-conditioning installations were not cheap; they often cost $5000 or more per passenger car. The public liked the new comfort, however, and soon many other lines were trying to keep up with Dan Willard's road. The Illinois Central ran its first air-conditioned train in the summer of 1932 on its Chicago to St. Louis route, and two years later the Burlington was adding such comfort to all of its first-class trains. Most other roads were soon providing such service on their best trains, and by 1940 more than 12,000 cars were air-conditioned.

Economy and the safety of railroad travel were stressed during the 'thirties. Intercity railroad revenue averaged 3.25 cents per passenger-mile in 1930, a figure just slightly lower than the average fares typical of the 'twenties. Fares were cut sharply during the depression, and by 1940 the average revenue per passenger-mile was down to 1.90 cents. Passenger fares in the southeastern states were much lower than those north of the Ohio or west of the Mississippi, and it was possible for a midwesterner going East, if he so desired, to make a deep swing into the South without adding to the cost of his rail ticket. Commuter fares for the suburbanite were already much cheaper, on a mileage basis, than regular intercity tickets, and during the decade they were only slightly reduced. Throughout the 'thirties commutation tickets cost just over a penny a mile.

Railroad passenger safety was improved at the same time that fares were being reduced. Railroad passenger fatalities exceeded one hundred annually for the years 1923 through 1926. During the decade there were, on the average, .28 fatalities per 100,000,000 passenger-miles, while in the 'thirties in only one year, 1938, did the fatality total exceed forty. Passenger safety was so greatly improved that the accident rate for the decade was reduced nearly 50 per cent to just over .14 fatalities per 100,000,000 passenger-miles. Railroad travel was many times safer than that by either airplane or automobile.

The railroads also upgraded their passenger service by introducing more frequent and faster trains. Only about 1100 daily miles of passenger service were operated at speeds of sixty miles an hour or more in 1930. A decade later daily runs at such speeds had been increased to some 75,000 miles, with perhaps one-tenth of this mileage made at speeds of at least seventy miles an hour. Most of this increase took place only when the railroad industry, with some reluctance, started to replace the traditional steam locomotive with new forms of motive power. While diesel-powered streamliners made most of the new railroad speed records in the 'thirties, railroads had actually experimented with new forms of power well before the depression. The Burlington had unsuccessfully tried gasoline power as early as 1898. A quarter of a century later, in 1922, the Burlington spent $17,500 for a Mack truck chassis which held a bus-type passenger compartment and ran on flanged wheels. This little hybrid was enough of a success to induce the Burlington, within a few years, to acquire more than fifty self-propelled rail cars powered by gasoline. Several other lines, including the Santa Fe and the Union Pacific, also found the "doodlebugs" to be economical and useful for branch line passenger service.

The Chicago Great Western Railway, a midwestern line known as the Corn Belt Route, went even further with gasoline power in the decade. The line had as president Samuel Morse

Felton, friend of the late E. H. Harriman and a railroad executive who had earned a reputation as "doctor of sick railroads."
Felton was determined to upgrade the passenger service on his
road, and he added a number of new trains and schedules during the 'twenties. His most extraordinary new train was the
Blue Bird, consisting of three lightweight McKeen gas-electric
cars powered by a 300 horsepower Electro-Motive gas engine.
The new train gave de luxe service between the Twin Cities and
Rochester, Minnesota, starting early in 1929, and some claim it
was the first American streamliner. The really unique feature of
the all-blue train was the last car, which was a parlor-club-café
car with four Pullman sections designed for the use of invalids
en route to the Mayo Clinic at Rochester.

With the stock market crash, and the death of Felton in 1930,
there was a reduction in the new passenger service on the Great
Western, and the *Blue Bird* was discontinued in 1931. But interest in fast lightweight passenger service did not die. There was
also a new interest in streamlining. Back at the turn of the century the author-inventor Frederick Upham Adams had persuaded the Baltimore & Ohio to build the Adams "Windsplit-
ter," a streamliner based on the patents of the inventor. The
unique train proved capable of speeds of nearly 100 miles an
hour, but its use was soon discontinued. Now in the 'thirties two
railroads, the Union Pacific and the Burlington, became interested in streamlined lightweight diesel-powered passenger equipment. In 1933 W. Averell Harriman, son of E. H. Harriman and
later diplomatic agent for many United States Presidents, announced that his Union Pacific had just ordered a high-speed
three-car streamliner which would revolutionize the railroad passenger business. The new train, the M-10,000, which would
weigh only 80 tons, would be of a new aluminum alloy and
would utilize recent advances from aircraft and automotive
technology.

That same year the top officials of the Burlington were deciding to introduce a streamliner of their own. They wanted a short
lightweight train which could be operated more economically

than the two-to-five car locals that made up about one-fourth of
all Burlington passenger train mileage. Ralph Budd, the soft-
spoken but energetic president of the Burlington, was impressed
by the newly designed 600 horsepower diesels which he had seen
at the General Motors exhibit at the Century of Progress in
Chicago in 1933, and he hoped that this new motor might furnish the power for the new train. Charles F. Kettering, vice
president of research at General Motors, had built and perfected the new two-cycle eight-cylinder diesel in the fall of 1932.
The really unique feature of Kettering's engine was its use of
alloys which permitted an amazing weight-to-power ratio of only
twenty pounds per horsepower. Ralph Budd was quick to realize
that the new motor was light enough to put in a locomotive
frame, and he formally ordered the new model in mid-June
1933. On the same day the Burlington president ordered from
the E. G. Budd Manufacturing Company of Philadelphia a
three-car streamlined train to be built of lightweight stainless
steel. Edward G. Budd, Sr. (no relation to Ralph Budd) was
given complete freedom in the new train's construction except
the gauge, clearance, and safety standards typical of more con-
ventional equipment. The new train, costing $200,000, 196 feet
in length, and with a seating capacity of 70, was delivered to the
railroad in April 1934. Kettering and his G. M. mechanics had
faced some tough problems in adapting the new diesel to railroad use. Later the talented G. M. research engineer, in recalling those numerous difficulties, said: ". . . I do not remember
any trouble with the dip stick." Ralph Budd was proud of the
new train, and thinking of a recent rereading of Chaucer's *Can-
terbury Tales,* decided to name the streamliner *Zephyr,* after
Zephyrus, the god of the west wind.

During April and early May 1934 the Burlington *Zephyr*
reached a speed of 104 miles an hour in a trial run, toured almost fifty cities, and was viewed by half a million interested and
enthusiastic people. In May Ralph Budd announced an unprecedented nonstop special run of the new train over the 1015-mile
route between Denver and Chicago. Budd promised that the lit-

tle speedster would make the run between dawn and dusk—some fourteen hours—even though the regular schedule was twenty-six hours. Many knowledgeable railroad men thought Budd was being reckless, but the daring rail executive went even further, and arranged for the *Zephyr* to arrive at dusk on the Lake Michigan shore, as the climax of the World's Fair transportation pageant, Edward Hungerford's "Wings of a Century."

The new train left Denver at 5:05 a.m., May 26, after mechanics at the last minute had replaced a cracked armature bearing with a new one borrowed from the obliging Union Pacific shops. As the speeding train rushed across the open plains toward Nebraska, Budd attested to the smoothness of the ride by shaving himself with a straight edge razor. Later in the morning the nonstop run was endangered when a steel door was accidently shut on a cable causing a short in the starting mechanism. The engineer shut off the engine, and the frantic efforts of the crew to splice the cable break succeeded only as an Electro-Motive mechanic, Roy Baer, jammed the two cable ends together with his bare hands. Baer burned his hands, but the engine started, and the nonstop run remained intact. Thousands of people watched the silver train glide past villages, cities, and the specially guarded grade crossings of the four states crossed in the trip. The *Zephyr* reached the Mississippi in the late afternoon, and at 7:10 p.m. (Chicago time) broke the timing tape at Halsted Street, covering the 1015 miles in thirteen hours and five minutes for an average speed of 77.6 miles per hour. During the day the silver streamliner had hit speeds of well over 100 miles per hour. An hour later the gleaming train rolled onto the stage of the World's Fair railroad show to the wild applause of the crowd.

Ralph Budd was proud of the performance his new train gave under pressure. One of the features he liked best was the *Zephyr*'s economy of operation. In its dawn to dusk run the train had traveled nearly three miles per gallon of fuel oil, and total fuel cost for the Denver to Chicago trip was under $15. The per mile operating costs of the new train, once in service, were to be almost 50 per cent less than the steam train it replaced. In the summer of 1934 the new diesel streamliner was sent on a western tour which included an appearance at the formal opening of the Moffat Tunnel, recently completed by the Rio Grande. On this trip the train followed the new transcontinental route later to be used by Burlington's *California Zephyr* when that train was introduced in 1949. By August the train was back on exhibit at the World's Fair, and after Labor Day played the leading role in a new RKO movie, *The Silver Streak*. Early in November the *Zephyr* was put on the 500-mile daily round trip from Lincoln, Nebraska, to Kansas City and back. Passenger traffic on the run increased so much that soon a fourth car was added to the little streamliner. The original *Zephyr*, soon to be renamed the *Pioneer Zephyr*, remained a workhorse for twenty-five years in the growing Burlington fleet of streamliners. In 1960 it was placed on permanent display at the Chicago Museum of Science and Industry, after having carried more than a million passengers and traveled well over 3,000,000 miles.

Other railroads noted the success of the new Burlington streamliners, and soon many lines were offering comparable service. The Union Pacific streamliner was actually delivered before the *Pioneer Zephyr*, but was slower to be placed in regular service. Carl Gray, the Union Pacific president, received the M-10,000 from the manufacturer on February 12, 1934, about two months before the delivery of Ralph Budd's streamliner. Gray's streamliner, later christened the *City of Salina*, was also a three-car articulated lightweight made of aluminum alloy, and powered with a Winton V-12 600 horsepower distillate motor. On January 31, 1935, the *City of Salina* was put into daily operation between Kansas City and Salina, Kansas.

The riding public during the 'thirties expressed a real preference for the new lightweights with their rounded rear ends, smooth roof lines, and shrouded wheels. Samuel Thomas Bledsoe, another railroad president who believed in improved passenger service, added the new type train to the passenger equipment roster of the Santa Fe. Bledsoe, a Kentuckian who had entered the legal department of the Santa Fe as a young man, was a railroad executive who believed in building up his railroad during hard times. In the middle 'thirties he spent over $4,-000,000 on track improvement before a single streamliner wheel turned. On May 12, 1936, Bledsoe's sixty-eighth birthday, the new *Super Chief* left Dearborn Station in Chicago for its first thirty-nine-hour run to Los Angeles. Powered by a two-unit 3600 horsepower diesel built by the Electro-Motive Corporation, a General Motors subsidiary, the new train broke by almost six hours the famous record run of Death Valley Scotty set back in 1905. At first the new train consisted of only standard Pullmans, but within a few months a brand new train of stainless steel streamlined cars had been supplied by Edward G. Budd's company. The Santa Fe soon added many additional streamliners, and for three decades the railroad, which for years was first in the nation in mileage, was also an acknowledged pace setter in the field of passenger traffic.

South of Chicago another line, the Illinois Central, also improved and speeded up its passenger service in the mid-'thirties. The depression had brought the Illinois Central so near the brink of bankruptcy that the company lawyers had drawn up the papers necessary for the filing of voluntary trusteeship under the Bankruptcy Act. Wages were reduced, employment drastically cut, and late in May 1932 the *Panama Limited*, daily flyer from Chicago to New Orleans and pride of the line, was discontinued. In 1933 and 1934 Chicago's Century of Progress helped bring some slight improvement in company traffic and earnings, and Illinois Central president Lawrence Downs was able to turn again to improving his freight and passenger service. On December 2, 1934, a brand new all-Pullman air-conditioned *Panama Limited* was returned to service on the Chicago to New Orleans run. Its schedule was eighteen hours for the 921 miles, two hours faster than any previous schedule. In May 1936 Downs introduced the line's first diesel-powered streamlined passenger train, the *Green Diamond*, for fast service between Chicago and St. Louis. In 1930 the Illinois Central had not run in any operating district a single passenger train whose speed, start to stop, had averaged 60 miles an hour. In 1936 the schedule showed eleven such trains, and by 1940 the number had risen to thirty-seven.

While western or southern lines probably led the passenger equipment and service renaissance of the 'thirties, railroads across the nation in general participated. Much of the success of the new trend was a direct result of the rapid acceptance of diesel power by the industry. Streamlining, lightweight equipment, and faster schedules, all seemed to naturally accompany the introduction of the new form of motive power. Increased use of diesels continued during the 'forties, especially after World War II. By 1951 almost half of the 655 named passenger trains in the nation were diesel-powered.

One man who definitely liked to ride the new trains in the 'thirties and 'forties was President Franklin D. Roosevelt. During his twelve years in the White House Roosevelt traveled an average of more than 20,000 miles a year by rail. Of course most of F.D.R.'s travel was in his heavy armored private car, the *Ferdinand Magellan*. The President liked trains for privacy, and for both the work and the relaxation which rail travel afforded him. In April 1940 on a special presidential B. & O. train from Jersey City to Washington a fuse on a new diesel blew out, causing a delay of half an hour. To Dan Moorman, the railroad official in charge of the train, Roosevelt explained: "Dan, the only thing that worries me about this delay is that you and the crew men may be disturbed by it. I don't want you to worry. The important thing is that you always take me where I'm going and bring me back safely and comfortably."

Trains in the 'thirties might have been safe, comfortable, and fast, but they were not profitable. The operating expenses for passenger service exceeded passenger revenues in 1930 for the first time. These passenger deficits continued for the next dozen years, and a profitable passenger business was regained only during World War II. Both the passenger operating deficits and

the passenger operating ratios grew progressively worse until
1935. The new attention given to upgrading the service did slow
the revenue decline, and generally after 1935–36 the deficits at
least grew no greater. Even so, the passenger deficits still averaged almost $250,000,000 a year from 1936 through 1941.

Railroad officials hoped that a full economic recovery from
the depression would go far to lick the problem of the passenger
deficit. But there was one aspect of passenger service—the dining car problem—to which there seemed to be no real solution.
Railroad passengers for a century or more, on all first-class
trains at least, have heard the familar call of the white-clad
steward or waiter: "First call for dinner—dining car ahead."
Americans in this century of course do not have the choice of
food and drink available to the travelers of the late nineteenth
century. The menu of the Chicago & North Western diner in
1887 on its Omaha train offered 13 different entrees, 6 kinds of
game, and a choice of 25 desserts. And the meal cost only 75
cents. When the late Wayne Johnston, long-time president of
the Illinois Central, said, "One of the pleasures of riding a train
is the opportunity it affords for dining in style," he may have
been thinking of the generous portions served on his own diners,
or of the special "King's Dinner" available on the *Panama Limited*. Today's diner menus are indeed spartan when compared
with those of an earlier day, but for half a century the nation's
dining cars have been losing money. The high price of food, increasing labor costs, and the inherent scheduling problems of always having the rolling restaurants on the right trains at meal-
time have all contributed to dining car losses. In 1937 the average meal check on the diners of the Pennsylvania Railroad averaged $1.24. The cost to the railroad per meal served that year
was $1.61.

Since the 'thirties the diner deficit problem has actually
grown worse. The dining car losses on the Pennsylvania were
not much over $1,000,000 per year in 1937 but by 1949 they
had increased to over $4,000,000 yearly. Wage increases con-
tributed greatly to the growing deficits, for hourly wages for

cooks more than doubled in the dozen years, and wages for waiters increased more than threefold. For every dollar of dining car revenue in 1954 the railroads of the nation were actually spending $1.44. The 1400 diners in service in 1957 grossed a revenue of $62,000,000, and ran up a deficit of $29,000,000 for the operations for the year. Some lines for short runs turned to pre-cooked meals, and both the Santa Fe and the Atlantic Coast Line sold meal tickets or coupons on certain trains. These efforts and the downgrading of diner service which resulted from the installation of automatic vending machines on some trains did little more than slow the growing deficits. Naturally the deficits have declined with the wholesale train discontinuances of recent years. Some railroads have continued to justify the losses as simply the cost of good public relations. The president of the Southern Railway in the 'fifties, Harry A. deButts, liked to claim: "There is no way that you can lose or pick up freight customers so fast as by the quality of the meal or the cup of coffee that you provide the traveler."

Even though passenger service deficits did return in 1946 after the four profitable years of World War II, railroad management generally was optimistic about the future of rail travel in a post-war America. One of the first railroad executives persistently to push toward improvements in post-war passenger service was Robert R. Young, chairman of the board of the Chesapeake & Ohio. Young, a lightweight physically (5 feet 6 inches and only 135 pounds), had early proved himself a match for the best financiers of the 'thirties. When in his early thirties Young had anticipated the stock market collapse in 1929, had sold short, and had quickly gained his first million plus a seat on the New York Stock Exchange. The C. & O., which Young controlled through his earlier acquisition of the Allegheny Corporation, did not run many passenger trains, but Young was quick to be critical of the status quo of the nation's rail passenger service. In full-page newspaper ads he labeled Pullman sleeping cars "rolling tenements," favored frequent renewal of all passenger equipment, and argued against the universal custom of locking train toilets during station stops. In his campaign to end the inevitable change of trains rail passengers made at Chicago, he called that city a barrier splitting America in half, and caught the fancy of the traveling public with his ad, "A Hog Can Cross the Country Without Changing Trains—But YOU Can't!"

Even as a few lines, in reply to Young, announced that Pullman passengers would soon be able to pass through Chicago without a change of cars, the entire industry decided to put itself upon display with the Chicago Railroad Fair. The sponsoring railroads spent $2,000,000 on the 1948 show which marked the centennial of the first railroad service in Chicago. Top feature of the fair was a transportation pageant, "Wheels A-Rolling," written by Edward Hungerford. Hungerford, long-time railroad author and publicist, had earlier written and created such railroad pageants as the B. & O. "Fair of the Iron Horse" (Baltimore, 1927), "Wings of a Century" (Chicago, 1933–34), and "Railroads on Parade" (New York City, 1939–40). Well over 2,000,000 visitors crowded the fair grounds on Chicago's lake front, the closing date was extended, and during the summer of 1949 the fair was reopened for a hundred days.

At the Chicago Railroad Fair much emphasis was put on the new streamlined passenger trains which were being added by most of the major lines in the late 'forties. By 1948, just fifteen years after W. Averell Harriman's announcement about the Union Pacific's first streamliner, the railroads of America had spent hundreds of millions of dollars to upgrade and improve their passenger service. By the summer of 1948 more than 250 streamliners, many of them diesel-powered, were being operated over a coast-to-coast network which touched every one of the forty-eight states. While the new trains were most evident on the transcontinental, the Granger, and the Atlantic coastal routes, everyone of the forty largest cities, plus hundreds of smaller towns and cities, shared in the new service. The 250 streamlined trains used 2500 new cars with another 2000 cars of the streamlined type on order. The trend toward the use and purchase of the new equipment was nation-wide; more than thirty-five different lines were buying the new trains. As of mid-century probably 30 per cent of all rail passenger travelers were riding the new equipment. No one at that time could honestly accuse American railroads of not wanting their full share of the passenger traffic.

The year 1949 saw railroad after railroad spend millions of dollars for the sleek new passenger equipment. Early in the year the Great Northern revealed that it was spending nearly $9,000,000 for sixty-six new cars to upgrade its *Empire Builder* and *Oriental Limited*. That same spring the Burlington-Rio Grande-Western Pacific introduced its high speed stainless-steel streamliner, the *California Zephyr,* for service between Chicago and San Francisco. In order to take full advantage of its breathtaking scenic route the fifty-one-hour schedule was arranged to permit day-time travel through both the heart of the Colorado Rockies and the Feather River Canyon in California. Six trains of eleven cars each were required to provide daily service over the route. The train was a fitting tribute to Ralph Budd's long sponsorship of Burlington *Zephyrs*. The *California Zephyr* was an instant success, and during its first decade established new records for daily occupancy. In the same spring months of 1949 the Pennsylvania was running new streamlined all-coach trains to St. Louis and Chicago, and out on the west coast the Southern Pacific was providing twelve-hour overnight service between Los Angeles and San Francisco with its all-Pullman luxury train, the *Lark*. The unique feature of the eighteen-car *Lark* was its Lark Club, a three-car articulated dining unit which cost almost a quarter of a million dollars. In this elongated 131-foot diner-club car free second servings of food, but not of liquor, were available.

Some of the new rail equipment which Americans were to use in the 'fifties was designed by the top-flight Fifth Avenue industrial designer, Raymond Loewy. This French-born designer had turned from fashion designing and working for such clients as Frigidaire, Pepsodent, and Coca-Cola, to railroad designing in the 'thirties. At that time, Martin W. Clement, president of the Pennsylvania Railroad, engaged Loewy to streamline the frame and body of the GG-1 electric locomotive. The designer suggested a welded rather than a riveted construction, and gave to the giant locomotive a streamlined simplicity which made the numerous GG-1 locomotives among the best known engines in the country. Raymond Loewy also designed passenger equipment for the Pennsylvania, and later worked for the Norfolk and Western, the Monon, and the diesel engineering staff of Fairbanks-Morse.

In the post-war years some passenger equipment was showing a new silhouette. The idea of an upper deck observation platform in a passenger car was perhaps first shown in the pages of *Scientific American* back in the early 'nineties, and a dozen years later the Canadian Pacific actually built and briefly operated a "vista-dome" passenger car. But it was a General Motors vice president, Cyrus R. Osborn, who first had the idea of the modern vista-dome car. During the summer of 1944 Osborn rode in the cab of a Denver and Rio Grande diesel freight locomotive through the Colorado Rockies. He was so impressed with the wide-open view which his ride gave him that upon his return to Chicago he constructed a model passenger car with a high-level glass observation compartment in the roof. When Osborn showed the small car to Ralph Budd of the Burlington, the C. B. & Q. executive ordered that a glass dome be built into the roof of a Burlington stainless-steel passenger coach. The new "Silver Dome" car was tried out on the Chicago to Minneapolis run in July 1945 and was an instant success. The public liked the new equipment so well that forty more of the cars were soon ordered for service on the Burlington.

Other roads quickly noted the popularity of the Burlington equipment. By 1949 the Baltimore & Ohio had added such a car to its new *Columbian,* a streamliner running between Chicago and Washington. The B. & O. car even featured a front instrument panel which contained a clock, altimeter, barometer, and speedometer. By the late 'fifties a dozen other lines were building and operating the new dome observation cars. Variously called vista-domes, astra-domes, or strata-domes, more than two hundred such cars allowed the railroad traveling public to view the scenic routes in America.

The Santa Fe thought so much of the idea that they went one step further with the introduction of "high-level" passenger equipment. Santa Fe president Fred G. Gurley had made his line one of the major early users of diesel motive power, and he also supported more strongly the railroad passenger than did some of his fellow rail executives. The new dome cars introduced on the *El Capitan* in 1956 did not give passengers the same forward view available on the regular vista-dome car, but the view was much less obstructed than that of the ordinary passenger coach. On the new Santa Fe cars the lower level was used for baggage storage, larger rest rooms, and other services. Another new type of equipment popular with the railroad passenger were the "Slumbercoaches" added to the consist (the make up of train equipment) of the *Denver Zephyrs* in October 1956. These new cars gave the coach passenger a private roomette with a bed for the night and toilet and baggage facilities. The passenger paid normal coach fare plus a modest charge for the roomette. The typical Burlington Slumbercoach provided for 40 passengers with 24 single and 8 double rooms. By 1963 the occupancy rate on new cars on the fast Chicago to Denver run averaged more than 83 per cent per car per trip. The new service was both profitable and popular, and by 1960 the Baltimore & Ohio, the New York Central, the Northern Pacific, and the Missouri Pacific were all including comparable economy sleeping cars on several of their top passenger runs.

All of this new equipment built and put into operation in the post-war 'forties and 'fifties cost a lot of money. The New York Central just after the end of World War II ordered over 700 new passenger cars at a total cost of $56,000,000. Alfred E. Perlman, president of the Central, recently pointed out that his railroad in the post-war years up to 1958 spent about $250,-000,000 on new passenger equipment and facilities. With the expensive new diesels up front, and passengers cars at $100,000 or more apiece, each new train could cost several million dollars. When the Pennsylvania placed the all-Pullman *General* in service for a sixteen-hour New York to Chicago run each new train cost about $3,300,000. When the same railroad in 1952 introduced *The New Congressional* for its New York City to Washington service, the eighteen coaches and electric locomotive had a price tag of $3,224,000. In 1914, an earlier *Congressional*, consisting of a steam locomotive and seven cars, had cost only $151,000.

By 1950 an economical new type of passenger train did appear with the new rail motor car, the RDC, offered to the industry by the Budd Company, the same organization that had helped introduce the first *Zephyr* back in the 1930's. The RDC was really a welding of the old gas-electric "doodlebug" of the 'teens and 'twenties with the streamliner techniques of a later day. This self-propelled car was powered by a pair of 275-horsepower diesel engines, and had a smooth acceleration which permitted a speed of 80 miles an hour in no more than four minutes. The new car was economical to operate, since it could run up to 3 miles on a gallon of 8-cent diesel oil. Further saving and versatility was possible since two or more cars could easily be operated in a single train. The Budd Company offered the air-conditioned 85-foot car in three versions: RDC-1 (all passenger), RDC-2 (baggage-passenger), and RDC-3 (baggage-mail-passenger). The passenger capacity thus ranged from 49 to 90 seats, with a price tag of only $128,750, f.o.b. Philadelphia. The car offered many railroads a chance to possibly preserve short passenger runs and branch line service. The Western Pacific, the New York Central, the Chicago & North Western, and the Chicago & Eastern Illinois all quickly ordered the new car. Within a few years the total purchases amounted to nearly $60,000,000 for 398 units. RCD could reasonably be operated with a two-man crew consisting of an engineer and a conductor. But many Brotherhoods in the 'fifties insisted that a brakeman, a fireman ("to watch for signals"), and sometimes even a flagman be added to the crew. Railroad labor thus was in great measure responsible for the fact that relatively few RDC units were in operation by the mid-'sixties.

The extensive innovations made by the railroads in passenger equipment and service in the post-war 'forties and early mid-'fifties would seem to refute the frequently heard charges that railroad management in recent years has not been interested in promoting the passenger business. In fact the railroad industry spent tens of millions of dollars to update and improve their passenger carrying capacity. It seemed at the time that many of the innovations, such as the vista-dome car and the slumber-coach, appealed to the traveling public. But the travel statistics of the 'fifties and since prove otherwise. In 1949, the year in which many lines were introducing brand new stainless steel and streamlined trains, the combined total of airline plus railroad travel amounted to just under 44 billion passenger-miles, with the railroads furnishing more than 80 per cent of the total. In 1950 the airline share rose to 24 per cent, continuing to increase year by year. A decade later in 1960, the airline share had grown to more than 61 per cent, and by 1968 it had climbed to 88 per cent of the combined air-rail passenger-mileage. Of course the total travel had increased during the post-war years. But even so, between 1949 and 1967 railroad travel, expressed in passenger-miles, had been cut more than in half, while air travel had grown more than tenfold in the same years.

Naturally, with the reduction of rail travel the post-war years were years of substantial financial loss for passenger traffic. According to the I.C.C. accounting rules the net railway operating loss from passenger traffic grew from $139,000,000 in 1946 to $704,000,000 by 1953. During the remaining years of the 'fifties the losses averaged about $645,000,000 per year. Losses were cut a bit in the 'sixties as more trains were cut off, but annual losses of $400,000,000 or more were normal throughout the decade. From 1953 on, again according to I.C.C. bookkeeping rules, passenger trains were operating at an average loss of $2 or more for every train-mile run. This in spite of hundreds of trains being discontinued and thousands of passenger-route miles being abandoned. In 1947 passenger trains were operating on 160,000 miles of road, or about 71 per cent of the national rail network. By 1957 passenger service was available on only 112,000 miles, or just over half of the railroads in the country. And in 1967 the passenger routes had declined to less than 68,-000 miles, or only 32 per cent of the total rail mileage. In the fall of 1967 the National Association of Railroad Passengers paid for a full-page magazine ad which asked, "Are people as important as pigs? This guy [the pig] can still travel by train from any station in the U.S.A. to any other station on our 212,-000 mile railroad system . . . without changing trains."

As trains and route mileage were reduced, so also were the rosters of the operating personnel for passenger trains. The number of road passenger conductors declined from 7678 in 1947 to only 2926 twenty years later. In the same score of years the number of road passenger engineers and motormen dropped from 9534 to 3489. The worker's pay of course has climbed as the roster of workers has grown shorter. The conductor's average pay of $4900 in 1947 had been increased to more than $11,300 by 1967. But there has been no comparable growth in the prestige of passenger train personnel. The conductor's job has certainly lost the dignity and glamour the position once possessed.

In an earlier day the gold watch in the vest pocket, the bright hash marks on the sleeve marking years of service, and the shiny brass buttons on the dark blue jacket all marked the well-paid conductor as an aristocrat among wage earners in the nation. This is not true today, especially on those railroads which are in financial difficulty such as the New York, New Haven & Hartford. A conductor on the New Haven line recently complained: "When I first came to this railroad over thirty years ago, a conductor was really a big man. No more." Today the future for passenger train personnel is so bleak that some conductors of commuting trains serving New York City have taken "moonlighting" positions in the city during the hours between their morning and late afternoon runs. The sleeping car or Pullman conductor is in equally bad shape. Since 1957 the number of Pullman cars in service has declined by nearly 75 per cent; today there are only a thousand cars in operation. Only three hundred Pullman conductors are working with any regularity, and the company has not employed a new conductor in more than a dozen years. This is not surprising, for passenger traffic figures reveal that since 1955 the number of revenue passengers using sleeping and parlor cars has declined by over 80 per cent.

Even the reduced railroad passenger service of the late 'sixties continued to produce uncomfortably large amounts of red ink in the balance sheets of the industry. Speaking before a Congressional subcommittee in the summer of 1968 Thomas M. Goodfellow, president of the Association of American Railroads, pointed out that less than 2 per cent of the traveling public used trains. This top industry spokesman continued: "There just isn't any future or need for passenger trains, except perhaps in heavily populated corridors like New York to Washington." Goodfellow stressed that the continuation of trains is really a service "the railroads, the shippers, and the public can ill afford." Top railroad officials like to point out that in the late 'sixties roughly two-fifths of the profits from freight operations are being consumed by the continuing passenger deficits.

Ten railroads, four serving the trunk-line region and six serving the western or southern regions, furnish most of the remaining passenger service today and also suffer most of the deficits. Each of the ten roads produces at least 3 per cent of the country's rail passenger traffic, and the group in total furnishes more than two-thirds of the national rail passenger-miles. First in passenger-miles for the nation, with more than 11 per cent of the total, is the Pennsylvania, followed closely by the Long Island, a line whose heavy commuter traffic creates an annual passenger revenue several times the size of its freight revenue. Third in passenger traffic in the trunk-line region is the New York Central, a road which had spent millions of dollars in the early post-war years to upgrade its passenger service. By the end of 1967 the president of the New York Central, Alfred E. Perlman, was clearly ready to abandon all long-haul trains. Referring to the new competition he said: "The supremacy of the jet airplane for long-distance travel lies beyond argument. And when we added the proliferation of limited access highways to the inherent convenience and flexibility of the private automobile, the demise of the long-haul passenger train was certain."

In the middle 'sixties the Santa Fe was the third in the entire nation in passenger service, and was well ahead of all other western or southern lines in annual passenger-miles. This was not too surprising since the Santa Fe, with almost 13,000 miles of line in twelve states, is the longest railroad in America. But the Santa Fe for a number of years has been a major friend of the railroad traveler, and much more willing to continue its support of passenger trains than most eastern and many western lines. Santa Fe executives sided with the minority of rail managers in saying that the I.C.C. formula for passenger expenses was probably exaggerated. It was an early purchaser of new passenger equipment after the war, including new high-level passenger coaches. While it did retrench and discontinue some trains during the late 'fifties and early 'sixties, its reduction in passenger service was noticeably less than other major western passenger roads such as the Burlington, the Southern Pacific, or the Union Pacific.

But the dollar losses in the mid 'sixties for the Santa Fe passenger service continued to run at about $30,000,000 a year, almost as large as those of the Pennsylvania and twice those of the rival Southern Pacific. When the Post Office Department in the fall of 1967 decided to remove nearly all of its Railway Post Office cars from Santa Fe trains, the reaction of John S. Reed, Santa Fe president, was prompt. A month later Reed announced that his railroad would seek to have discontinued all passenger service except for three top trains: *Super Chief/El Capitan* (Chicago-Los Angeles), *San Francisco Chief* (Chicago-San Francisco), and *Texas Chief* (Chicago-Houston). In explaining this drastic discontinuance request Reed said: "Santa Fe has not abandoned the traveling public—travelers show an increasing preference to drive or fly."

In the same winter of 1967–68 other railroads were also making news with requests for the cutting of passenger service. The I.C.C. permitted the Monon to drop its last remaining train, the *Thoroughbred*, serving Chicago and Louisville. This reduction added the 541-mile "Hoosier Line" to the growing list of freight-only railroads. The Burlington succeeded in dropping its *Texas Zephyr*, ending a Dallas to Denver passenger service which had started back in 1882. The Northern Pacific, the New York Central, and the Southern Pacific all sought to abandon additional passenger trains, citing in every instance the additional dollar loss being suffered when additional Railway Post Office cars were removed from service. In making his plea for the train-off petition of the *Lark*, an overnight train between Los Angeles and San Francisco, Passenger Traffic Manager Robert M. Jochner of the Southern Pacific said: "We have to run a whole train—which requires a total crew of 21 on a single run from San Francisco to Los Angeles—to carry the passenger equivalent of little more than half a jet airliner, or less than two buses." Back in the Mississippi Valley, the new president of the Illinois Central, William B. Johnson, was endeavoring to maintain his passenger service with a new look at the feasibility of high-speed trains over middle distances of 200 to 300 miles, and the possible use of food bar coaches to cut down the losses of dining car service. Johnson emphasized his open-mindedness by saying: "The Illinois Central is determined to offer the kind of passenger service the traveling public wants—and uses." He was probably speaking for many other railroad executives when he said that it may be unfair to expect a financially hardpressed industry to continue a money-losing service which so few customers continue to patronize.

8

"Why Can't It Be Done Here?"

Since the 'forties, and perhaps before, the American people have been contributing to the decline of railroad passenger service. As taxpaying citizens they have favored, or at least condoned in a negative way, the appropriating of billions of dollars of federal and state money for airway and highway transportation. Americans have generally deserted railroad passenger trains, except as a standby service to be available in the emergency of blizzard or airline strike. In the past twenty years, or since 1948, noncommuter rail travel has dropped by more than two-thirds, from 35 billion passenger miles to under 10 billion passenger miles annually. Many Americans, as they noted the canceled trains, dirty coaches, and indifferent rail service in their country, have remembered the fine fast trains of Europe, of Canada, and of Japan. Many Americans seem to be asking, "Why can't it be done here?"

To observe the magnitude and dimension of the problem of the disappearing railroad passenger coach in the 'sixties is easier than correctly to assess the relative importance of the reasons normally given for this development. Greedy railroad labor, a government too generous in its financial support of competing highway and air services, a callous railroad management indifferent to the needs of the traveling public, a poor public relations image, and the inherent technological backwardness of the industry itself—these and other reasons have been put forward as causes of the sad state of railroad passenger traffic.

The speed of the jet, convenience of the automobile, and the run-down condition of the average railroad day coach suggest to much of the public that the railroad passenger train should be relegated to the museum along with the stagecoach. But other people often ask why American passenger trains cannot be more like those of Canada or Japan. Friends of rail travel like to point to the success, financially and otherwise, of the Japanese New Tokaido Line running between Osaka and Tokyo. True, in its year of completion (1964) the new line had an operating ratio of 141 per cent and lost $22,000,000. But the popularity of the fast new 125-mile-an-hour service grew, and daily usage increased from 60,000 passengers a day to nearly 300,000. By 1966 the operating ratio was down to 82 per cent, showing a profit of $5,000,000. In fiscal 1967 the operating ratio dropped to 69 per cent, and profits climbed to $96,000,000. Critics of American railroads have wondered why this country cannot have something like this speedy three-hour service between two Japanese cities 320 miles apart. The answer quite simply is that Japan and the United States are very different countries. Japan is a crowded little country of short distances and dense population where air travel is not common and privately owned automobiles are the exception rather than the rule. In the United States we have one automobile for every 2.5 people, while in Japan, in the year the line was completed, only one person in fifty-seven owned a car. In this nation only 5 per cent of our rail revenue comes from passenger traffic, while in Japan such traffic produces 69 per cent of the total revenue. Of course it is true that the Japanese government spent something like $1.3 billion to construct and equip the Tokyo to Osaka road. In contrast the United States government is spending only $12,000,000 for the new high-speed train service between New York and Washington.

And many Americans look with approval upon railroad passenger developments in areas nearer home. Travelers south of the Rio Grande often note that the trains of the National Railroads of Mexico have a better "on-time" performance than passenger trains in the States, and are cleaner and better maintained as well. But an even greater interest is generally found in the rail service of Canada, where the Canadian National, since the early 'sixties, has gone out of its way to woo and win the traveling public back to the railroads. From 1962 on the government-run Canadian National has pushed passenger travel with Red, White & Blue special fares, free meals for sleeping car and parlor passengers, complimentary coffee hours, faster trains, and almost any other gimmick which might bring in that extra passenger. The schemes worked, and by 1965 the Canadian National had produced more annual passenger-miles than in any year since 1948. As one top official said: "What we seek is the elimination of the railway passenger deficit, not the elimination of the rail passenger business." In the middle 'sixties, while United States railroads were retiring hundreds of passenger cars, the Canadian road was buying new equipment and upgrading older passenger equipment. In 1965 they introduced the *Rapido*, which provided five-hour service for the 335-mile run between Toronto and Montreal. This train was so popular that a still faster "Turbo-Train" made its first runs in the winter of 1968–69.

The passenger traffic on the Canadian National has definitely grown in the past decade, but it still has deficits. Passenger revenues on the line dropped 15 per cent in 1968 after reaching a peak of $84,000,000 in the centennial year of 1967. By the summer of 1969 there was even talk of abandoning some CN passenger service. But the influence of the Canadian National can be seen in the attitude of its subsidiary line, the Grand Trunk Western whose main line runs from Chicago to Detroit and Port Huron, Michigan. This road's effort to reverse the downward trend in rail travel could be seen in the fall of 1968 when it established passenger train stops in East Lansing for the convenience of Michigan State University students. But the chances of many American railroads following in these footsteps are not good. Canada may well possess some inherent characteristics which favor railroad travel. Train travel may be preferable to car travel because of winters which are longer and colder than they are in the United States. Also the relatively lower number of motor vehicles in Canada further increases that country's dependence upon the railroad.

One of the most pressing and nagging problems facing American railroads is the high cost of labor. This is in spite of a downward spiral of declining rail employment during the last forty years. In the fall of 1968 fewer than 592,000 railroad workers were gainfully employed, a number less than half of the 1950 total, and well under the number employed in 1890. For the last decade and a half the decline in rail employment has averaged more than a hundred jobs lost every day. The number of passenger train personnel naturally has also declined with the discontinuance of hundreds of trains in recent years. By 1967 the total number of passenger conductors, ticket collectors, baggagemen, brakemen, flagmen, engineers, motormen, and firemen had dropped to 15,428, only one-third of the number employed in such work at the end of World War II. Passenger train personnel, while declining in numbers, are not poorly paid. Their average compensation in 1967 was very close to $11,000 a year, and their straight-time hourly earnings of about $6.40 an hour was within pennies of the hourly pay of the 15,500 railway executives, officials, and staff assistants, men at the very top of the industry. And yet in spite of their high pay, the average passenger conductor or trainman frequently presents a picture of grouchiness and complaint to the traveler in the day coach. Faulty air-conditioning, a cold breakfast in the diner, or a balky footrest, all are readily blamed by crew members upon an unfeeling railroad management that "doesn't care."

Certainly passenger personnel cannot complain about long hours of work. For decades the basic work day for passenger train firemen and engineers has been 100 miles of operation. For brakemen and conductors it is only 150 miles. The result is a story of "featherbedding" which has greatly increased the cost of passenger service, and the size of the annual passenger deficits. Engineers who had fast runs on first-class trains could do a month's work in a remarkably short time. In the late 'fifties railroad executives, as they entered a new round of labor negotiations, told each other of the lush run of a passenger-train engineer out in Kansas. Eighty hours in the engine cab each month earned him $800, leaving him ample time to run a 700-acre farm whereby he received another $800 a month from Uncle Sam for not growing wheat.

A "day's work" for a passenger engine crew on a fast train is indeed short. On a Chicago to Denver sixteen-hour run the train stops about every two hours to change crews, and the engine crews receive, on the average, over a day's pay for about two hours up in the cab. Down on the Southern Pacific the engineer and the fireman on the *Sunset Limited* receive about a day and a half's basic pay for the 145-mile run (3 hours and 16 minutes) between New Orleans and Lafayette, Louisiana. On a number of poorly patronized trains the size of the aggregate train crews (counting all crew changes) is greater than the total passenger list.

A graphic portrayal of the passenger train labor problem was recently presented to a Denver luncheon club by William J. Quinn, president of the Burlington. Quinn compared the revenues, costs, and labor expenses of a tri-jet Boeing 727 with the *California Zephyr* in their rival service between Chicago and Denver. Quinn pointed out to his audience that 72 passengers, on the average, took the two-hour air trip, while the *Zephyr* typically carried 166 revenue passengers on its longer 18½ hour run to Denver. Trip revenue for the train was $5073 ($30.50 per passenger), while the jet took in $3454 ($48 per ticket). Even though the train's occupancy was high, the *Zephyr*, on the average lost $334 for the trip, while the airline was making a profit of $943. Biggest reason for the poor profit showing of the train was its high labor cost. While labor consumed only 16 per cent of the jet revenue, on the train the figure was 42 per cent. With frequent crew changes, the train required the services of 47 different workers for a total wage bill of $2288. In contrast the 6-member jet crew cost the airline only $391 in wages. It is small wonder that Quinn told his audience that high railroad labor costs could "threaten to finish off the passenger train."

Of course another cause of this unfavorable rail passenger

picture is something the public often forgets—the continuing and generous financial support given by the government to air, highway, and water transport facilities. The public never seems to forget the half billion dollars or so of land grant aid given to the railroads in the nineteenth century. This aid has been repaid several times over in reduced freight and passenger charges for government business in the century prior to 1946, when the special rates finally ended. In contrast federal, state, and local aid to the competition seems to go on at an ever increasing rate. The Chicago to Denver jet which comes off so well when compared with William Quinn's *California Zephyr* is part of an airline industry which receives millions of dollars of annual aid.

In 1966 federal, state, and local aid for airways and airports, and cash subsidies to airlines amounted to $1.4 billion. In 1966 the air carriers of the nation produced 69 billion passenger-miles of passenger traffic, while the railroads produced about one-quarter as much, or 17 billion passenger-miles. If a government subsidy of $350,000,000, or one-quarter of the aid given to airlines, had been provided for the railroads, this assistance would have taken care of seven-eighths of the $400,000,000 railroad passenger service deficit incurred in 1966. Such a subsidy would certainly assure the retention and continuation of the present minimal railroad passenger service.

A more specific instance of the air-rail subsidy problem can be seen in the Southern Pacific's *Sunset Limited*, which provides that line's sole remaining service over the 2000-mile route from New Orleans to Los Angeles. In recent years the *Sunset* has lost much of its business to rival air service between these two cities and currently is operating with an annual deficit of about $2,-000,000. During fiscal 1969 the federal government was scheduled to spend some $3,280,000 in airport aid for eight cities along the route of the Southern Pacific train. With total governmental expenditures for highway, waterway, and air facilities currently running at $19 billion (1968) per year, it might seem reasonable to expect that Uncle Sam's largesse should also include something for the nation's hard-pressed rail passenger service.

The railroad passenger problem is certainly made worse by the hostile and critical opinion the general public has of American railroads. The man in the street views the railroads which serve him as the original pork-barrelers still living back in the days of the land grant, and as common carriers who hate passengers. Enchanted with jet travel and the air age, he is apt to think that today's railroading still has a Vanderbilt at the throttle of a wood-burning steam locomotive. To a remarkable degree the railroad problem today is not so much what it actually is, as what the American public thinks it is. A prime example of the unfriendly attitude of the American news media toward railroads can be recalled when on June 8, 1968 a twenty-one car special train of the Penn Central carried the body of Senator Robert F. Kennedy from New York to Washington for burial in Arlington Cemetery. Negativism and errors in reporting were commonplace. A TV reporter for CBS pointed out that the train was nearly as anachronistic as the horse, and a national news magazine reported that the sad journey was "a rolling catalog of the physical discomforts that have turned U.S. passenger railroads into the nation's most unpopular form of mass travel."

Even though 90 per cent of the railroad business is with shippers and freight rather than passengers, the general public seems to be mindful only of the sad plight of the passenger train. Santa Fe's executive vice president, John C. Davis, put it quite well when he said: "We are deluding ourselves if we don't consider that despite all the affirmative action being taken by the railroad industry, the bulk of the people in this country still think of the railroads only in terms of the movement of people." Much of the public agrees with the advertising agency executive who recently observed that railroads might just be a dying industry. When challenged with references to recent innovations made in shipping and freight, the advertising man, no doubt recalling an unhappy train trip, in effect said: "So what? This doesn't touch me."

Railroads cannot afford much industrial or company advertising because they do not make much money. Their rate of return on net property investment was only 2.45 per cent for 1968, and for the 1959–68 the rate averaged only a little higher, 2.83 per cent. With such meager profits it is the rare company that can afford much advertising. But sometimes a railroad, even with a limited budget, gets its message across with a touch of humor. During the summer of 1968 the Seaboard Coast Line, referring to the frequently hijacked planes that were being rerouted to Cuba, had a clever 14-word ad: "If you want to go to Miami without a stopover in Havana, call us." And recent Northern Pacific ads have also managed a dig at the airlines. In stressing the pleasures of scenic travel in vista-domes served by a railroad stewardess the ad read: "The scenery is magnificent when you're flying at 14 feet. . . . She does everything but fasten your seat belt. No seat belt."

But too many representatives of American railroads have spent their public relations effort and dollars on the crying towel, citing chapter and verse of the many problems facing the industry. It is no wonder that recently a New York business-man remarked: "Why is it, that when you listen to an air-line man talk about his industry, you feel like rushing right out and buying airline stocks—and when you listen to a railroad man talk about railroads, you also feel like rushing out and buy-ing airline stocks?" Currently top railroad personnel are facing up to this problem. One such executive is Thomas M. Goodfel-low, longtime president of the Long Island Railroad, who be-came the new president of the Association of American Rail-roads in 1967. Goodfellow saw three factors—crying, quarrel-ing, and negativism—as responsible for the poor railroad image. Goodfellow challenged his colleagues to: "Shout proudly . . . and weep no more." In reviewing the poor performance of his industry, he said: "Our gnashing of teeth, our wearing of sack-cloth and ashes, brought attention to our cause—but not vic-tory. We should continue to fight. But not with the crying towel."

Goodfellow has quickly moved to make America more aware of its railroad industry. His A.A.R. has raised its annual advertising budget and started to spend money for TV and magazine ads. This was indeed different from previous practice, since for years the railroads have given little priority to advertising. In 1966 two major airlines, United and TWA, each spent as much money on newspaper publicity as the entire railroad industry. In the new campaign Goodfellow sought to present the rail industry as a forward looking segment of the American economy whose chief chore was the movement of freight rather than the movement of people. One such ad emphasized computer usage by railroads and carried the line: "There's more room on the road for the kind of driving you like . . . when highway trailers ride piggyback—the modern *rail* way."

Regardless of the relative significance of the several factors contributing to the decline of rail passenger travel, no one could deny at the end of the 'sixties the basic truth of Howard Hosmer's 1958 prediction. The I.C.C. hearings examiner had foreseen the end of Pullman service by 1965 and coach traffic by 1970. The man in the street was well aware of the vanishing day coach and the abandoned rail service. He noted the dreary railroad depots with dimmed lights, closed lunch counters, and absent Redcaps. Railroad executives felt fortunate when they could profitably convert their once busy terminals into less costly facilities. New York City's famed Pennsylvania Station was relegated to an underground terminal, a fraction of its former size, with a sports center and office building rising on the former site. Plans are well advanced in Washington, D.C., to transform the beautiful Union Station, located just north of the Capitol Building, into a National Visitors Center for tourists and sight-seers. Hosmer had predicted that the passenger car would join the stagecoach in the museums of the land. When travelers, on those rare days when ice or bad weather grounded the ubiquitous airliner, sought the standby service of vanished trains they felt that Hosmer was probably correct. Down in Fort Lauderdale, Florida, a historic Pullman car, marked "U.S. No. 1" and named the "Ferdinand Magellan," did indeed become a museum exhibit piece early in 1967. This magnificent

Presidential Special had for sixteen years been the traveling office of Roosevelt, Truman, and Eisenhower. Like the general public, the family in the White House has joined the jet set.

By the end of the 'sixties the traveling public was convinced that most railroad managers were no longer interested in passenger traffic. This was not entirely true, of course. The Pennsylvania was co-operating fully with the government-sponsored project for a new high-speed passenger service (with speeds up to 110 miles an hour) between New York City and Washington. The Pennsylvania prepared for the new service by installing continuous welded rail over most of the 227-mile route, by ordering fifty new high-speed self-propelled electric cars, and by building new high-level platforms along the route. After numerous delays this high-speed Northeast Corridor Project Service was started on January 16, 1969, with the new Metroliner running between the two cities. But it was also the Pennsylvania Railroad which many Americans associated with dirty cars, indifferent train service, surly ticket agents, and the discontinuance of money-saving round trip tickets. And it was this line, now the new merged Penn Central, which early in 1969 was reported to have announced that it would no longer handle passenger baggage, or haul newspapers and corpses.

The railroads have clearly tried to woo and win the American public. In the last generation they have spent hundreds of millions of dollars on air-conditioning, streamlining, lightweight modern cars, and clean diesel power. They have tried innovations such as family rates, movies on trains, slumbercoaches, and vista-dome cars. And all to little effect. Every new railroad effort seemed to result only in more crowded highways and airways. As Stuart K. Saunders, top man on the Pennsylvania, said in 1966: "The railroads have not left the passengers, the passengers have left the railroads." In 1965 and 1966 the late Lucius Beebe and co-author Charles Clegg made their last contribution to the American railroad fan, with their two-volume *The Trains We Rode*. Considering the state of railroad passenger service today, it was fitting that the title was put in the past tense.

America will never be able to regain the extensive and complete rail passenger service so graphically recalled by the pen and camera of Lucius Beebe. But some limited passenger service will continue in spite of the pessimism of Howard Hosmer. Both Alan Boyd, secretary of transportation under Lyndon B. Johnson, and John A. Volpe, secretary of transportation under Richard M. Nixon, believe that the passenger train cannot be allowed to disappear totally. Just before his retirement Boyd in a television interview stressed the fact that the nation *needs* passenger trains and that the nation was going to *have* passenger trains regardless of the cost. Naturally, Boyd was thinking of a limited passenger service which would require government aid of some sort. The high-speed rail service between New York City and Washington of course has some federal support.

In the 'sixties several state and local governmental units have given increasing financial support to urban transit projects. And in Japan, Canada, and Europe every upgrading of passenger service has had total governmental sponsorship. Early in 1969 the American railroad industry finally decided to support a joint industry-government project to sustain some passenger service. The A.A.R. president, Thomas M. Goodfellow, said: "The railroads are willing and anxious to do what they can—within their means—to help solve the public transportation crisis. . . . But where we're forced to operate money-losing trains, we feel the government should assume the obligation to share in the cost." As American railroads look toward the possibility of federal financial aid, they must never forget that voters and taxpayers make up the general public, and in turn any program sold to Congress must first be packaged and presented to a taxpaying public. As America enters the decade of the 'seventies it seems quite probable that Alan Boyd's view of a continuing, but limited, rail passenger service is more likely to prevail than the earlier sweeping prophecy of Howard Hosmer.

9

"Tote That Bale"

For a number of years rail executives have been trying to impress the American public with the notion that the chief business and concern of American railroads is the movement of freight. Certainly in their new advertising campaign of the late 'sixties the Association of American Railroads has played up the freight business and consciously avoided references to passenger traffic. The man largely responsible for this new effort in good public relations claims that his industry has made itself "lean, hard, and efficient" for the job of moving freight. Early in 1968 Goodfellow said: "Thoughtful people . . . know that railroads are going to be in the business of hauling goods, not people." Clearly Goodfellow believes that the future song of American railroads must be "tote that bale."

Even in the days when the "varnish" was carrying a money-making number of passengers, railroads made most of their revenue hauling goods rather than people. Today freight traffic produces roughly 90 per cent of all operating revenue. It is profitable enough to pay taxes, bond interest, high wages, *and* annual passenger deficits which have averaged nearly half a billion dollars per year during the last decade. In the last generation the railroad freight business has suffered as barges, trucks, and pipelines have captured much of the profitable traffic. Less-than-carload freight, farm produce, household goods, and large shipments of manufactured goods now move on rubber and concrete. Pipelines and barges have been equally successful in taking over many of the shipments of oil, coal, grain, and other bulk products. But in recent years the railroads have fought back with such innovations as piggyback service, unit trains, the delivery of motor vehicles on open rack cars, and a whole new spectrum of larger freight cars built to the needs and specifications of individual shippers. By the middle 'sixties the long-time decline in the rail share of all intercity freight traffic had leveled off, and in 1968 the railroads carried an all-time high of 743 billion revenue ton-miles. In the process new records in operating efficiency in rail freight service were also achieved.

More than a half-century ago, in the days before World War I, the railroads had only minor competition in the movement of goods and freight. Good roads did not exist, horse-drawn drays were only for short hauling, pipelines were short and of small size, and river and barge traffic generally seemed out of date. In the middle 'teens about four-fifths of all intercity freight moved by rail. The steam locomotive with its string of red wooden box cars, slatted stock cars, tank cars, and vari-colored reefers served all America. Two and one-third million freight cars delivered the many products ordered earlier by merchants and store-keepers from the thousands of drummers and traveling salesmen. Pancake flour and cigars, washboards and writing paper, boys' clothing and garden tools—all were delivered to the busy freight houses and team tracks of the nation. Less-than-carload freight was booming and was increased further by the efforts of the new mail order houses. The small town depot agent spent as much time with shippers and freight customers as he did with his ticket buyers or his telegraph instruments. The dependence of the American consumer upon railroad freight service was most noticeable in the farm villages of western America. Blizzards or prolonged spells of bad winter weather might occasionally isolate such towns for days on end before the automobile existed.

Rail freight traffic volume had simply exploded in the half-century of industrial expansion after the Civil War, growing from 10 billion ton-miles in 1865 to 366 billion ton-miles in 1916. Although the population roughly doubled every generation; rail business, on the average, easily doubled every decade.

Thus per capita freight service in the country expanded from only 285 ton-miles in 1867 to 1200 ton-miles in 1890, and 3600 ton-miles per person in 1916. With the development of new competition for the railroads in the 'teens and after, this rate of growth has naturally slowed. While the total freight needs of the country have continued to grow, pipelines, trucks (both commercial and private), and a revitalized river barge traffic seem to have taken over much of the new business. Thus the per capita rail freight traffic has gone above 5000 ton-miles per year only once, during the emergency of World War II. The record 743 billion ton-miles of railroad freight in 1968 was no more than 41 per cent of the nation's aggregate commercial freight movement, and the 3700 ton-miles of rail freight per capita was only slightly above the figure of half a century earlier.

As trucks, pipelines, and barges took a growing share of rail freight in the decades after World War I there were major shifts in the make-up and composition of railroad freight. Livestock, animal products, and oil started to move on rubber and concrete, or underground in pipes and as a result, the demand for certain types of freight equipment dropped off. The number of tank cars owned by Class I railroads dropped from just under 11,000 in 1925 to just over 5000 by 1968. Between 1928 and 1942 new tank cars were built in only two of the thirteen years, and by 1960 the tank car's average age of 34.5 years was older than any other type of freight equipment. Railroad stock cars declined in number from 87,000 in 1925 to 17,000 in 1968, and few new ones were built during the 'thirties. Comparable reductions occurred in the number of railroad-owned refrigerator cars. Two types of freight equipment, gondolas and hoppers (used for the carrying of coal, ore, and coke), continued in common use. The number of such cars in use today is nearly as great as in the 'twenties, and constitutes roughly half of the total freight equipment.

The railroads still carry much of the nation's coal and mine products. Unfortunately for the railroads, such traffic is a low producer of revenue. In the early 'sixties such traffic was being carried for about $3 a ton against a total average of nearly $7 a ton for all freight traffic. The competition, especially that of intercity trucks, has naturally chosen to carry freight paying higher rates. Since the 'twenties the railroad traffic in livestock and animal products has declined by two-thirds. This traffic which the railroad has managed to retain pays a profitable average rate of about $22 for each originated ton. Naturally the trucking industry, whether private or commercial, prefers such high revenue freight over the poorer-paying coal or ore shipments. The same sort of traffic loss by rail lines has taken place with general merchandise or less-than-carload (L.C.L.) freight. In the 'sixties less-than-carload rail freight was paying an average rate of more than $40 per originating ton. The trouble is that such shipments by rail have almost disappeared. L.C.L. freight declined from 53,000,000 tons in 1920 to 15,000,000 tons in 1940, 3,000,000 tons in 1960, and under 1,000,000 tons in 1968. Even though such freight has always paid high rates, most railroads in the 'fifties and 'sixties found L.C.L. freight to be more trouble than it was worth. Truck competition has increasingly forced railroad freight traffic to be characterized by bulk, heavy volume, long-distance movements.

But even with the losses of freight to the competition, railroad freight revenues have managed to grow slowly. Annual freight revenue, which had averaged about $3 billion annually during the 'thirties, more than doubled to reach more than $7 billion in 1944, the best year during World War II. In the 'forties and 'fifties rail freight revenue soon hit and kept a plateau of between $7 and $9 billion. In the early 'sixties it dropped to under $8 billion, but a definite upward trend began in 1963, which reached an all-time high of $9.7 billion for the year 1968. Between 1944 and 1960 the rail share of all intercity freight traffic had declined from 68 per cent to 44 per cent. Since 1960 this decline has slowed, and the rail share of all freight seems to have become stabilized slightly above 40 per cent.

Freight rates have certainly not risen, in constant prices, since World War II. From 1945, when the average rate was just under one cent a ton-mile, until 1958, when it had risen to 1.4 cents a ton-mile, freight rates did not quite keep up with inflation. This bargain in rates has been made even greater in the last decade. Since 1958 average rail freight rates have dropped by a tenth, declining from 1.46 cents a ton-mile to 1.31 cents a ton-mile. In the same decade the consumer price index has gone up 20 per cent. It should be pointed out that in this same decade prices paid by the industry for fuel and material have risen, and that wages paid railroad workers have climbed by 40 per cent. Certainly some of this substantial drop in real average freight rates has resulted from the continuing success of trucks in getting and retaining much high rate freight. But a considerable factor in explaining the low rates has been the successful and continuing efforts of the entire industry to increase the basic efficiency of their freight service operation.

A major reason for the resiliency of the railroad industry is the inherent efficiency of the flanged wheel on a steel rail. The public may feel that the railroads constitute an antiquated industry run by reactionary old fogies, but the railways of America really have a lot going for them. Their basic economy cannot be refuted. Like the Indian travois or the Japanese jinrikisha, railroads do not carry but rather pull their load. The minimum friction of steel on steel plus the maneuverability of a string of cars guided by flanged wheels permits a maximum load to be propelled with a small amount of power. A two-unit 6000 horsepower diesel can readily pull a freight train with a net load of 2000 tons, which is a typical load in the late 'sixties. Neither the truck nor the airplane can come close to this ratio of roughly three horsepower per ton of cargo. H. L. Smith, the chief engineer of the electro-motive division of General Motors, figures that a diesel with three horsepower per ton of freight can on level track get up to a speed of 71 miles per hour. Smith points out that a Chevrolet, using this same horsepower to weight ratio, would have only a five horsepower motor, hardly sufficient to reach speeds of 70 miles an hour. Smith estimates that modern heavy duty highway trucks require 7 to 8 horsepower per ton of cargo to be efficient.

The freight train is clearly far ahead of the competition in ton-miles of transportation produced per gallon of fuel consumed. The typical freight train can produce close to 200 ton-miles of freight movement per gallon of fuel, while the average truck can produce roughly one-third as much. Also, even with the railroad work rules which permit featherbedding and excessive crew size, the railroad today outproduces the truck in ton-miles of freight per worker by a margin of three or four to one. The same high efficiency of rail freight movement can be seen when one recalls that in the late 'sixties railroads were carrying almost twice as much intercity freight, in ton-miles, as trucks, but receiving only about one-fifth as much revenue for their service.

But railroad freight service even with its inherent efficiency, faces certain problems, some of which are beyond the industry's control. Railroads can do very little about the affection the average American has for the automobile and truck. Nor can the industry match the convenience, adaptability, and extensibility of door-to-door highway transport. The 3,000,000-mile highway and road network of the nation gives the truck a flexibility of service the freight train can never hope to equal. But there are other problem areas where one might expect the railroad industry to have been more successful. Unfortunately in such areas as surplus plant, the loss and damage to freight, the labor dilemma, and the lack of freedom in rate making, little real progress has been made in recent years.

Considering the present heavy emphasis on long-haul through freight, and the loss of much short-haul freight to the highway, it seems clear that the present railroad plant is larger and more extensive than it need be. When the iron rail network was built to completion in the half-century before World War I, the nation needed nearly every railroad that was constructed. Every little valley could afford a branch line. In a day when the farm wagon was the main mode of transport closely spaced lines with depots located every few miles made real sense. In 1967 the Class I railroads of the nation were operating almost 213,000 miles of line. Unlike passenger service, nearly every mile of line was used for freight traffic. Freight trains were running on almost 212,000 miles of the total network. Since 1916 about 40,-000 miles of line have been abandoned. The density of traffic on the remaining network is most uneven. Some rusting branch lines see only an occasional short freight, while other miles of well-maintained and ballasted welded rail may have dozens of long freights every day. The nearly completed Interstate Highway system of little more than 40,000 route-miles will soon be carrying the bulk of all truck traffic. Some transportation experts feel that in this day of unit and integral trains the nation's rail network need be little more extensive than the projected Interstate Highway network. This is not a realistic claim, since the new Interstate Highways are clearly supplemented and supported by hundreds of thousands of miles of national, state, and secondary roads. But nevertheless it is true that a really healthy national rail system should probably give up thousands of miles of uneconomic trackage.

A change has appeared in the railroad landscape of many small towns as rail lines have been either abandoned or seldom used in recent decades. The depot has either disappeared or been converted to other uses. Causes other than abandonment may account for the closing of local stations. Few branch lines today have any passenger service at all. In fact passenger trains are running on only 67,000 miles, or less than one-third of the 213,000 miles of line in the country. Thus many small ticket offices have been closed. Some village stations have been torn down, but others have been converted to a different commercial use, serving as feed stores, implement shops, or warehouses. In a few eastern towns the village "depots" have been converted into antique shops or bakeries. In Stockbridge, Massachusetts, an old station became a discotheque, and down in Oklahoma one became a combined church and parsonage. The depot at Allen,

Kansas, was moved intact to an adjacent lake where it now functions as a fishing lodge. In Indiana an Illinois Central depot at New Harmony was moved into the center of town as a tourist center for a village made famous by two groups of Utopians in the nineteenth century. And in Peoria, Illinois, a larger depot was transformed into a quality restaurant.

On many roads the station agents serving in musty and little-used depots on branch lines often have wondered how much longer their offices would remain open. In 1966 and 1967 the Burlington came up with an imaginative solution to the problem of derelict stations on branch lines in northern Illinois. R. G. Johnson, Burlington General Manager—Lines East, introduced four Ford truck mobile-office units to replace more than a dozen local stations on branch lines. The red, white, and black mobile units with a two-way radio and complete office furniture are fully equipped with heating and air-conditioning. The new mobile service means that Burlington shippers may transact railroad business in their own establishments rather than making a trip to the station. From their van the mobile agents can contact dispatchers and conductors, as well as the permanent agent located in a station in the center of the route. On a fifty-mile branch line north of Galesburg, Illinois, one permanent agent and one mobile agent in a van serve five towns, each of which formerly had its own depot. The new service has created new freight traffic, has often sped up service, and also has improved the morale of the remaining agents who now feel greater job security. General Manager Johnson is contemplating an expansion of the service to other branch lines, and other railroads are viewing the experiment with interest. Some such solution must be forthcoming since most railroads are still maintaining scores of village depots which are not paying their way.

Another more pressing problem, still unsolved late in 1969, is that of firemen on freight trains. Half a century ago the problem was simply one of whether the fireman's back was up to the job of moving mountains of coal into a locomotive firebox which had an insatiable appetite. In the days before the appearance of the automatic stoker the fireman's job was back-breaking work, and competition was keen for the better paying and easier work of controlling the throttle on the right hand, or engineer's, side of the cab. Even with the stoker the fireman in a steam engine was kept busy watching the fire and checking boiler controls. But the work of the fireman changed with the coming of the diesel locomotive in the 'forties and 'fifties. Fuel is fed automatically to the diesel, and there are no boiler controls to watch. When the first diesels appeared and began to replace steam the National Diesel Agreement was already in effect and the job of the fireman was protected by contract. Thus, even though there were no fires to tend or significant duties to perform, thousands of "firemen" worked on the diesels of American railroads. By 1959 there were 28,000 diesel locomotive units and 750 steam engines on the locomotive roster of the nation. In that same year there were 17,000 freight firemen and helpers, and 18,000 yard engine firemen and helpers employed in the entire industry.

In 1959 the railroad industry made a concentrated effort to ease or reduce the entire problem of "featherbedding." As the industry faced the problem Daniel P. Loomis, top executive of the Association of American Railroads, said of American railroads: "Featherbedding is seriously curtailing efficiency and service, and may eventually drive us into bankruptcy—or into the arms of the government. The time is now to put an end to rules that limit work or output." Specifically the railroads sought a redefinition of a "work day" for operating personnel, the removal of "excess crew" laws in more than a dozen states, and the orderly elimination of firemen in freight and yard diesel locomotives. This last objective of removing firemen in engines without fires had high priority. The industry estimated that this change in work rules would ultimately save $200,000,000 a year in wages. The managers felt they had a strong precedent in the fact that a royal commission in Canada in the late 'fifties had held that diesel firemen were not needed in freight service. Firemen had also been dropped in many European countries, even from some passenger trains. Rail executives generally answered questions about safety considerations by pointing out that there would still be an "extra pair of eyes" in the engine, since the head-end brakeman shares the cab with the engineer.

Between 1959 and 1963 several different presidential commissions and boards were set up to arbitrate this dispute. Such well-known figures as James P. Mitchell, former secretary of labor; Samuel I. Rosenman, New York jurist and special adviser to Franklin Roosevelt and Harry Truman; and Clark Kerr, president of the University of California; were members of the several boards. Without exception these several findings supported the railroad view and called for the general elimination of freight and yard engine firemen. Without exception the Brotherhood of Locomotive Firemen and Enginemen refused to accept the several recommendations. The threat of a railroad strike resulted in Congressional action in August 1963 under which one final arbitration board, appointed by President John F. Kennedy, agreed with railroad management against labor. Labor again appealed to the courts, but unsuccessfully, and Arbitration Award No. 282 finally became effective on March 31, 1964. The award, to continue in force for two years from the effective date, permitted eventual elimination of all but 10 per cent of the firemen assignments on freight and yard diesels.

Starting in April 1964, most of the railroads of the nation developed an orderly program of reducing the number of freight and yard firemen. Efforts were made to minimize any adverse effects upon the workers, and many reductions were obtained by the policy of not replacing men when death or retirement created a vacancy. Comparable railroads jobs were offered to many junior firemen, and others were provided with generous severance pay. This practice was further expanded on the Illinois Central in the summer of 1964 when substantial severance allowances were offered engineers 65 years of age and older, men already eligible for full pensions. This program had the effect of allowing many firemen to obtain earlier promotion to the right hand side of the cab. In the next few years the industry managed to cut the number of firemen by 18,000 across the country.

One of the major objections to the job reduction made by the firemen was the matter of safety. Many engineers and firemen claimed that the "deadman's control" was not a foolproof device. Engine crewmen and their union officials have also alleged that the frequency of accidents has increased since the award was placed in effect. The railroad's reply is to refer to the evidence given by such men as C. J. Coughlin and Charles A. Webb. Coughlin, the first assistant grand chief engineer of the Brotherhood of Locomotive Engineers and a member of a board which studied the operation of locomotives without firemen, reported in January 1965 that: "No single case available for evaluation produced concrete evidence that any accident was the result of the elimination of a fireman, or that any accident could or would have been avoided had a fireman been a member of the crew or crews involved." And in the same year a former chairman of the Interstate Commerce Commission, Charles Webb, stated that ". . . the Commission has investigated no accident . . . in which it was found that the absence of a fireman was a contributing or the proximate cause."

Nevertheless the firemen's union, the Brotherhood of Locomotive Firemen and Enginemen, on November 15, 1965, called for a reversion, after the expiration of the two-year period of the award to the manning practices which had earlier prevailed. In many ways the rather insistent attitude of the firemen and their union is not surprising. They work for an industry in which employment clearly is in decline. In the 'fifties the total number of railroad workers had dropped from 1,220,000 to 780,000, and firemen (passenger, freight, and yard) had declined from 51,000 to 38,000 men. Enginemen point out that there are fewer choice "red apple" train assignments than the claims of rail management would suggest. They correctly argue that the preferred high-pay runs go only to the older men with "whiskers" and long years of seniority. And the unions point out that all operating personnel fail to receive extra or overtime pay for work at night or on holidays and week ends. Further they must pay their own expenses when away from home during their wait for a return run.

Thus the firemen in the years since the spring of 1966 have alternated between strikes or strike threats and continuing court appeals. The strike efforts have resulted in a majority of lines surrendering to the unions, restoring many of the vacated firemen jobs. Other roads such as the Louisville & Nashville, the Chicago & North Western, the Illinois Central, and the Belt Railway Company of Chicago have been reluctant to capitulate to the union demands. Meanwhile the court decisions have not conclusively upheld the right of the railroads to keep the fireman's seat vacant, and the entire problem still remains unresolved.

Another problem that is a financial drag upon the profitability of rail freight traffic is the continuing cost of loss and damage claims made by shippers against the railroads of the country. In recent years these have been climbing faster than freight revenues. In 1955 loss and damage payments, often shortened to L & D by railroaders, were less than $100,000,000 and little more than one per cent of total freight revenues. By 1967 L & D had climbed to $167,000,000 and were just under 2 per cent of the total freight revenue. The cost and wastage of loss and damage on his own line has recently inclined G. H. Baillie, vice president of the Canadian Pacific, to call it, "probably the greatest junk-purchasing program of all time." The size of L & D is made the more meaningful when one recalls that it amounted to almost one-fourth of the total net railway operating income in 1967. Of course faster speeds and heavier loads typical of recent years help explain the increase in loss and damage and resulting claims. But the growth in L & D claims and costs is especially unwelcome since railroads in recent years have made many efforts to reduce these losses through such innovations as cushioned cars, improved load tie-down systems, moveable-bulkhead flatcars, foam insulation, and improved retarding and switching methods.

Some experts in the field believe the real costs of the less than perfect care and handling of rail freight are greater than the immediate out-of-pocket costs. The general manager of the Illinois Central figures that L & D costs on his line easily amount to a dollar and perhaps two dollars per share of stock. It is hard to measure the dollar value of an angry shipper or the ill-will and lost tonnage that must be charged up to the inability of the industry to improve the quality of its service. But often the shippers themselves should share in the blame for damaged freight. Containers that are too large, packages that are too flimsy, poor handling by fork-lift trucks, loading pallets that are beaten up or the wrong size—all are contributory factors generally beyond the control of the railroad. L & D prevention men recall the story of the big tomato shipper in California who consistently used flimsy cartons, and just as consistently had full cars delivered with squashed layers of tomatoes at the bottom of every car.

It often is difficult to place specific blame for L & D. There is a great temptation to pass the buck. The railroad would like to blame the shippers and in turn the shippers, generally having the last word, naturally blame the railroad. Within the industry itself many in the front office like to blame the switchmen and yardmen for bashing cars together at excessive speeds. Otto H. Zimmerman, vice president and general manager of the Illinois Central, and a switchman himself thirty years ago, believes that switchmen are only partially at fault. He notes that across the country, train wrecks and derailments account for millions of dollars of loss every year. Nor can theft losses be charged against switching crews or hump yard classification work. Other millions of dollars of L & D are just written off as undetermined or unlocated loss. Regardless of the placement of fault or responsibility, it is the railroad cash box which in the end must pay. In spite of the best railroad efforts at quality control and increasingly sophisticated methods of prevention, L & D claims seem to be an inevitable part of freight operations on American railroads.

Nor have the railroad managers and top brass succeeded in

making much headway in another area—freight rates. Just as the work rules for labor are hopelessly out of date, so too is the basic stance and posture of governmental regulation of railroads. The development of a rather complete regulatory control over the nation's railways appeared more than half a century ago during the Progressive Era. In the days of Teddy Roosevelt and William Howard Taft the railroads had a clear-cut monopoly of freight traffic. The stench of nineteenth-century corruption and the chicanery of men like Fisk, Gould, and Vanderbilt were still present, and the rail lines were vulnerable to a heavy-handed regulation. Today some government regulators often act as if they were still dealing with the rail problems of the prewar 'teens. Conditions of transportation in America have changed drastically since World War I. While rail service is still a public service meeting a major public need, there is today no requirement for a regulation as rigid as that provided by present law. This is particularly true since the major competitors for freight traffic go so largely unregulated. About two-thirds of all truck traffic and nine-tenths of inland water traffic are today operating free of governmental rate regulation.

Thus a railroad cannot cut off a train, close a station, or raise a freight rate without regulatory approval. Nearly all requests for rate increases are trimmed by the Interstate Commerce Commission. Hearings and decisions are often slow. As an executive on the Boston and Maine once described them, "Every rate case is a carnival of oratory." When the inflation and increased costs of the late 'sixties hit the railroads, they requested in March 1968 a new schedule of rate increases ranging from 3 to 10 per cent. By the summer of 1968 the I.C.C. permitted an interim increase of 3 per cent, but did not give its final decision and approval for the rate increases until January 1969.

The Commission has also often been reluctant to let railroads reduce their rates. Government regulations and regulators have often required rail lines to keep their rates high enough to assure the competition (i.e. barges or trucks) a fair share of the total traffic. In a sense the emphasis seemed to be shifting from a stance of protecting the public against abuses to a posture of protecting other forms of transportation against free competition. And the I.C.C. was slow. Not too long ago the efforts of a major line to cut freight rates—reductions that would have saved shippers millions of dollars—were subjected to four long years of court and regulatory proceedings. Legislation of 1958 was intended to remove this rate "umbrella" from the less efficient carriers, but the operation of this law has been something less than perfect.

But while American railroads continue to have some problem areas in the movement of goods, there are in fact many other stories of progress, significant innovation, and improved freight service. In the years since V-J Day the "pluses" of such innovations as dieselization, improved track maintenance, the use of computers, "piggy-back" service, unit trains, and new unique freight equipment far exceed such "minuses" as L & D, the freight fireman issue, or the closing of hundreds of local stations.

Probably the most significant innovation in American railroading since World War II has been the revolution in motive power which came with the introduction and rapid acceptance of the diesel-electric locomotive. Tremendous increases in operating efficiency, and corresponding declines in costs of motive power and fuel, resulted in the post-war years as the new motive power completely replaced steam locomotives. The shift from steam to diesel-electric power has been swift. In 1941 only one per cent of the freight service, 8 per cent of the passenger service, and 12 per cent of the yard service was by diesel. Twenty-five years later the new form of motive power accounted for 99 per cent of all rail service, with the small remainder performed by electric locomotives.

Rudolph Diesel, a French-born German mechanical engineer, invented the diesel locomotive in the 1890's. A rich brewer in St. Louis, Adolphus Busch, purchased the American manufacturing rights for the invention in 1898. Busch had a modest interest in railroads and was a pioneer in mechanical refrigeration, but he never applied the new engine to transportation. In the early twentieth century several companies including the Burlington, the Santa Fe, and the Union Pacific had some success with self-propelled rail cars driven by gasoline engines. But the first efforts to use the diesel engine for such service failed. The General Electric Company solved the problem by combining a diesel engine with an electric generator which in turn ran a traction motor. In 1925 a sixty-ton 300 horsepower diesel-electric locomotive was sold to the Central Railroad of New Jersey. The new locomotive was placed in switching service in a freight yard in New York City, where the engine's ability to develop maximum power at starting and slow speeds made it very useful. Within a few years several dozen light diesel switchers were in operation.

The success of diesel power in the streamlined passenger trains of the Burlington and the Union Pacific during the 'thirties has already been noted. In 1941 the Santa Fe was the first line to use diesel motive power for freight service. This new freight locomotive was a far cry from the light switchers built back in the 'twenties. The Santa Fe engine was a giant consisting of four units, each with a 1350 horsepower V-12 diesel motor. The combined units measured 193 feet in length, weighed 464 tons, and the 16 driving axles produced a total of 5400 horsepower. The new motive power was so satisfactory on the Santa Fe that before the end of the year the Milwaukee, the Great Northern, and the Southern were all ordering comparable locomotives from the Electro-Motive Corporation.

The new diesel-electrics of the 'forties and 'fifties had numerous advantages and few disadvantages as compared with steam locomotives. Certainly the new diesels were not cheap. The average unit cost ran from $125,000 to $200,000. Compared with steam engines, both in original cost and in dollars per horsepower, the diesels were expensive. But in the low consumption of fuel, reduced costs of maintenance, and long hours of service per day, the new engines provided immense economic advantages. The economy in fuel consumption is significant. A diesel engine generally can furnish as much transportation service with a tank car of oil as a steam locomotive can provide with six to eight cars of coal. While probably not quite capable of hauling a ton of freight a mile on a spoonful of oil, diesel power on the average does provide 200 ton-miles per gallon of fuel. The rising price of coal in the post-war years made many railroad managers look with interest at diesel power. Fuel costs for locomotives declined from 8 per cent of the total revenue in 1948, when only one locomotive in five was a diesel, to less than 4 per cent in 1967, when active steam locomotives in the industry had dropped to only twenty-one units. Compared to thirsty steamers the diesel uses very little water. When complete dieselization was achieved by the late 'fifties, the railroads were able to retire about $50,000,000 worth of water-supply tanks and equipment previously needed for the steam locomotives.

Shop repair and maintenance costs for diesels are also low. Many railroads soon found that diesels required only about one-quarter as many man-hours of maintenance service as steamers. The new engines did not require the extensive daily servicing and attention the firebox and boiler of steam locomotives did, since diesels can run thousands of miles without major servicing. The replacement parts for most diesels are standardized, so most repairs can be accomplished quickly. Diesels are available for long and hard use. The Chicago & North Western ran a twin-unit diesel on an 838-mile round trip between Chicago and Minneapolis for 733 days without missing a single trip. A steam locomotive requires an hour or two of "firing up" before it can move out under its own power. In contrast the diesel can achieve full power very quickly from a cold engine. The high horsepower at low speeds permits faster starts and improved schedules. The lower center of gravity also allows faster speeds on curves, and the lack of reciprocating parts in the diesel tends to reduce stresses set up in the track by the steam locomotive. All of these advantages permitted the new diesel to haul larger loads at faster speeds. By the early 'fifties many railroad managers were discovering that diesel motive power might allow three freight cars to do the work of four cars behind a steamer.

The diesel locomotive, like the electric locomotive, can reverse its electric motors, using them as brakes. This braking effect is generally sufficient to hold a train's speed within proper limits on a 2 per cent descending grade. This dynamic braking effect was well illustrated as the first Santa Fe diesel locomotive took a heavy train down the steep western grade below Cajon Pass toward San Bernardino, California. The veteran Santa Fe engineer in the cab, Jack Burke, discovered that he could descend the hill with only an occasional use of his air brakes. And at the foot of the long hill not a wheel was smoking from hard-used iron brake shoes. The Santa Fe people soon discovered that the new diesel dynamic braking methods were to save them hundreds of tons of iron brake shoes every year.

The economy and operating superiority of the diesel was so great that soon it was replacing electric motive power as well as steam. In the early twentieth century a score of lines had electrified more than 6000 miles of road, the Pennsylvania, the New Haven, and the Milwaukee being the chief users. By World War II days over 850 electric locomotives were in use in the nation. Offering most of the advantages of electric motive power without the worry of maintaining electrified track, the diesel quickly began to replace the electric units. Such engines numbered under 600 units by 1957 and only 321 in 1967.

But it was the steam engine which really capitulated to the efficiency of the new motive power. Some of the change-over started during the Second World War. In 1941 only 1200 (or about 3 per cent) of the 41,000 engines in the locomotive roster were diesels. By V-J Day the number had climbed to 3800 units. The diesels were already proving to be motive power warhorses, for in 1945 they performed 25 per cent of the yard switching, 10 per cent of the passenger service, and 7 per cent of the freight service. In the post-war years most railroads were soon concentrating their engine procurement upon diesel units. In the first post-war decade the industry purchased 21,000 engines for $3.3 billion. In the same years fewer than 400 new steam locomotives were built for domestic use. In 1952, for the first time, there were more diesels than steamers listed in the roster of motive power. Not a single steam locomotive was purchased by American railroads after 1953. More than fifty major lines in 1955 owned no steamers at all. By 1957 diesels were furnishing 96 per cent of the switching, 93 per cent of the passenger service, and 92 per cent of the freight service. Most of the remaining steam locomotives were soon placed in storage, even the immense 7000 horsepower "Big Boys" of Sherman Hill fame out on the Union Pacific. The steam engine roster dropped below a hundred in 1962, and in 1967 only twenty-one were included on the nation's list of motive power. By the early 'sixties it was easier to find a steam locomotive in a museum or a city park than operating on an American railroad. And the lonesome sound of the steam whistle that had meant so much to generations of Americans had given way to the raw bleat of the diesel horn.

Since the appearance of diesels the number of tons of freight moved one mile during an hour of freight train operation has doubled: 17,623 net ton-miles per hour in 1943; 36,091 in 1968. Not only diesel power, but larger cars, longer trains, and increased freight train speeds have all helped make this improved service possible. In the last twenty-five years average freight train speeds have gone up one-third. In 1968 trains averaged 20.4 miles an hour from original to final terminal, including the time spent to pick up and set out cars enroute and meet opposing trains.

Higher speeds require better tracks and improved roadbed. Not many years ago a commuter remarked to a fellow passenger that railroads, like their tracks, never seemed to change. He was somewhat taken aback when his seat mate, who was the president of the railroad, listed more than a dozen ways in which track had been improved. Recent years have seen the use of heavier rail become standard. Before World War II almost two-thirds of all rail weighed less than one hundred pounds per yard. Today almost two-thirds weighs more than one hundred pounds per yard. Much of the new rail put down is continuous welded rail. More than 2600 track miles of such rail were laid in 1967. Some companies find that they save $1000 a mile per year with welded rail.

Since World War II many new machines for improved track maintenance have appeared. Powered spike hammers, new track-laying machines, and detector cars to locate hidden flaws in rail have brought increases in operating efficiency and economy. The variety of the new track maintenance equipment is so great that when the machines are lined up to go out on the road they often are referred to as "the circus train." Periodically track ballast can be raised, cleaned, and carefully tamped back around the ties by mechanical ballast tampers and cleaners. Machines guided by complex electronic devices can rapidly raise and align the track. Not many years ago there was a rule of thumb that a section hand could replace one tie in an hour. Today modern mechanized equipment can replace two ties in a minute. This new equipment, though expensive, has cut down on labor costs and maintenance-of-way personnel. In the early 'fifties some 167,000 men (section men, extra gang men, and section foremen) were needed to maintain the track of American railroads. By 1967 this number had been reduced to 45,000 men, or only one man on the average for every five miles of line. This saving of 120,000 men, at perhaps $6000 a year (the averag 1967 wage), would certainly pay for a great deal of modern mechanized track and roadway equipment. Critics of the railroads are not happy about this reduction in maintenance personnel. They see it as a major factor in the recent increase in freight train derailments, noting that between 1961 and 1967 derailment accidents increased by 85 per cent.

Comparable improvement—the result of years of research—can also be seen in many new switching and classification yards in America. Transfer points in rail shipments are expensive and troublesome, sometimes constituting one-third of the total transportation cost. Since World War I many improvements have

been made in the old style "flat" switching yard where a locomotive pushes a train of cars into a set of tracks controlled by
numerous hand switching and braking operations. In 1926 the Illinois Central put into operation near Chicago a giant new classification facility named Markham Yard after Charles H. Markham, a longtime president of the line. The new yard, one of the
largest in the nation, was more than 3 miles in length, and its
113 miles of track had a capacity of 9000 freight cars. Eastern
roads made comparable improvements in the same years. The
Pennsylvania spent $34,000,000 in the years after World War
II on a mammoth freight yard near Conway, Pennsylvania. The
new yard not only sped up shipments, but was scheduled to save
up to $11,000,000 per year in operational expense.

One of the most recently completed yards is the new Union
Pacific Bailey Yard in North Platte, Nebraska, named after the
U. P. president Edd H. Bailey. Finished in the fall of 1968 the
$12.5 million facility includes 62 classification tracks which can
handle 800 cars an hour in its departure yard. In the most modern yards today a computer tells wheel retarders on the declining hump track how much pressure to apply in order to be certain that the cars will couple at a speed of no more than four
miles per hour. The man in the tower can program five or six
car movements in advance with much of the work being done by
computer. Radar measures car speed, other devices determine
the rollability of the car after a track scale has weighed the
moving car. The computer may even take into account the force
of prevailing winds. Other automatic machines check cars for
any dangling equipment, while electronic devices note loose
wheels or damaged flanges. Such equipment may be expensive
but it results in lower labor costs, reduced loss and damage
claims, and faster freight shipments.

Railroads have long made use of radio and TV in the area of
railroad communcations. The Lackawanna used radio in an experimental fashion as early as 1914, and after World War I in
1922 the Nashville, Chattanooga, and St. Louis also tried. But
the major developments came in the 'forties; by mid-century

some 190 railways and terminal companies had F.C.C.-licensed radio stations. Thousands of cabooses, locomotives, and offices are equipped for radio service, and hundreds of walkie-talkies are also in use. The Pennsylvania Railroad in 1954 was the first line to use industrial television. The Pennsy employed TV to aid in the switching of mail cars at Pittsburgh, but soon TV was being tried for identifying incoming freight cars, the general supervision of yard and terminal work, and even as an aid in protecting railroad crossings. It soon proved so helpful that one rail manager boasted that TV "watches without coffee breaks or overtime pay and doesn't complain about rain or snow."

By the 'sixties microwave transmission was rapidly replacing pole-line telegraph and telephone communication along many rail routes in the country. Hundreds of tall towers with dish-like antennas were erected along the main-line routes of most of the major railroads. Using the very high frequency radio waves, focused in narrow beams from tower to tower, railroad men can talk to each other on direct-dial telephones. The new microwave systems are needed partly because railroad communication requirements are growing by one-third or more each year. As the railroads of the country increasingly depend on computers for information and decision-making, more and more data must move back and forth through the microwave transmitters.

By 1968 there were over 22,000 route miles of railroad microwave in use, and some experts believe this figure will double in the next decade. Led by its new president William B. Johnson, who is committed to the new rail technology, the Illinois Central has recently completed a 976-mile microwave system between Chicago and New Orleans. This $2,600,000 system was started in 1967 at the southern end of the line, with a New Orleans to Jackson, Mississippi, segment built to replace wires knocked down by Hurricane Betsy. A total of 44 repeater towers, each about 25 miles apart and some as high as 340 feet, provide a Gulf to Lakes communications link for the Illinois Central. The system helps to provide complete control over train movements, information on car location, information for the hot box detector system, and high speed transmission of operating and administration messages. Much data also move over the microwave network to computer headquarters in Chicago.

Nearly all of the major lines are endeavoring to upgrade and improve their freight service through an increased dependence on new information systems made possible by the computer. At the end of 1968 the industry was using nearly 250 computers, almost half of which were the sophisticated third-generation models. Railroads of all sizes are using computers. The giant Southern Pacific has committed itself to an ambitious $21,-000,000 computer information program planned to touch all the basic paperwork operations of the entire 13,000 mile system. At the same time the much smaller 734-mile Delaware & Hudson has determined to employ the advanced computer technology along with the larger lines.

Computers from the first have been used by railroads to help handle the mountains of paperwork that accompany nearly every railroad operation. Thousands of complicated rates, bills of lading, way bills, tickets, wage rates, car per diem rates, accounts with other railroads—all mean millions of pieces of paper for the average railroad. Increasingly computers are being used to digest these masses of paper.

Specific operational problems facing railroads have often been analyzed by computers through simulation. A railroad may find it hard to decide whether to concentrate on shorter and more frequent trains or longer ones running less often. Programmed into a computer such simulation studies can introduce and judge such variables as tonnage, speed, locomotive power, and railroad grades. The speed of the computer allows a study of an almost infinite number of "mixes" of such variable factors. As computers are tied to actual rail operations for the monitoring of train movements the accumulation of data soon permits the computer to be of great assistance to the dispatcher. Computers clearly have the capacity at present to help railroad managers relentlessly to seek out inefficiencies, gain new business by providing better service, and generally increase the utilization of manpower and equipment. Before long they may be taking over even bigger tasks.

One of the significant uses of the new electronic and computer equipment in recent years has been the growth of freight car tracing and location systems. By the summer of 1968 more than three dozen railroads had car tracing and location systems in operation. Although installed for the benefit of the shipping public, they have also permitted the line to utilize its freight equipment better. Nearly all of the systems permit shippers to call into company traffic offices to gain information about car locations, information generally provided by computers. The system used by the Chicago & North Western is so effective that John J. Kane, vice president of sales and marketing, claims that customers are now given service in a few seconds which formerly took hours. Proud that they knew the location of every one of their 40,166 freight cars, the Burlington ran ads in the winter of 1967–68 which asked: "Want to know where any car is on the Burlington route? Ask our pair of IBM 360 computers. Get an instant answer." The Southern Railway claims as much, contending that having 283 recording locations and the use of computers allows them to locate any car on their system in two seconds. *Trains* magazine in October 1968 challenged the Southern to back up its claims; the railroad's computers responded admirably. When the computer in Atlanta was asked the location of fifty different cars earlier spotted throughout the South, the Western Union machine quickly printed out the location of all but three of the designated freight cars.

Actually, the entire rail industry, under the leadership of the Association of American Railroads, is completing plans for a national computer car-locating system which should be in full operation by the winter of 1969–70. Basic to the system is the universal use of a system of automatic car identification, called ACI. In this nation-wide program every piece of railroad rolling stock—locomotives, passenger cars, freight cars, cabooses, railroad service, and work cars—will be identified with a plastic label placed on the side of each car or engine. The label, 20 inches high and 6 inches wide, will consist of 13 strips of brightly colored plastic which will identify the car by type, ownership, and number. At a cost of about $10 per unit, the industry will spend at least $20,000,000 to so label and identify the 2,000,000 cars and engines which serve Canada and the United States. The second part of the ACI system is a trackside scanner capable of reading the plastic car labels through snow, rain, and fog, and at speeds of up to 80 miles per hour. The scanners will be located at dozens of strategic locations on every line, including interchange tracks, switch yards, and car and locomotive repair shops.

The information picked up by the scanners across the continent will be fed into local, regional, and national rail computers. Pooling data and equipment from all railroads, this TeleRail Automated Information Network (known in the industry as TRAIN) will be able to head off car shortages, spot "lazy" systems and methods, and furnish equipment where most needed. The Association of American Railroads believes that the new system, once in operation, may well boost freight car utilization by as much as 25 per cent. This could provide service equal to the addition of 450,000 cars to the nation's rail fleet.

The railroad industry should welcome any innovation which works toward greater utilization of its equipment, especially of freight cars. Freight cars have been noted for their low daily average use and mileage. In the early 1930's the average freight car mileage was below 23 miles per day. Even today the average car is on the road only about 11 per cent of the time, traveling just over 50 miles in each 24-hour period. Average freight car usage has climbed rapidly with the new unit train idea. While average freight cars may make only 20 trips a year, the cars placed in unit trains often make up to 150 or more trips in 12 months.

Someone has called the unit train "one car repeated many times." The unit train idea started with coal, a commodity which for years has been first in bulk, and carloadings, of all railroad freight. After World War II the coal traffic was in decline as an increasing number of homes and factories shifted from coal to oil and gas. Even the railroads contributed to the decline as they traded in coal-burning steamers for oil-driven diesels. Between 1947 and 1961 railroad coal traffic dropped from 9,000,000 carloadings of coal to just over 5,000,000 cars per year. In the late 'fifties several cost-conscious steam power utility companies decided that coal moving via slurry pipelines might be cheaper than the current coal freight rate then charged by the railroads. In 1959 a 108-mile slurry pipeline was built in Ohio, and soon others were planned. At this point several railroads reacted by inventing the unit train. An early sponsor of the new type of train was Jarvis Langdon, Jr., president of the Baltimore & Ohio and a man eager to break with tradition. Soon Langdon was joined by other eastern lines.

The unit train idea is useful where large tonnages of a single product are shipped regularly to a single destination. Whole trains of permanently coupled cars could avoid switching delays and speed up schedules. The Denver and Rio Grande Western, a very well-managed road in recent years, naturally went in for unit trains. Soon the D. and R. G. W. was carrying coal in unit trains from mines in Colorado and Utah to U. S. Steel's Geneva works near Provo, Utah. The officials of the mountain road soon found that 625 hopper cars were doing the work previously done by 1000 cars. In speaking of the complex co-operation required, John E. Timberlake, division superintendent on the line, remarked: "All segments of the operation must interlock so that the total system functions like clockwork." Unit train service is further improved when shippers and customers install special high-speed loading and unloading equipment.

The coal-bearing unit trains which were running from mine mouth to utility power plant were soon so economical that coal rates were substantially reduced. This was especially true when unit trains could make long hauls on a regular schedule of several trips each week. Some unit trains were able to carry coal at a rate as low as a half-cent per ton-mile. The public utility companies were soon saving a great deal of money. Detroit Edison, which earlier had planned a slurry coal pipeline, gave up the idea once railroad unit coal trains were making possible annual savings of $3,800,000. By the mid-'sixties unit trains were hauling more than one-third of the nation's coal and had lowered coal freight costs by nearly $100,000,000 a year. D. W. Brosman's Southern Railway found that bigger coal-carrying cars plus unit trains increased its coal revenues, even at reduced rates. The Southern increased its coal revenues almost 30 per cent between 1957 and 1962. Brosman's road in the same years was trying the same technique with large shipments of grain (a minimum of 450 tons) in its newly constructed larger "Big John" box cars. Rival barge lines, who did not like the new tough rail competition, protested to the courts and the Interstate Commerce Commission, but eventually the cheap bulk grain rates offered by the Southern Railway were approved.

Unit trains were soon used for other products as well. Hot steel slabs, chemicals, ore, and pulpwood were all soon moving via the new shuttle train method. Soon food chain associations were talking of solid unit container trains which could move lettuce and other garden truck from the fields of California to markets in the New York metropolitan area in four days rather than the normal seven. As American cities in the 'sixties faced the perplexing problem of the daily disposal of thousands of tons of trash and garbage, they finally thought of the unit train. Early in 1969 unit trains started to carry San Francisco's daily trash collections from the Bay City to convenient desert locations in the interior.

In the late 'sixties several roads made real efforts to speed up their freight service. The Illinois Central started a new overnight container service on the fast freight, the *Hustler,* which they claimed was only two hours slower than air freight. The Illinois Central even offered to cancel the premium charge when failing to meet the promised delivery time. The Denver and Rio Grande Western decided to provide faster service with shorter more frequently scheduled freights. Using 12,000 horsepower multi-unit diesels the D. and R. G. W. was able to pull 40 to 50 car freights through and over the Rockies at speeds as high as 65 miles per hour. Rio Grande freights were often moving as fast as the *California Zephyr*. Another line which practiced a speed-up of freight traffic was the Milwaukee. By early 1968 the road's eastbound *Thunderhawk* and westbound *XL Special* had cut 26 hours off the earlier schedule between Chicago and the Pacific Northwest. To the south the Santa Fe also introduced faster freights early in 1968. Sixty-odd years ago Death Valley Scotty, the rich eccentric from California, had paid $5500 to have a special train rush him from Los Angeles to Chicago in under 45 hours. A generation later Santa Fe's new streamliner *Super Chief* had cut the time to under 37 hours. Early in 1968 the speed record went to a new freight train, Santa Fe's *Super C* —a through freight consisting of high priority piggyback and container cars. On January 17–18, 1968, the Chicago to Los Angeles 2202-mile run was made in 34 hours and 36 minutes. The new Santa Fe freight train, like fast freights all over the country, was given running rights over passenger trains. After all, freight traffic was paying the bills for the entire industry, not passenger business.

Even before its record *Super C* run, the Santa Fe had co-operated with the New York Central in an experimental coast-to-coast run of a through freight consisting of 36 loaded Flexi-Van containers. The special transcontinental freight ran from New York City to Los Angeles in a record-breaking 54 hours and 20 minutes. Another western line, the Northern Pacific Railway, became interested in the "land bridge" idea of helping to speed freight between Europe and the Orient. Early in 1969 the Northern Pacific used double page "We're Playing Bridge" magazine ads to tell the story of its new service. The road, which likes to call itself the "Main Street of the Northwest," claims that its containerized freight land bridge service across the United States from Europe to the Orient can beat the steamship route around the Cape of Good Hope by twenty days, and Panama Canal service by ten days. Another road pushing combined ocean and rail international shipments is the Southern Pacific, whose vice president-traffic, F. E. Kriebel, points out that Southern Pacific is the original promoter of land bridge traffic. The Central Pacific first introduced the idea a century ago, shortly after the 1869 Golden Spike completion date.

The high tonnage train, a trend of the late 'sixties, was more a result of unit trains than of extra-fast schedules. Long trains, of well over a hundred cars, were not unknown in the era of steam, but only with diesel power has the long high tonnage train became commonplace. The Pennsylvania in 1966 boasted of a 300-car ore train, and a year later claimed a 341-car train grossing 36,000 tons and pulled by eight diesel units furnishing a total of 25,000 horsepower. Almost before the public knew about Pennsy's big train the Norfolk and Western routed a 450-car coal train grossing 44,475 tons through the mountains of West Virginia. Later the same road dispatched a 500-car coal train from West Virginia to Portsmouth, Ohio, traveling 157 miles in less than seven hours. In this movement the Norfolk and Western used three radio-controlled "slave" diesels near the center of the train.

Still another instance of innovation in improved bulk railroad freight was the introduction of the "rent-a-train" by the Illinois Central. In 1967 John W. Ingram, Illinois Central's assistant vice-president-marketing, proposed that his company take the principle of the unit coal train and transform it for the use of the big oats, corn, and wheat farmers of Illinois. Since Illinois is one of the largest grain exporting states in the country the idea seemed a natural. Ingram estimated that a single 86-car "rent-a-train" used for grain carriage in an orderly fashion the year round could roughly do the work of perhaps 5000 box cars at the harvest season. Some officials feared that the Illinois Central request to replace car-mile rates with special low train-mile rates would not be approved by the Interstate Commerce Commission, the I.C.C. having been most reluctant a few years earlier even to approve the low rates requested by the Southern Railway for grain moving by way of the new huge "Big John" hopper cars. Surprisingly, the Commission approved the new "rent-a-train" rate request, and officials of the new Department of Transportation offered congratulations on the new service as the "boldest step yet made" to promote farm production and prosperity in the region.

Taking a page from automobile rental companies, Ingram and his fellow officers figured out a range of alternative rates for big shippers who might wish to use either their own cars or those of the railroad. When the big grain company, Cargill, Inc., made its grain hauling contract with the Illinois Central the rate was $800,000 a year plus a small ton-mileage charge. The grain company supplied its own cars pulled with Illinois Central crews and motive power. Normally, such a shipper may make an unlimited number of trips annually from a single originating point. The first such "rent-a-train" movement was made in late October 1968 between the Cargill grain elevators in Gibson City, Illinois, and Baton Rouge, Louisiana, where the corn was put on the grain vessel, the *Captain W. D. Cargill,* bound for Amsterdam. The first train was loaded with 400,000 bushels in 115 cars and ran on a 25-hour schedule. The success of the early grain shipments encouraged the Illinois Central to plan for an extension of "rent-a-train" service to export shipments of soybean meal and oil, grain sorghums, and barley.

But one of the brightest spots in the rail freight picture in the past fifteen years is the story of piggyback service, or the intercity transporting of truck trailers on special railroad flat cars. While this modern development started in the early 'fifties, some instances of "wheels on wheels on rails" go back to the early years of railroading. In 1833 an early instance of such service on the Baltimore & Ohio was noted in the pages of *Niles' Weekly Register.* In 1855 the piggyback hauling of farm wagons was tried on a short railroad up in Nova Scotia. Half a dozen years after the Civil War the great showman P. T. Barnum put his huge circus and menagerie on rails. Barnum shifted from using 600 horses to 65 brightly painted railroad cars for the between city movement of his circus wagons and vans. During the 1880's a number of Long Island farmers started loading their garden truck and produce wagons on Long Island Railroad flatcars for the trip into the markets of New York City. The farmers' teams went along in box or stock cars on the same train so that they could be used on the streets of the big city. The first rail movement of loaded motor trucks was started in 1926 when the Chicago, North Shore & Milwaukee started such a service between Chicago and Milwaukee. A decade later comparable piggyback service was offered by the Chicago Great Western Railway.

In the early 'fifties half a dozen different lines started to offer the new piggyback trailer service. The innovation offered a two-pronged approach: not only would it provide new freight revenue for the industry, but it would show that railroads could serve truck shippers and customers as well. In 1953 one railroad alone carried over 50,000 trailer loads on its flatcars. The next year the Interstate Commerce Commission permitted railroads to carry trailers without the necessity of gaining certification as motor carriers. The I.C.C. also approved several separate plans for piggyback operations. Among railroads first interested in the new traffic were the Southern, the Missouri Pacific, the Chicago & North Western, and the Pennsylvania. James M. Symes, who became president of the Pennsylvania in 1954, was an early booster of the service and soon was building 500 new extra-long trailer carrying flatcars for his road. Taking a different approach, the president of the Missouri Pacific, Paul J. Neff, started his service by hauling only the trailer or truck body on ordinary flatcars. The new piggyback service boomed, and by 1959 fifty-seven different lines were moving trailers in every one of the forty-eight continental states. Between 1955 and 1960 piggyback service climbed from 168,000 to 550,000 carloadings.

The Milwaukee soon was moving bulk mail from Chicago to Wisconsin in Flexi-Vans on passenger trains, and the Chesapeake & Ohio also added piggyback flatcars to some of its passenger runs. Much of the new traffic consisted of meat and other perishables moving in refrigerated trailers. The Baltimore & Ohio by the early 'sixties had 40 per cent of its piggyback trailers carrying meat, and the Chicago Great Western estimated that meat and other perishables often made up 75 per cent of its traffic. Since they so often carry premium or high value freight, piggyback trains are forced to keep to tight and dependable timetables. Thus piggyback trains normally have fixed departure times and run at high speeds, generally bypassing yards and all local stops. The Illinois Central put its trailers on the Chicago to Memphis run on a special all-piggyback train scheduled at passenger train speed, and called it *Fastback*. The increase in the utilization of equipment on such trains is often great. One railroad admits that though special piggyback flatcars may cost one-third more than ordinary box cars, they often travel three times as far each year and produce six times as much revenue. Many shippers also find piggyback service allows them to cut down on warehousing expenses. Of course many railroads have been put to some extra expense to make possible the new movements. Some lines have had to modify their rights-of-way, even eliminating tunnels in order to accommodate off-size or extra-large trailers. Most lines have had to build new yards, or modify old ones as terminals for the handling of the trailers and the new truck traffic. The Chicago & North Western spent a million dollars on its Proviso Piggyback Plaza, a new Chicago facility capable of handling 700 trailers per day. The Baltimore & Ohio, like many other roads, uses special cranes to lift trailers off and on flatcars at terminal points. The best of these giant cranes can unload a trailer from a flatcar in no more than 90 seconds.

In the 'sixties piggyback traffic, now often called TOFC (Trailer On Flat Car), continued to climb, increasing in several years by 12 to 15 per cent. Between 1960 and 1968 TOFC carloadings increased from 554,000 to 1,337,000 cars. TOFC traffic was up nearly 11 per cent in 1968, and amounted to 4.7 per cent of total carloadings for the year. Clearly piggyback service had become far more than the "passing fad" which some critics had predicted back in the early 'fifties. Today it is one of the brighter spots in an industry whose future in recent years has often seemed bleak. In placing trucks on flatcars the rail industry has provided a prime example of the co-ordination possible between rival and competing modes of transport.

A near cousin of piggyback is container freight or COFC (Container On Flat Car), a service which in recent years has started to challenge TOFC. Container freight has many advantages, since an unopened sealed container can easily be shifted from one mode of transport to another. Standard sized containers are 8 feet wide by 8 feet high and either 20 or 40 feet in length. Fitted with rear wheels, called bogies, they quickly can become trailers. They can as easily be loaded into ships, and will also soon be traveling as air freight. Containers, which are well secured and locked, make pilferage almost impossible. The savings in handling costs and insurance, as well as L & D, are so great that one executive recently claimed, "it's the most workable, useful, intermodal tool available for cheaper, faster, and safer movement of goods."

Container freight, like piggyback, is best used in long-haul, medium-to high-value shipments which place some premium on fast schedules. Container traffic also is a natural complement to "land bridge" or combined ship and rail freight. Both the Northern Pacific and the Union Pacific have recently opened freight offices in Tokyo anticipating increased container freight eastward via ship and rail. As with TOFC, shipments of fruit and produce often move by container. Containers have been used to bring pineapple products from Hawaii to midwestern markets, and returned to the islands with canned goods. Special cooled containers have been used to move fruits (by rail and ship) from California to Britain in just over two weeks.

Many lines have experimented with COFC, but the Southern Railway and the New York Central were the early major sponsors of the new service. With its introduction of "Flexi-Van" containers the New York Central became an early leader in container freight, and by 1967 found that its Flexi-Van shipments were increasing far faster than the piggyback growth in the industry at large. One of the advantages the New York Central put forward for container service was the lower center of gravity and higher speed possible, as compared with piggyback. Alfred Perlman, president of the New York Central, also has contended that Flexi-Van containers, in avoiding the air turbulence created in the wheel space between trailer bottom and flatcar floor, permit fuel savings of as much as 10 per cent. Certainly container freight was serving Perlman's road well by the mid-'sixties. In 1965 container and Flexi-Van cars amounted to only about one per cent of the line's freight equipment. In that same year container freight on the New York Central amounted to 6 per cent of the freight revenue and 15 per cent of the profit.

The Southern Railway is equally enthusiastic about COFC. This line has adopted a flexible stance on rail-highway transport, having built since 1965 a big fleet of all-purpose flatcars which with equal ease handles wheeled trailers or wheelless containers. At the same time freight executives on the Southern generally favor container traffic and try to follow a principle that "wheels on wheels is a waste." W. Graham Claytor, Jr., the Southern's new president and legal expert who helped win the so-called Big John hopper car rate case, also likes container freight. Claytor believes that "Vast amounts of traffic now moving entirely by highway are subject to recapture by the railroads as the use of containerization increases. . . ."

Another favorable freight development of recent years has been the increased shipment of new motor vehicles by rail. In the early days of the twentieth century railroads carried nearly all new automobiles from factory to market. "F.O.B. Detroit" meant that the manufacturer would pay for laboriously stuffing three or four new automobiles into box cars to be shipped to dealers across the nation, where the difficult unloading task would often be accomplished with damage to the vehicles. Slow delivery, delays in yards, damage in transit, and loading problems made both factories and dealers eager for a better way. By the 'thirties it was discovered that special highway rack trucks, each holding five or six new cars, could deliver new cars to dealer showrooms more economically. The railroad share went down to under a million cars moving by rail annually in the middle 'fifties. By 1958–59 less than 10 per cent of new motor vehicles were being shipped by rail.

The Frisco and the Santa Fe were among the early lines to attempt to regain this lost traffic. The Frisco first used piggyback in addition to local truck delivery. Soon it developed a tri-level rack car capable of carrying a dozen to fifteen new cars. In 1960 the Santa Fe and the Burlington were using comparable rack cars for the new auto traffic. Soon more than half of the Class I railroads were offering such service, and by 1961 the rail share of new auto traffic started to climb. Seeing their business going to the railroads, many truckers complained to Congress, and Teamster Union president James Hoffa even warned of massive unemployment. The economy of the new service was obvious, since rail rack car delivery generally ran $25 to $60 less per automobile than shipment by highway. Private car owners could appreciate not only this saving, but also the fact that each train of rack cars kept hundreds of trailer trucks off crowded highways. Often solid trains of new vehicles went by rail. By 1965 the New York Central was running a daily train east out of Detroit, with each trip carrying 1800 new autos worth perhaps a total of $5,000,000. In that same year new motor vehicles shipped by rail climbed to 40 per cent of the auto production for the year. The rail rack cars were also being used for the shipment of tractors, small trucks, farm machinery, boats, and auto trailers. By 1968 the railroad share of new auto traffic was 5.4 million trucks and automobiles, or about half of the annual production. This new rail freight service, like piggyback and the unit train, illustrates what railroads can sell best: wholesale transportation.

The auto rack car was typical of the innovation and diversity found in recent freight equipment. A long generation ago, in the post-war 'twenties, the average freight car had a capacity of 40 tons and cost perhaps $2000 to build. Today the average cost of new cars is around $15,000 to $16,000, and the average capacity is 80 tons. A typical railroad in the 'forties owned perhaps seven or eight kinds of freight equipment, while today it may own more than three dozen types of cars. The revolution in freight equipment really started after the Transportation Act of 1958, which clearly eased regulatory pressures on the industry. In the last dozen years American railroads have spent hundreds of millions of dollars to equip themselves for competing in the modern world of business.

The new generation of freight cars has been tailored to meet the special or particular needs of shippers. Beyond the two fixed limits and standards of height of coupler and track gauge, almost any idea in car design was possible. The larger average size has also permitted heavier loading and "incentive" or lower freight rates. Whale-shaped new tank cars, often called Pregnant Whales, hold 30,000 gallons or more. High-cube box cars became so large as to almost cause clearance problems. "All-door" cars permitted easier loading and unloading. New special covered hopper cars were tailored to hold dry bulk loads of great variety: pumice, salt, cement, grain, dry acids, or ore pellets. The Southern's Big John grain cars were joined by the Southern 100, a four-section articulated hopper with 16 wheels and a capacity of 260 tons—more than half a million pounds. Another innovation is a stock car called a "pig palace" large enough to accommodate more than 300 hogs. Some specially equipped cars have schedules so certain that they permit industries to cut back their inventory. Such are the cars which carry auto parts in special racks and rigs to automobile assembly plants. The diversity of the new freight equipment and service was recently well described by Herman H. Pevler, president of the Norfolk and Western, when he said: "We are selling service the way a barber or a beauty shop sells—how do you want it? Plain or fancy, short or long, all the variations."

The new cars are expensive because they often include new equipment such as cushion-type underframes to reduce shock, improved draft gears for easier coupling, or cargo-securing devices to reduce L & D. Stainless steel, aluminum, and new car coatings combine to give the new cars reduced maintenance and lighter weight. Many of the new cars, including the Southern 100, are equipped with roller bearings. But even today only one-quarter of all freight equipment runs on roller bearings. In the last decade immense progress has been made in eliminating "hot boxes," or over-heated journal bearings which require that cars be set out and removed from trains between terminals. In 1957 more than five cars per million car-miles were set out because of "hot boxes." Infra-red detection devices placed along side the track now can determine the heat of every bearing and journal as a freight train passes by. Such detection devices plus improved lubrication have reduced the 1957 figures by nearly 90 per cent, and in 1967 only six-tenths cars were set out for each million car-miles run.

Naturally the new freight equipment has to be utilized in order to justify its high cost. Auto rack cars, piggyback flats, and cars built to speed the flow of parts to automobile assembly lines are all on the road more days per year than the tired old red boxcar of yesteryear. But ordinary box cars still make up a major share of the national freight fleet of 1,800,000 cars—enough equipment to span the country five times in a train 15,-000 miles long. But even including old box cars, which may not fully share in carrying the load, American railroads have made impressive gains in freight service in the last two decades. Between 1947 and 1967 the average freight carload climbed from 41 to 51 tons, and the cars per train increased from 52 to 70. In the same twenty years the average freight train speed, between original and final terminals, went from 16 to 20 miles per hour. In the twenty years the increases contributed to a virtual doubling of net ton-miles per train-hour, which climbed from 18,126 tons in 1947 to 35,549 tons in 1967.

Obviously the potential for future improvement in efficiency is very great. An example of the ultimate in pure railroading might well be the privately run railroad of the Reserve Mining Company in Minnesota. A 47-mile double track line from open pit mines down to ore boats on Lake Superior, the Reserve Mining line is so efficient that it is practically a conveyor belt running on steel flanged wheels. Moving more than 30,000,000 tons of crude taconite a year down to the ore boats, this mining railroad originates almost as much tonnage as is obtained annually by several midwestern Granger roads. In ton-mileage per year the Reserve Mining road exceeds by 10 per cent the freight traffic of the Pittsburgh and Lake Erie, a road which carries vast amounts of coal and iron ore in the Pittsburgh region. The ore trains naturally are unit trains in a very real sense, since the cars are never turned or uncoupled. Rotary couplers permit dumping of the ore at dock side while the cars remained coupled. The utilization of equipment is high, with the average car running 135 miles a day in comparison with an industry-wide average of just over 50 miles. Of course the Reserve Mining line has tremendous advantages over ordinary common carriers. It has no passenger train losses, L & D claims, interchange delays, or punitive regulations to live with. Its labor force does not work under 1919 rules, and it is paid by the hour (a basic eight-hour day) rather than by the mile. It is small wonder that this private railroad up in Minnesota can provide 130,000 ton-miles of freight service per train hour, a figure nearly four times the national average for American railroads.

Yet American railroad freight service has recently made innovations the industry can be proud of. Late in 1966 the president of the Norfolk and Western, Herman H. Pevler, noted these changes when he said: "In terms of years, railroads are one of America's oldest industries. The first track was laid more than 135 years ago. Yet there have been more changes in our business in the past 15 years than in all of the previous 120. In fact, the average train you see today along our lines did not exist 15 years ago." Dieselization, computerized operations, unit trains, piggyback and container freight, and the continuing revolution in the size and type of freight rolling stock—all seem to confirm the optimism expressed by the president of the Norfolk and Western. In recent years American railroads have shown rather conclusively that they are continuously finding new and better ways to "tote that bale."

10

Tomorrow's Railroads

In spite of the traffic inroads of trucks and pipelines, in spite of the dire passenger train predictions of the I.C.C. examiner, Howard Hosmer, the nation's railroads are not going to vanish from the American scene in the near future. The inherent efficiency of the flanged wheel running on a steel rail would seem to assure a continued dependence of the national economy upon our railroads for some decades to come. Recent innovations in freight traffic would seem to suggest that American railways have at long last turned away from the past and are looking to the future. Their share of a freight traffic consisting of large loads moving long distances should grow as rapidly as the national economy. Even a minimum continuing passenger service, probably subsidized by the government, and geared to medium-distance mass urban transport, seems a probable prospect.

It is difficult to predict the future of American railroads, especially in the post-Sputnik jet age of the 'sixties. But in three areas—commuter service, railroad mergers, and diversification—recent trends and developments would seem to make certain predictions less precarious. The role of the government has been, and will be, of paramount importance in all three phases of railroad development. In recent years the moving force of state and federal tax money, and direction, has been of prime importance in upgrading and retaining several vital commuter systems. Clearly, the future growth and improvement of urban mass transport will go forward only with the aid of further governmental subsidy. Railroad mergers of the past have all required the approval and supervision of the Interstate Commerce

Commission, and future combinations must travel the same route. Finally, diversification, either of the intermodal transport variety or the kind in which railroads branch out into other fields of business, will naturally always be under the watchful eye of governmental regulations and regulators.

The number of passengers commuting by rail has generally declined in recent years, but the decrease has been much less than the drop in coach or Pullman traffic. From 1947 to 1962 commuter traffic dropped one-third, from 6 billion passenger-miles to 4 billion passenger-miles. In the same fifteen years the noncommuter passenger business fell from 40 billion passenger-miles to just under 16 billion passenger-miles. Since 1962 commuter traffic has increased about 10 per cent, standing at 4.4 billion passenger-miles in 1968. In the same half-dozen years coach and Pullman traffic continued to fall, dropping to just over 9 billion passenger-miles in 1968. Year in and year out about three-quarters of the commuter travel is in the Eastern District, a railroad traffic area located east of Chicago and north of the Ohio River and the state of North Carolina. Most of the remaining commuters reside in the Chicago area or out on the California coast.

Commuter fares per passenger-mile have climbed quite rapidly in the last three decades. Just before World War II the average commuter ticket cost just over one cent a mile, while coach tickets were 1.6 cents, and first-class travel cost about 2.25 cents a mile. By 1968 commuter tickets were up to an average of 3.49 cents a mile, or 8 per cent above the average coach ticket which cost 3.24 cents a mile. Even with the hike in suburban commuter tickets the typical railroad is supplying such service at a loss. In 1965 Stuart Saunders, top executive of the Pennsylvania, told his stockholders that "there is no way on earth" to make the operation of commuter railroads show a profit. At the nub of the commuting problem is the simple fact that commuter lines must maintain large rosters of expensive equipment for what is essentially a twenty-hour week consisting of a couple of two-hour peak periods of traffic per day for only five days a week. The automobile, suburban shopping centers, and evening television have combined to deprive the railroad of most of its one-time off-hour, evening, and weekend suburban commuter business. As Saunders told some United States Senators early in 1966: ". . . fewer and fewer people seem willing to use commuter trains for any purpose other than traveling to and from work."

As intercity rail travel declined in the 'fifties the number of commuter passengers surpassed the total number using the day coach or sleeper. In 1968 about two-thirds of the 296,000,000 revenue passengers were commuters. In the middle and late 'sixties, eight railroads—five in the East and three in the Chicago area—provided the lion's share of all commuter service. These eight roads sold 83 per cent of the commuter tickets. In order of traffic density the major eastern commuter lines are the Long Island, the Pennsylvania, the New York Central, the New York, New Haven & Hartford, and the Erie-Lackawanna. The Long Island provides one-quarter of all commuter service in the nation, and far exceeds the combined efforts of the recently merged Penn Central. The major roads serving Chicago traffic are the Chicago & North Western, the Illinois Central, and the Burlington.

The Long Island Rail Road, like all other commuter lines, has had to compete with parallel expressways and highways. But even with the competition of automobiles, the Long Island carries roughly a million commuters a week. Unlike the typical American railway, the Long Island depends almost entirely on passenger business. Long Island freight traffic in fact is so marginal that it resulted in a $6 million deficit for 1967. Its passenger terminal at Jamaica, a dozen miles east of midtown New York, is one of the busiest in the world. Like all eastern commuter roads, the Long Island has been a consistent money loser. During most of the time since being taken over by the Pennsylvania in 1900, the Long Island has been Cinderella—without a fairy godmother.

Dirty cars, late trains, and wrecks were rather standard on

the line, and in 1949 it declared bankruptcy. The president of the road from 1956 to 1967 was Thomas M. Goodfellow, who had served for thirty years in the engineering and operating departments of the Pennsylvania. In the 'fifties and 'sixties commuter fares were raised half a dozen times, and with heavy financial support from the state of New York a multi-million dollar equipment modernization program was undertaken. New York state also offered to forgo $2,000,000 in annual taxes, and the Pennsylvania Railroad agreed to forgo an equal amount in yearly bond interest. The Long Island continued to lose money, and finally in early 1965 Governor Nelson A. Rockefeller asked his legislature for money to buy the commuter line. In view of the poor financial condition of the road, the purchase terms of the sale announced in June 1965 were indeed generous. The state paid the Pennsylvania Railroad $65,000,000 for the property, allowed future tax reductions for both Pennsylvania Station and Grand Central Terminal, and permitted the Pennsylvania to retain certain Long Island freight yards and terminal facilities in Brooklyn. When someone suggested to Governor Rockefeller that his new purchase was in reality "creeping socialism," he grimly replied that there seemed to be no other alternative.

An entirely different point of view seems to pervade commuter lines in the Chicago area. There the three roads which daily carry most of the suburbanites into Chicago do not lose money on the operation. The Burlington and the Illinois Central have shown modest but rather regular profits during the 'sixties. But the Chicago & North Western Railway has made some real profits from its commuter traffic. It really started when Ben W. Heineman was elected chairman and chief executive officer on April 1, 1956. The pipe-smoking 42-year-old chairman at once started to get out of the intercity passenger traffic and to upgrade his commuter service. Between 1955 and 1965 the noncommuter passenger revenue declined from $14,-000,000 to $3,000,000 as dozens of passenger trains were discontinued. In the same decade commuter revenue climbed from

$7,000,000 to $15,000,000, as Heineman started to upgrade his suburban service before asking for a hike in fares.

Heineman emphasized new equipment, especially the purchase of new double-decker air-conditioned, comfortable coaches, each with a capacity of 160 passengers. Between 1956 and 1968 the North Western spent more than $50,000,000 for 267 of the new gallery-type commuter cars. Other roads such as the Milwaukee, the Burlington, the Rock Island, the Illinois Central, and the Southern Pacific have followed Heineman's lead in buying the new cars. Heineman's investment has paid off. In the year he became chairman the C. & N. W. was seventh in volume of commuter traffic and was losing big money. By 1959 the line was fourth in suburban traffic, and the bookkeeper used black ink, not red. In 1967 the three commuter routes to Chicago's west, northwest, and north suburbs showed a profit of $2,500,000, and the C. & N. W. was second behind the Long Island in passengers carried. While other commuter lines were losing passengers Heineman's line was gaining new business. Between 1956 and 1968 the daily haul of commuters grew from 55,000 to 84,000. The C. & N. W. top executive sold his tickets by the month, rather than by the mile and also insisted that his trains be on time. Crew members who consistently brought in late trains were expected to have good excuses.

When Heineman was asked to explain the success of his commuter operations, he replied that he simply follows the first rule of good merchandising: "Sell a good product, advertise it, and satisfy the customer." He has kept his riders satisfied by taking the canned music out of the stations, the advertising cards out of the coaches, and by billing the riders for the monthly tickets which arrive by mail before the first of each month. Heineman advertises his service on the radio, and on rainy days has even supplied his passengers with umbrellas as they left the station for the wet streets of Chicago.

Unfortunately, there are not many commuter railroad executives like Ben Heineman. For the industry at large the Long Island story is far more typical than that of the North Western.

Certainly the few who tried to emulate Heineman were in the Chicago area rather than in the East. Harry C. Murphy, railroad section hand who rose to be president of the Burlington during the 'fifties and early 'sixties, upgraded his suburban service with the new bi-level cars and made some modest profit. The Illinois Central was making small returns in the early 'sixties on the remarkably dependable and on-time performance of its fleet of ancient electric cars serving the South Side of Chicago, and in 1966 introduced a new automatic suburban revenue collection system in which commuters used magnetic tickets to activate automatic ticket gates. But when it came to replacing its 41-year-old fleet of suburban cars with new bi-level commuter coaches, President, William B. Johnson, insisted that most of the purchase price should come from the federal government.

The commuter story in the East, now and in the foreseeable future, is one of government subsidy and assistance. The stance of the Pennsylvania is clearly one of deserting commuters, raising fares, and obtaining all possible public aid. The New York Central was so eager to get rid of its money-losing commuter traffic that in the middle 'fifties it eliminated some Hudson River ferry boat service in order to be able to abandon its West Shore commuter service. Alfred E. Perlman, New York Central president, was willing to use some new stainless steel air-conditioned commuter coaches, especially since they had been purchased by the New York Port Authority. So many financial pirates had worked over the New Haven that to attempt to continue its commuter service in the 'sixties without massive transfusions of government assistance was impossible. Governor Nelson Rockefeller of New York, and Governor John Dempsey of Connecticut, made available state aid of various sorts to enable the New Haven suburban service into New York City to continue. In other parts of the East, the cities of Boston and Philadelphia and the states of Massachusetts, New Jersey, and Pennsylvania, individually or collectively, initiated programs of tax reduction and financial support which have allowed commuter services to continue to function. Quite clearly, most commuter service in the 'seventies will be available only with substantial support by the American taxpayer.

Another proof that urban and commuter transport is expensive can be seen in the recent experience of the San Francisco area. Back in the 'fifties the urban transportation planners in the Bay City region organized the Bay Area Rapid Transit, or BART. This 71-mile regional system consisting of subways, surface lines, aerial lines, and a Trans-Bay tube was intended to take care of future transportation needs. In 1962 the voters of three counties in the Bay area voted to approve a $792,000,000 bond issue, and the state of California agreed to turn over more than $100,000,000 in surplus bridge tolls to help with construction costs. In 1968–69 the nearly completed BART system was hoping for additional money from Washington which would bring total federal aid to $80,000,000, and asking Governor Ronald Reagan and the California legislature for a new local sales tax increase which would meet a contemplated $146,000,000 deficit. As the billion dollar plus project neared completion, two things were obvious: (1) major urban transport projects cost big money, most of it supplied by the taxpayer; and (2) money can probably be saved when existing rail facilities can be retained and upgraded by the use of federal, state, and local subsidy programs.

A major proponent of new and imaginative approaches to today's urban transportation problems is Claiborne Pell, Democratic senator from Rhode Island. Pell was the moving force behind the $90 million High-Speed Ground Transportation Act, which was signed into law by President Johnson on September 30, 1965. This legislation showed that the federal government was willing to invest modest sums of tax money over a period of years to improve and strengthen passenger service in the Boston to Washington corridor. In 1966 Pell wrote a book, *Megalopolis Unbound,* in which he speaks out in favor of a dynamic approach to the transportation problems of tomorrow's supercities. Obviously Senator Pell favors the spending of public tax money for projects which will aid urban and mass transportation programs.

Pell is also a firm believer that rapid transit railroads can serve large cities much better than highways. According to Pell, a single-lane urban expressway will permit up to 2200 passenger cars per hour to enter a city. Filled to capacity these cars might deliver 10,000 commuters an hour, but the national average of seats filled would suggest no more than 3000 occupants. A single railroad track, by contrast, can accommodate 30 ten-car trains an hour, or a maximum of 50,000 to 60,000 commuters arriving per hour. Thus the suburban rail line is from 15 to 20 times as productive as the expressway. And the commuter railroad can also help eliminate parking problems and crowded street traffic. Many estimates suggest that the average speed of vehicles moving in midtown New York City today is no higher than that of the horse-drawn traffic at the turn of the century.

Urban or commuter rail transport is also efficient when compared with air travel. This is especially true of the railroad's economical use of valuable land space. The Commerce Department estimates that the hourly passenger capacity of a single rail line is roughly equal to the hourly traffic flow at a major air terminal. In New York City the rail terminals win easily for size of terminal in relation to traffic flow. Grand Central Terminal and Penn Station together occupy 124 acres of land and annually accommodate 105,000,000 passengers. The three largest air terminals in New York occupy 780 acres, more than twelve sections of land, and care for only 30,000,000 passengers a year. And the combined acreage of the three airports is roughly equal to a double-track railroad right-of-way 65 feet wide running 950 miles from New York City to Chicago.

A number of factors would suggest that suburban commuter problems will continue to be with us for sometime, and that American railroads will have to shoulder their share of meeting this urban transportation problem. All indications are that suburbia will continue to grow in the future, and that the wage earners living there will continue to work in the inner city. Present urban traffic and parking problems make it highly unlikely that expressways can assume a larger share of future urban transit needs. Speaking of urban congestion, John A. Volpe, the secretary of transportation said in March 1969: "Some type of mass transportation has got to get into operation pretty rapidly or we do face the real possibility that either we have to shut off to rubber tires certain limited areas within a city or charge a fee to come in there." Concern over air pollution may also result in a certain cutback in highway travel in congested urban centers. At the same time the inherent efficiency of railroad urban transportation may well result in a growth of rail passenger traffic, especially in the metropolitan corridor areas. Most railroads today seem reluctant to use their own money to finance present or future urban transit improvement programs. The experience of the Long Island Rail Road, or BART in San Francisco, seems to be far more probable for the future than that of the Chicago & North Western. There just are not many Ben Heinemans around anymore. Tomorrow's commuter railroads will definitely be seeking and obtaining massive financial support from cities, states, and the federal government. As Stuart Saunders, president of the Penn Central, recently said: "The U.S. Government is spending virtually nothing to assist 73 million people to get to and from their jobs, while putting up $25 billion to send three men to the moon."

A second development, both of current and future importance, is the trend toward the merger or consolidation of American railroads. The number of individual railroad companies in existence in the last century seems almost without limit. When the centennial issue of *The Official Guide of the Railways* appeared in June 1968 it contained thirty pages listing in small type the names of old and new railroads in existence since the first issue of the *Guide* appeared in 1868. More than 4000 individual rail lines made up the list. The trend toward consolidation was strong in the years just before and after the turn of the century, and by 1916 the record 254,000 miles was divided up among 1243 different companies. By 1920 this number had declined to 1085 different railroads.

Between 1920 and 1957 the number of roads dropped by more than 40 per cent to 635 companies, 116 of which were Class I railroads (above $3,000,000 in annual operating revenues). Much of this decline resulted more from the total abandonment of short roads than because of major mergers. The extensive railroad consolidation plans as proposed by the Transportation Act of 1920 had not been mandatory, and little enthusiasm had ever appeared for the program in the industry. Perhaps nine-tenths of the 60 roads which Professor William Z. Ripley of Harvard planned in the early 'twenties to consolidate into 19 major systems still remained as independent separate companies in the late 'fifties. Most of the present merger activity has occurred in the last dozen years. By 1968 the number of individual companies had declined to 375 lines. In the spring of 1969 there remained only 76 Class I railroads (defined after January 1, 1965 as lines with above $5,000,000 in annual operating revenues) in the United States.

As American railroads in the mid-twentieth century suffered a relative decline both in traffic and financial health, the advantages available through consolidation or merger were obvious. With the new operational and equipment advances of the 'fifties and 'sixties the railroad plant was larger than necessary. A good merger could cut out unneeded parallel tracks and trains. Five main lines compete for the freight traffic available between Omaha and Chicago. Chicago in the mid-'sixties was still served by twenty railroads with more than eighty different freight yards in the area. Consolidation could result in the elimination of costly small yards, and in the use of fewer really large yards which were automated. Chicago in the mid-'sixties was still served by six major passenger stations, far more than the dwindling passenger traffic could justify. Consolidation could result in the cheaper purchase of supplies and an over-all reduction in required inventories. Savings in the utilization of motive power and equipment would also result from well-planned mergers. In

1965 it was estimated that a reduction of the nearly one hundred lines into fifteen or twenty large and really efficient systems could result in annual savings of nearly a billion dollars.

The modern merger trend started in 1955 when the Louisville & Nashville asked the I.C.C. to approve the merger of the Nashville, Chattanooga and St. Louis into the L. & N. In the dozen years since this proposed merger, which was approved in 1957, some fifty-two merger applications have been sent forward to the Interstate Commerce Commission. Thirty-three of these proposed mergers have been approved, five have been denied, six have been withdrawn or dismissed, and eight are pending. A number of the consolidations have been of small lines, but several have been mergers of major companies. In 1959 the Norfolk and Western, one of the larger coal carriers, gained approval for its control of the Virginian Railway, a 600-mile line which was practically a conveyor belt for 16,000,000 tons of coal moved yearly from the mines of West Virginia eastward to Norfolk. In 1959–60 two-century-old eastern lines, the 960-mile Delaware, Lackawanna & Western and the 2200-mile Erie merged into the Erie-Lackawanna.

The merger trend continued in the 'sixties. Between 1960 and 1963 the prosperous 5000-mile Chesapeake & Ohio took over the larger 6000-mile Baltimore & Ohio, a road that was in some financial trouble. The B. & O. was able to use the good credit rating of the C. & O. to finance major purchases of much needed new equipment. Rather significantly the two eastern lines complemented each other in regions served, since the merger tended to be of "end to end" rather than parallel lines. By 1964 Walter J. Tuohy was the chief executive officer of a combined 11,000-mile system which hoped to be able to save $35,000,000 annually through merger. Between 1964 and 1968 another coal carrier, the 800-mile Western Maryland, was added to the C. & O.-B. & O. system. Further south two major southeastern lines, the Atlantic Coast Line and the Seaboard Air Line, started active merger talk as early as 1960. Both roads were of about equal size and generally were competitive lines in the major cities of the states of Virginia, North Carolina, South Carolina, Georgia, Florida, and Alabama. When the merger was finally made effective in mid-1967, the new 9000-mile Seaboard Coast Line expected to achieve yearly savings of $38,000,000. This new competition in the Southeast soon forced the Southern Railway, which had achieved almost equal size back in 1963 when it acquired the Central of Georgia, to consider further merger plans.

In the same years the Norfolk and Western continued to expand. The man responsible for N. and W. growth and expansion was the hard-working lawyer, Stuart Saunders, who was with the N. and W. for twenty-five years before moving on to the Pennsylvania. Saunders had arranged for the take-over of the Virginian in 1959, in the first year of his N. and W. presidency. Early in the 'sixties Saunders pushed for the acquisition of the Wabash and the Nickel Plate, two moderate sized roads which served mid-America from Buffalo to Detroit, Chicago, St. Louis, and Kansas City. This merger was approved in 1964 by the I. C.C. just as Saunders was getting settled in his new position as chairman and chief executive officer of the Pennsylvania. The new enlarged Norfolk and Western in 1964 was a 7600-mile line with total assets of $2 billion, and an annual gross operating revenue of $560 million. As the N. and W. saw the new giant Penn Central appear, it sought even another consolidation. As proposed late in 1965 this latest rail grant would include the Norfolk and Western, the Chesapeake & Ohio-Baltimore & Ohio, the Erie-Lackawanna, the Delaware & Hudson, and the Boston and Maine. This proposed new Norfolk and Western, if and when approved by the Interstate Commerce Commission and the federal courts, would consist of a 27,000-mile system which would be even larger than the new Penn Central.

By far the largest of the recently completed rail mergers is that of the New York Central and the Pennsylvania, which became official early in 1968 with the reading of a 37-page opinion by Justice Abe Fortas of the United States Supreme Court. In approving the creation of the new Pennsylvania New York Central Transportation Company, generally called the Penn Central, the Supreme Court brought to an end a frustrating decade of negotiations, hearings, petitions, and court proceedings. The first merger talk between the two rail giants had taken place in 1957 between Robert Young of the New York Central and James M. Symes, Saunders's predecessor at Pennsy's Philadelphia headquarters. The formal merger petition to the I.C.C. was made in 1962, followed four years later by the Commission's approval. The rail marriage seemed an unnatural one, for the two partners-to-be had been rail rivals for decades. The Central claimed a Water Level Route, while the Pennsy took a shortcut over the mountains. The Central preferred gray and the 4-6-4 Hudson steamers, while the Pennsylvania favored tuscan red and 4-6-2 Pacifics. The Central liked Flexi-Vans, while its rival pushed piggypack service.

After Stuart Saunders became head of the Pennsylvania in 1963, he pushed for consolidation with real vigor, convincing Alfred Perlman, the Central president, that merger could eventually mean yearly savings of at least $80,000,000. When the merger became official on February 1, 1968, Saunders became chairman and chief executive officer of the new Penn Central, with Perlman, one of the best operating men in the industry, becoming president. The Penn Central is by a wide margin the largest American railroad in mileage, assets, and revenue. Its 21,000 miles of line makes it 8000 miles longer than the Santa Fe, first in mileage for decades. The Penn Central has total assets well above $4 billion, and annual gross operating revenues in excess of $1.5 billion.

To merge two such huge and complex organizations as the Central and the Pennsylvania was not a simple task. As the merger became effective Saunders had few illusions about an easy transition, for he had earlier remarked: "The Pennsy itself is a tough property to operate." And Allen J. Greenough, Saunders's number two man and Pennsy president, was heard to say of the new enlarged railroad: "This is a big dog with a lot of

fleas. . . . We'll be scratching for a long time." Some of the
problems were caused by the different style with which the two
big roads had been operating in recent years. Perlman during
the mid-'sixties had introduced or supported several innovations
such as aggressive freight selling, sophisticated computerization,
numerous new electronic yards, and increased Centralized
Traffic Control. On the other hand the Pennsylvania Railroad,
once thought of as the pacemaking or "standard railroad" of the
nation, had recently presented a rather tarnished image to the
shipping and traveling public.

A number of problems plagued the first months of Penn Central operations. There were savings as duplicate freight routes
were eliminated and transit time was cut on several major
routes. But often there was confusion in the routing and billing
of shipments and freight cars. This was most common in cities
originally served by both lines and therefore having different
Central and Pennsy yards. When a Penn Central waybill arrived in one yard with the car appearing in the other yard on
the other side of town, the car might eventually wind up any-
where. There was also confusion caused by the incompatibility
of the two electronic data and computer systems. It was difficult
as well to mesh the operation of locomotives since Central diesels had one type of cab signal and Pennsylvania units another.

There were comparable problems in uniting the two freight
traffic departments. The freight marketing staff of the Central
was young and aggressive, while the comparable group of the
Pennsylvania followed older and more traditional patterns. In
the pre-merger talks Saunders had promised labor that no one
would be fired because of the consolidation—that employment
totals would be reduced only with retirement or death. The
Penn Central was a bit surprised when in the first months of the
merger they spent nearly $18 million for the separation allow-
ances of 2500 employees who voluntarily quit. Some experts
early in 1969 were guessing that Penn Central had actually lost
$100 million in rail operations during the troublesome honey-
moon merger months of 1968. Considering the size of the total

operation—the Penn Central employed 90,000 workers who operated 4200 locomotives, 5000 passenger cars, and 200,000 freight cars—it was really surprising that the newly merged giant railway did not have even greater problems. The extensive savings and economies that naturally result from consolidation will soon be accruing to the Penn Central.

The excess capacity of American rail facilities plus the tough competitive stance of other forms of transportation make it rather certain that the years ahead will see further mergers. Many potential combinations exist in addition to the giant system which would result from the approval of a union between the Norfolk and Western and the C. & O.-B. & O. lines. One of the oldest merger bids, starting back in 1961, has been the contemplated union of the Great Northern, the Northern Pacific, and the Burlington into a mammoth 23,000-mile system to be called the Burlington Northern. Early in 1969 the Supreme Court did not seem much more sympathetic to the proposal than an earlier court had been in the Northern Securities Case in 1904. In the late 'sixties there were several eager suitors for the hand of the Rock Island, even though that line was suffering certain financial problems. Further south the Louisville & Nashville was seeking to acquire the Monon, while the Illinois Central was hoping to merge with the Gulf, Mobile and Ohio. Clearly the future of American railroading lies in the direction of merger. American railroads may both survive and prosper by a decline in number and a growth in size.

The last of the three suggested areas of current and future significance to American railroads is the development of diversification. *Business Week* in the fall of 1967 pointed out that few companies are as difficult to modernize as "a hidebound railroad." But in recent years several railroads have broken with tradition in moving into two types of diversification: (1) integrated or intermodal transportation, and (2) the conglomerate technique of branching out into nonrailroad enterprise. The role of governmental regulation has been quite different in these two forms of rail diversification. Historically and currently, the restraints of federal regulation through the Interstate Commerce Commission often tend to retard or prohibit any major movement of railroads into other forms or modes of transportation. On the other hand the recent tendency of some railroads to venture into nontransportation business has not been seriously restricted by the government.

Federal regulation of course does permit some intermodal transport by railroads. In years past railroads have on occasion ventured away from rail service. The Pennsylvania, the New York Central, and the Union Pacific all had modest highway bus investments back in the 'thirties. The Burlington in 1935 established a truck freight service which by 1941 had expanded to nearly 4000 route-miles in the states of Illinois, Minnesota, Iowa, and Missouri. The rapid expansion of both piggyback and container service in the 'fifties and 'sixties illustrates the advantages of intermodal freight service using long rail hauls combined with flexible truck service at each end of the line. Still another example of intermodal freight which promises future growth is the land bridge operation which several transcontinental lines are presently offering for cargoes moving between Europe and the Orient.

In the West and South the Southern Pacific is a major proponent of intermodal freight. In the spring of 1969 Benjamin F. Biaggini, president of the Southern Pacific, stressed the need for legislation permitting a completely integrated transport when he said: "We see one-package service as the answer to the nation's growing transportation needs. . . ." The Southern Pacific. has already started to do just that. Currently it is operating a pipeline and its highway trucks serve over 25,000 route-miles. The S.P. tried unsuccessfully to buy a barge line and has an application before the Civil Aeronautics Board asking to engage in the forwarding of air freight. North of the border the Canadian Pacific is doing the same thing, claiming to be the "world's most complete transportation system." This is not an idle boast since the Canadian Pacific does offer rail, highway, sea, and air service in a single integrated company serving Canada from

Nova Scotia to Vancouver Island. The new Penn Central owns the Buckeye Pipeline Company, which the Pennsylvania acquired back in 1964. This carrier of petroleum products in the same states served by the Penn Central is a good money maker, and in the late 'sixties was annually earning $13,000,000 for the parent company.

In spite of certain legal limitations on intermodal transport it will no doubt be expanded in future years. Governmental officials, railroad labor, and industry spokesmen all seem to favor such an expansion. A. Scheffer Lang, federal railroad administrator in the Johnson administration, believes that if railroads did use additional modes of transportation it would benefit the shipper and also improve the quality of railroad management. Lang, however, does see certain inherent geographic limitations in such intermodal transport. When railroad diversification proposals were before Congress back in 1960, testimony favoring such legislation was given by brotherhood union leaders Guy L. Brown and W. P. Kennedy. Kennedy, president of the Brotherhood of Railway Trainmen, felt that a diversified rail service might be as successful as piggyback. The president of the Association of American Railroads, Thomas M. Goodfellow, also was enthusiastic about an across-the-board service. Early in 1969 he said: "The railroads don't want to get out of the railroad business; they just want to get into the transportation business." The same point was made several years ago by the Burlington in its ad which read: "Lou Menk Says Railroads Should Get Out of the Railroad Business." Louis W. Menk, the Burlington president's point was that railroads should first think of themselves as part of a distribution system working for the good of their customers. The larger merged railroads of tomorrow may well have the opportunity to be broad-gauged transportation companies.

Many railroads in recent years have been even more active in the other type of diversification, in which railroads move into enterprises having no connection with transportation. Ben Heineman's holding company, Northwest Industries, is a good example. In 1968 Heineman's company obtained less than half of its $700,000,000 revenue from railroad operations. Wearing apparel, boots, chemicals, and steel are all included in the new interests of this Granger railroad. Early in 1969 Heineman was even reported to be interested in a big investment in one of the nation's major rubber companies, B. F. Goodrich. Probably a dozen other Class I railroads have formed conglomerates of one form or another, often by forming holding companies. Included are the Southern Pacific, the Norfolk and Western, the Union Pacific, the Santa Fe, the Illinois Central, and the Penn Central. Frequently the same railroad has ventured into diversification along the dual routes of intermodal transportation and conglomerates.

In 1968 it clearly was the nonrailroad earnings of the Penn Central that kept that newly merged company in the black. Not only is Penn Central the largest American railroad and among the largest six or seven corporations in the country, but it is one of the nation's largest real estate companies, owns a 7500-mile pipeline, and has major investments in industrial parks, resort hotels, sports facilities and assorted other corporate holdings. And these nonrailroad ventures are making money. Chairman Saunders has denied that the Penn Central is going to de-emphasize its rail operations, but he recently did state: "We are attaining a better balance of earnings to make us less dependent upon the fluctuations and extremely low rate of return from railroad operations." Most of the money available for these nonrailroad ventures has come from the recent liquidation by the Pennsylvania Railroad of its major holdings of Norfolk and Western stock.

The Illinois Central is another major railroad conglomerate. Back in 1963 the late Wayne A. Johnston convinced the owners and directors of his railroad that they should create a new holding company, Illinois Central Industries, in order to diversify the line's activities into new income-producing areas. The railroad was the major property of the holding company, but Johnston had plans for the future. In 1966 the Illinois Central won a long court fight which gave the railroad full legal title to air rights on the Chicago lake front—property whose value was estimated by some to run as high as $150 million. In that same year it elected a new president, William B. Johnson, Wayne Johnston being named chairman of the board. Under the dynamic new leadership of Johnson the nonrailroad interests of the Illinois Central were to be greatly increased. In the year 1968, for the first time, manufacturing operations produced more income than railroad operations. The manufacturing ventures included the recently acquired Abex Corporation, the Waukesha Foundry Company, and the Chandeysson Electric Company. This total complex included 63 different plants in the United States, Canada, Mexico, and Europe, manufacturing a spectrum of products ranging from automobile tires to baking equipment to moonshot hardware used by the Apollo astronauts. In addition, Johnson's Illinois Central Industries also had large real estate holdings, including high-rise residential and office buildings to be built on the Chicago lake front, an industrial park project on the east bank of the Mississippi in New Orleans, and the real estate development of a new town, Park Forest South, located south of Chicago. In 1969 Johnson was matching these nontransportation ventures with an imaginative and bold direction of his rail operations.

While diversification developments like those of the Penn Central and the Illinois Central will no doubt continue in the years ahead, several railroad leaders have some reservations. Some rail executives suggest that it makes rather poor economic sense to continue to put money in railroad improvements when the same money placed in nonrail enterprises might return 10 to 15 per cent yearly, a yield several times the normal railroad rate of return. Jervis Langdon, Jr., president of the Rock Island, clearly had such doubts when he recently said: "I wonder to what extent conglomerates . . . can afford to pump into their railroad subsidiaries the kind of money that is required, particularly when there are so many attractive investment opportunities outside the railroad business." Some critics fear that the trend toward railroad conglomerates may finally result in outright nationalization being the only way of maintaining a viable railroad industry.

American railroads in the Golden Spike Centennial year (1969) are viable, but certainly not in the best of health. In size and significance the railroads of the nation have been in decline for some decades. A century ago American railroads were really the only "Big Business" on the American scene. No other institution in the 1860's employed such numbers of men of varied skills, did business on so vast a scale, or financed themselves from such a variety of sources. The proof of the high place which the industry held in the late nineteenth-century American economy can be seen in the way railroads dominated the stock market activity of the period. Things had changed by the 1960's.

In its annual survey of America's largest corporations *Fortune* magazine gives few top billings to railroad companies. True, the newly formed Penn Central is at the head of the list of transportation companies, but its size is dwarfed by a number of industrial and utility concerns. American Telephone & Telegraph has total assets which are one-third larger than the net investment for the entire rail industry. Standard Oil of New Jersey, the biggest of the industrial corporations, has annual revenues of $13 billion, or roughly one-quarter larger than the combined yearly revenues of all 76 Class I railroads. General Motors, second of the industrials, has annual revenues nearly double the total railroad income. G. M. employs one-quarter more workers (725,000) to build Cadillacs, Buicks, Oldsmobiles, Pontiacs, and Chevrolets, than are employed in the entire rail industry. The second of the big motor corporations, Ford, has annual sales as large as the entire rail industry and has a work roster four times that of the Penn Central.

The man in the street is certain that American railroads are going down the drain. He only has to remember the loss of railroad passenger service to be certain of it. If he is bald or getting gray, he is old enough to recall the onetime good passenger service of the Pennsylvania, a line which for years led all Class I railroads both in revenue and in passenger mileage. Twenty-five years ago a fat 42-page timetable showed fourteen different daily Pennsylvania trains scheduled for the Chicago to New York City run. Today a timetable consisting of a single large folded sheet reveals that only four trains serve the same route. And of course in these same years the Pennsylvania has cut off from other routes dozens of through trains and hundreds of locals. A century ago Mark Twain wrote his little piece and jingle about the train conductor, the chorus of which ran: "Punch, brothers! Punch with care! Punch in the presence of the passenjare!" Today the average American believes that the railroads have lost their passenger trains, their conductors, and their punch. And the railroads do not seem to care too much about their public image. The 1969 advertising campaign of the public relations department of the Association of American Railroads will hardly reverse long-standing public indifference or even hostility. Few individual railroads spend much on advertising. Recently *Trains* magazine reported that for the year of 1968 the total of railroad advertising in the *New York Times* was but 20 pages, while the total of the airline industry was 791.

But no one can deny the American railroads their significant role in the rich national history of the past century and a half. The locomotive whistle and the small town depot were part of the very warp and woof of nineteenth century America. As iron rails were laid to the Pacific, the railroads hastened the settlement of the trans-Mississippi frontier, and shaped the lives of western cowboys, miners, and farmers. In the decades after the Civil War, railroads helped to transform an agrarian-based, second-rate industrial society into the complex industrial nation we know today. In the last fifty years the competition of new forms of transportation has caused a serious decline in rail traffic, especially in passenger service. Today for every passenger carried one mile, our railroads are hauling 57 tons of freight that distance. Railroads may be in decline, but the inherent economy of the flanged wheel running on a steel rail is so great that American railroads are still viable today. Tomorrow's America will still have many transportation chores which can most efficiently be performed by railroads.

Acknowledgments

Advice and suggestions given by Professor Bernard A. Weisberger of the University of Rochester, and by Professor Alexander B. Callow, Jr. of the University of California at Santa Barbara aided in the original planning of this book. Once again I am indebted to Professor Richard C. Overton of the University of Western Ontario, whose generous advice has so often helped writers of railroad history. Throughout the writing of the volume I also received much assistance from Dr. Thomas J. Sinclair of the Association of American Railroads. Time for some of the early work on the book was made possible by a sabbatical leave taken during 1967, and by a travel grant provided by the Purdue Research Foundation. The review of twentieth-century railroad development was facilitated by the abundance of statistics that result from the exhaustive accounting requirements of the Interstate Commerce Commission. And the pages of such publications as *Trains, Railway Age, The New York Times,* and *The Wall Street Journal* were all of invaluable assistance in obtaining a full and varied view of current railroad events. Also I owe much to the understanding patience and counsel of Sheldon Meyer of Oxford University Press. Finally, I wish to acknowledge the services of three very competent secretaries: Mrs. Grace Dienhart, Mrs. Joyce Good, and Mrs. Kathryn McClellan.

Selected Bibliography

The volumes listed below represent but a small fraction of the existing railroad literature. In the last century and a half several thousand works on railroad progress and history have appeared, and the list is annually being increased by more than two hundred new titles. This brief selected bibliography ranges from picture books aimed primarily at the rail buff to more technical volumes on such subjects as railroad economics or steam locomotive construction. Several works on individual railroads are included. A number of the titles cover nineteenth-century development and the golden age of railroading between the Civil War and World War I. The books on more recent railroad history are fewer in number, since the period of railroad maturity and decline in the mid-twentieth century has been of no great appeal to railroad historians. Two periodicals, *Railway Age* and *Trains,* while not included in the following list, are excellent sources of information for anyone wishing to keep abreast of current railroad developments.

Athearn, Robert G., *Rebel of the Rockies: The Denver and Rio Grande Western Railroad,* (New Haven: Yale University Press, 1962).

Beebe, Lucius, and Charles Clegg, *Hear the Train Blow: A Pictorial Epic of America in the Railroad Age,* (New York: E. P. Dutton & Company, 1952).

Beebe, Lucius, and Charles Clegg, *The Trains We Rode* (Berkeley: Howell-North Books, 1965–66), 2 vols.

Benson, Lee, *Merchants, Farmers and Railroads: Railroad Regulation and New York Politics, 1850–1887,* (Cambridge: Harvard University Press, 1955).

Black, Robert C., III, *The Railroads of the Confederacy,* (Chapel Hill: University of North Carolina Press, 1952).

Botkin, B. A., and Alvin F. Harlow, eds., *A Treasury of Railroad Folklore,* (New York: Crown Publishers, 1953).

Bruce, Robert V., *1877: Year of Violence,* (Indianapolis: Bobbs-Merrill Company, 1959).

Chandler, Alfred D., Jr., *The Railroads: The Nation's First Big Business,* (New York: Harcourt, Brace & World, 1965).

Cochran, Thomas C., *Railroad Leaders, 1845–1890: The Business Man in Action,* (Cambridge: Harvard University Press, 1953).

Corliss, Carlton J., *Main Line of Mid-America: The Story of the Illinois Central,* (New York: Creative Age Press, 1950).

Craib, Roderick, *A Picture History of U. S. Transportation,* (New York: Simmons-Boardman Publishing Corporation, 1958).

Fogel, Robert W., *Railroads, and American Economic Growth,* (Baltimore: Johns Hopkins University Press, 1964).

Grodinsky, Julius, *Transcontinental Railroad Strategy, 1869–1893: A Study of Businessmen,* (Philadelphia: University of Pennsylvania Press, 1962).

Harlow, Alvin F., *The Road of the Century: The Story of the New York Central,* (New York: Creative Age Press, 1947).

Henry, Robert S., *This Fascinating Railroad Business,* (Indianapolis: Bobbs-Merrill Company, 1946).

Hilton, George W., and John F. Due, *The Electric Interurban Railways in America,* (Stanford: Stanford University Press, 1960).

Holbrook, Stewart H., *The Age of the Moguls,* (Garden City: Doubleday & Company, 1953).

Holbrook, Stewart H., *The Story of American Railroads,* (New York: Crown Publishers, 1947).

Hungerford, Edward, *Men of Erie: A Story of Human Effort,* (New York: Random House, 1946).

Hungerford, Edward, *The Story of the Baltimore & Ohio Railroad,* (New York: G. P. Putnam's Sons, 1928), 2 vols.

Johnson, Arthur M., and Barry E. Supple, *Boston Capitalists and Western Railroads: A Study in the Nineteenth Century Railroad Investment Process,* (Cambridge: Harvard University Press, 1967).

Kerr, K. Austin, *American Railroad Politics, 1914–1920: Rates, Wages, and Efficiency,* (Pittsburgh: University of Pittsburgh Press, 1968).

Kirkland, Edward C., *Men, Cities and Transportation: A Study in New England History, 1820–1900,* (Cambridge: Harvard University Press, 1948), 2 vols.

Kolko, Gabriel, *Railroads and Regulation, 1877–1916,* (Princeton: Princeton University Press, 1965).

Lane, Wheaton J., *Commodore Vanderbilt: An Epic of the Steam Age,* (New York: Alfred A. Knopf, 1942).

Lewis, Oscar, *The Big Four: The Story of Huntington, Stanford, Hopkins, and Crocker, and of the Building of the Central Pacific,* (New York: Alfred A. Knopf, 1939).

Lyon, Peter, *To Hell in a Day Coach: An Exasperated Look at American Railroads,* (Philadelphia: J. B. Lippincott Company, 1968).

McAdoo, William G., *Crowded Years.* (Boston: Houghton Mifflin Company, 1931).

McCague, James, *Moguls and Iron Men: The Story of the First Transcontinental Railroad,* (New York: Harper & Row, 1964).

Marshall, James, *Santa Fe: The Railroad that Built an Empire,* (New York: *Random House,* 1945).

Moody, John, *The Railroad Builders: A Chronicle of the Welding of the States,* (New Haven: Yale University Press, 1920).

Nelson, James C., *Railroad Transportation and Public Policy,* (Washington, D. C.: The Brookings Institution, 1959).

Overton, Richard C., *Burlington Route: A History of the Burlington Lines,* (New York: Alfred A. Knopf, 1965).

Pell, Claiborne, *Megalopolis Unbound: The Supercity and the*

Transportation of Tomorrow, (New York: Frederick A. Praeger, 1966).

Riegel, Robert E., *The Story of Western Railroads: From 1852 Through the Reign of the Giants,* (New York: The Macmillan Company, 1926).

Stover, John F., *American Railroads,* (Chicago: University of Chicago Press, 1961).

Taylor, George R., *The Transportation Revolution, 1815–1860,* (New York: Rinehart and Company, 1951).

Taylor, George R., and Irene D. Neu, *The American Railroad Network, 1861–1890,* (Cambridge: Harvard University Press, 1956).

Turner, Charles W., *Chessie's Road,* (Richmond: Garrett & Massie, 1956).

Turner, George Edgar, *Victory Rode the Rails: The Strategic Place of the Railroads in the Civil War,* (Indianapolis: Bobbs-Merrill Company, 1953).

White, John H., Jr., *American Locomotives: An Engineering History, 1830–1880,* (Baltimore: Johns Hopkins University Press, 1968).

Winther, Oscar O., *The Transportation Frontier: Trans-Mississippi West, 1865–1890,* (New York: Holt, Rinehart and Winston, 1964).

Index

A

Abandonment of rail lines: since 1916, 153-57; during 1920's, 155-56; during 1930's, 156; since World War II, 156; mentioned, 112-13

Abbott, William Hawkins, 149

Abex Corporation, 290

Accidents, on railroads, 9, 12, 21, 22, 76, 77, 274

Adams, Alvin, 22

Adams, Charles F., Jr., 16, 92

Adams, Frederick Upham, 205

Adams, John Quincy, 8

Adamson, William C., 120

Adamson Act (1916), 120

Advertising, railroad, 229-30, 231, 292

Advisory Commission of the Council of National Defense, 121, 160, 161, 181

Aiken, William, 11

Air brakes, 71-73

Air-conditioning of trains, 203, 232

Air Force One, 126

Air freight, 148, 287

Air-rail passenger service, 145

Air rights, Chicago lake front, 290

Air transport: growth of, 143-49; safety of, 148; air freight, 148; receives federal subsidies, 200; compared to rail service, 218, 224, 227; extensive advertising by, 292; mentioned, 124, 125, 126, 193, 201

Aircraft, private, 147

Airline hostess, 145-46

Airmail service: first American (1918), 116, 145; extension of routes, 144

Airports, 146, 228, 279

Allegheny Corp., 212

Allen, Horatio, 11, 12, 19, 20

Allen, William F., 69

American Airlines, 145

American Central Line, 38

American Railroad Journal, 10

American Railway Association, 67, 69, 160

American Railway Union, 89

American Telephone & Telegraph Co., 291

American-type locomotive, 20, 73, 78

Ames, Oakes, 79, 80

Anaconda Copper Mining Co., 109

Andrews Raid, 44

Arlie, Earl of, Scotland, 52

Armed forces, interest in aviation, 144-45

Armour, Philip D., 108

Army Appropriation Act (1916), and railroads, 160, 164

Army engineers, survey Pacific rail routes, 36-37

Arthur, Chester A., 92

Ashtabula, O., wreck, 77

Association of American Railroads, 69, 181, 189, 220, 230-31, 234, 257-58, 288, 292

Astor, John Jacob, 125, 143

Atcheson, Topeka and Santa Fe R.R.: construction of, 54-55;

B

C

D

E

G

H

I

L

M

N

O

P

Q

R

S

T